THE DOMESTIC THEATRE HANDBOOK

Instant plays, anywhere, any time

Beth Shaw and Martin Bould were born in the same year, grew up in Hertfordshire, met briefly as teenagers at Quaker summer camp and both studied history at university. They started writing plays together in 1990, remained firm friends and have settled down within walking distance of each other in North London.

Special thanks

To Ellie Bould, Penny Cloutte, Dora Clouttick, Paul Dalton, Martin Jakes, Jackie Beim and Richard for their stories and their contributions to plays.

To Madeleine Casey, Janet Smith, Peg and Derek Jakes, Caroline Penney and Geoffrey Bould and the late Kathleen Bould, Lower Shaw Farm and all those who have regularly supported domestic theatre in its first twenty years, especially Kath Shaw-Urlich for inspiration with cakes and props; Lucy Goodison for editorial support and encouragement to publish; Patrick Hogan, Emily Ayto and David Morgan for assistance with proof-reading; Malcolm Taylor at the Vaughan Williams Library for help with research.

To everybody who appears in the photographs and to Sue Bineham and Carlos Guarita for permission to use their photographs.

Acknowledgements

John Boyd Hyland for permission to adapt his 'Ladies' Mumming Play'.

The late Shaun Sutton for permission to adapt his children's BBC television play 'The Queen's Champion' (shown in 1958) and for sending us the novel that it became (as the original TV scripts had been lost long ago).

Lisa Thiel for permission to include adapted lines from her song 'Spirit of the Plants'. Professor David Wiles for permission to include text from *The Early Plays of Robin Hood* (1981)

THE DOMESTIC THEATRE HANDBOOK

Instant plays, anywhere, any time

Beth Shaw and Martin Bould

Published in Great Britain by
Just Press 2011
www.justpress.co.uk

Just Press offers books, DVDs, art works and lectures/exhibitions that
provide a platform for exchange between different generations and
interests. In areas including history, religion, theatre, health, politics,
art, poetry and fiction, we honour unsung aspects of human experience
and celebrate the unorthodox. Just Press is a non-profit project.

ISBN 978-1-907352-04-1

Design, typesetting and cover design by Catherine Weld
www.catherineweld.com

Printed and bound in Great Britain by
Advantage Digital Print, Dorchester

Contents

This book is dedicated to our respective partners,
Patrick Hogan and Helen Richards.

1. Introduction

What is domestic theatre?

Domestic theatre is theatre in the comfort of your own home or garden, performed by you and the friends you invite, from a script, with no learning lines, no auditions, no rehearsals and no special stage.

The players are you and your friends: those who don't have lines take part as the audience. The stories are simple, usually well-known, and told in rhyming couplets. People get up and read their lines from a script, with the minimum of preparation. And yes, you need a few improvised costumes to add liveliness and create a sense of performance.

Think of domestic theatre as the opposite of a grand theatrical event: instead of hard-won preparation and formality, it captures a spontaneous feeling, where everyone shares in the occasion and the fun.

What this book is about

Beth created domestic theatre with the help of friends. This is the first book about it, telling you why we think it is relevant today (Chapter 2). It is a handbook telling you how to arrange a production in your own home, or at a friend's place – just like organising a party, with a bit extra that we can guide you through (Chapter 3). At the end there are 26 scripts that you can try out.

Once you've got the hang of it, you may want to take it further – varying the script and experimenting with different styles (Chapter 4) – until you reach the point when you realise you could just as well choose your own story and turn it into a play for domestic theatre (Chapter 5).

In Chapter 6 you can learn about some other settings where you can try out the domestic theatre approach. These are usually gatherings where an audience has a shared purpose and people are willing to step up and take a part, such as community celebrations or weekend conferences, or maybe even as part of the 'works pantomime'. But they never go as far as paying entry or rehearsed productions – or else where are the spontaneity and sense of community?

In Chapter 7 we provide more information on the well-springs of domestic theatre such as the seasonal festivals of the year, and in Chapter 8 we introduce the plays and the scripts.

Who this book is for

Anyone can use this book. With a bit of enthusiasm, you can organise a party and put on a play. As we explain, domestic theatre has never been known to fail. So you could be any of the following:

- Like us, too poor to pay to go out as often as we'd like for professional entertainment.
- People who enjoyed dreaming up plays and showing off when they were children.
- People who want to celebrate seasons and festivals in a more active manner.
- Anybody with a birthday or special occasion who wants a new way to mark it.

You don't need special skills, acting abilities, grand houses or expensive equipment for domestic theatre – you can turn whatever you lay your hands on into material for a production.

Beth: how it all started

Beth Shaw is the founder of domestic theatre. She tells how she came to create her first domestic theatre performance over 20 years ago, and how the idea for this handbook gradually came about:

'From the late '70s we sometimes organised play-readings with friends. We did *Under Milk Wood* by Dylan Thomas several times. In 1989 I was becoming more and more interested in the traditional seasonal festivals. For Halloween that year I had gathered people together for apple-bobbing and a Halloween-themed cabaret. We were planning a Twelfth Night party and I was wondering what activity to arrange. On the last shopping day before Christmas, I was crossing Hampstead Heath with two friends when one mentioned that she had never forgotten playing the Turkish Knight in the Christmas mummers play when she was a child. I was so impressed by how vividly she remembered the experience that I rushed off and managed to get hold of a copy of the text that same day. I took it to a party the following evening. People acted it out with umbrellas for swords and a kitchen sieve for a dragon mask. It was so popular that ten days later I put it on again for New Year's Eve at Lower Shaw Farm, an activity centre in Wiltshire. For this performance, my sister Kath organised splendid props and costumes, and this meant people slipped easily into their roles.

Over the next year I researched mummers plays for the seasonal festivals and tried them out at parties in my living room and at Lower Shaw Farm. In 1990 Martin began working with me, and together we updated plays, tidied up rhymes and adapted stories. This meant that by 1991 we had a full cycle of plays for every season, and the confidence to develop our own.

Martin introduced domestic theatre performances into the garden party he organises in June each year with his daughter Ellie. Gradually we got into the habit of researching and writing a new play each year, to perform once in the summer and once in the autumn at my flat. Over the years, other friends would put on plays in their own houses, sometimes using their own story, sometimes borrowing a ready-made script. One year we wrote a Christmas mummers play in two versions, traditional and topical, and went round to three houses on Christmas morning, demanding mince pies in return for our performance.

People often said, why don't you make a video, write a book or set up a website? So we experimented with a few things such as a film for a TV arts show and a play script posted on the website of St Pancras Almshouses to mark their 150th anniversary. We have found that people always enjoy the plays, and often they encourage people's own creativity elsewhere in their lives. So we thought it was time to produce the handbook.'

Martin: domestic theatre and me

'The first time I was invited to domestic theatre, I was very relieved that I could be "audience", that is, I was not obliged to have a part in the play. But I was intrigued by Beth's description, and, as a weekend parent to my five-year-old daughter Ellie, I was keen on social gatherings where there were other children.

In the event my misgivings disappeared. I found that the play added verve and energy to the party, and that both Ellie and I could meet and make friends with a wide range of people. When Beth began a year of plays to mark the seasons, I became a "small part" regular, and then, when she asked for help finishing off a playscript, I volunteered.

One of Beth's great talents is to help people believe in their own creativity and find unique ways to express it: that's what domestic theatre is all about. In a way, that's what happened to me.

At first, all that was involved was finishing up some rhymes. I remember how pleased Beth was when, editing *Demeter and Core*, we came up with a couplet for the Sun God to explain to the weeping Demeter how Core was abducted:

> *I respect you greatly and honour your grief*
> *But Zeus is the culprit and Hades the thief.*

From there, I became interested in using rhymes to carry the action and entertain. The next step was to include a play in my summer garden party. I am lucky to have a secluded garden, shared with the neighbours in the small block of flats where I live. Because the party is near my birthday in June, we usually have good weather and always follow the play with strawberries, cake and cream. (Nowadays the plays finish with a reference to this.)

My first idea was to adapt a medieval tale, *Aucassin and Nicolette*. This had been recommended by an inspirational tutor at university, because of the way it reverses courtly chivalric values: it makes Aucassin – rather than a questing hero – a wimp who finds happiness through a strong woman. The story offered a quirky approach, plenty of dramatic interest, and characters such as the Topsy Turvy King. The play was a great success for all my friends and neighbours, as well as for the children, who enthusiastically hurled rolled-up socks in the "topsy turvy" battle. Then, with Beth's help, I went on to adapt another medieval favourite, *Sir Gawain and the Green Knight*, which has a Christmas setting and a startling challenge to chop off the Green Knight's head.

Eventually writing the plays with Beth became part of my own annual cycle. From late summer I would nurture the germ of an idea, begin research in autumn and then meet Beth in January or February to talk through the structure and the themes of the play. In spring we would gradually develop the plot, storyboard and text. By the morning of the play, Ellie and friends would be marking up the scripts. Then in October, Beth would bring the play to life once again for her birthday. With only occasional repeats, we have put on plays in this way for over two decades.

Often we chose stories for Ellie – *Little Girl with the Kind Heart* was for her, and later we did a Beatles play when she grew to like their music. However, I gradually realised that as well as offering vivid narratives, the stories often echoed the hopes, fears and patterns in my own life – for example, step-parents in the *Little Girl with the Kind Heart*, the strong women in *Nicolette and Aucassin* and the complicated seductions and ever-present danger of losing your head in *Sir Gawain and the Green Knight*.

Beth and I began to look for the subtexts or hidden themes of the stories we adapted, so we could highlight them and make the plays more entertaining. Or we simply looked for topical relevance: for example, giving *Great Expectations* a political theme in 1996, before the following year's general election, and finishing with an audience vote on Dickens' alternative endings. If we could go further and bring to life less well-known stories such as the suffragettes, so much the better. We felt we were echoing eternal themes and current events, with a touch of subversion, for a modern audience, as the original mummers had done for their times.

The plays remain a great way to meet friends each year and have become an annual focus for my neighbours. When those further up the street hear the plays and get curious, we invite them next time. The plays are suitable for everyone and have literally featured all ages from nought to ninety. As Ellie has grown older, we have had fewer young children, but there has always been a role for her in organising the party and taking photographs.

The actual co-writing of the plays still requires the daunting effort of facing a blank page, but can be rewarded by finding a deft (near) rhyme or a concise plot summary, such as my favourite from *Great Expectations*, where Miss Havisham says of Estella, the hero's love object:

> *She is the brightest star in the firmament.*
> *You'll love her, Pip: it'll be permanent.*

The corny humour and crowd-pleasing rhymes also extended into the world of work through office pantomimes and end-of-year reviews. In the pub with fellow training course members, I devised an end-of-course entertainment relying on in-jokes and a simple hero-and-three-challenges storyline.

Everyone welcomes the plays, finding them stimulating and unaffected. Each year, a few more people experience domestic theatre, and bring some suggestions of their own. It seems the most natural thing in the world to go on doing it.'

Paul's story

The door knocker clacks like an express train on a wooden bridge as more guests arrive with food, costumes and props. This is people entertainment in action. Everybody has a part – actor, singer, chorus. This creates an even greater bond between us. There are people who come to Beth's parties as total strangers to each other. Yet in an evening they have fought to the death or embraced longingly and passionately or even had babies by each other – and watched them grow up. Beth is able to transform a serious intention into a romp with pomp. Even the first-time visitor is embraced in an atmosphere of bustle, purpose and excitement. With a pumpkin pie in one hand, Jack O'Lantern will be trying to pull on his tights with the other. Or Ceres, the goddess of corn, will waft past in a diaphanous dress, her hair tumbling like a mountain stream bejewelled with a waterfall of diamonds.

2. Active entertainment for our times

Why do domestic theatre?

Why do domestic theatre? Fun – that's the first reason for putting on a play in the comfort of your own home. By its nature, it's accessible, democratic, free, portable, and a bit different. We want to explore just why it is so appropriate today.

Domestic theatre has active energy – there's no slumping in an armchair, no subdued click of a computer mouse. Quite the opposite: you are declaiming lines in improvised fancy dress. It brings an immediacy to your individual preferred style of entertainment, with the added excitement of theatre itself – telling a story and evoking feelings. Whereas watching television, no matter how good the story, cannot offer real, human contact.

Plays give a great opportunity to see another side of friends, family members, work colleagues and neighbours, and provide the experience of cooperation towards a common goal.

Domestic theatre is fun because it's out of the ordinary, and entirely your own. Everyone will remember the performance and talk about it for days afterwards. They will have experienced something special, something different, and something created in an ordinary home. And this feeling is even more remarkable when you are the one who has planned the occasion and acted in the play. It is like creating a 'temporary community' in your own front room.

A new kind of party

People love parties, but even a tried-and-tested approach can become jaded. Remember that sinking feeling of a drink in your hand, asking, 'Who are you, what do you do for a living'? There comes a time when a change is in order. Now is your chance to find out what people are really like, and let their qualities shine through their domestic theatre performance. Imagine saying, 'I'm the Sun God, what part are you playing?' or, 'You were a terrific villain – so angry!' You are starting quite a different conversation.

Your party-goers arrive with anticipation about what is to come, and a trace of uncertainty about whether they will be able to go through with it all. Each person has an important role – even those who choose to be 'audience' – and everyone surprises her- or himself when they carry it off. Their last-minute panic is taken over by a pleasurable thrill as they realise that nobody else knows, either, what is going to happen next. But after the play, the chatting, dancing, munching and chatting-up carries on according to whatever is your normal style – but in the delicious afterglow of shared energy and shared enterprise. When everyone has something brand new to talk about, your party goes with a new kind of swing.

Too good to leave to the children

Even if they have forgotten all about it until now, most people played dressing up games as children. Many will have invented and performed sketches for parents. In some families the tradition was to act out whole plays. Or there were school plays or performances in youth groups. This impulse is never lost, just buried, and most party-goers will recall these events as exciting or pleasurable.

A domestic theatre performance in your own front room revives all these memories and family rituals. It helps people remember that taking part in a performance is something they once did, and can now do again. When they were young, dressing up, improvising props and acting out adventures was fun and exciting.

So in domestic theatre we say, let's take this up again with the greater resources of adults. It is too much fun for children to have the monopoly.

Long and honourable traditions

And why did we let these traditions go – not only family performances, but our community celebrations? For no good reason. We somehow drifted into doing other, less participative things, or left traditions to the experts. So let's see if we can reclaim them. Domestic theatre is one of the community activities that can update these traditions and make them happen today. And it is ready and waiting to try out! No grants, room hire, committees, constitutions or performing rights are needed.

In fact, traditional customs actively contribute to the domestic theatre experience. Seasonal celebrations are one way to connect with the different times of the year and recreate local festivals that bring another dimension to our lives, now that our community and collective life has been eroded and barely exists in the way that it once did. Existing festivals and the plays associated with them provide a ready-made short cut (as we describe in Chapter 7). They can help us to tune into the rhythms of life and the traditions of centuries whose meanings are no less important to our collective well-being today. They are real and add a little bit of unpredictability, providing alternatives to commercialised Halloween, Christmas tinsel or Easter choc-fests.

Boosting confidence and creativity

For most people, confidence benefits from a solid platform, and creativity is fostered by gentle encouragement. Domestic theatre provides both.

Standing up and speaking lines in front of other people is naturally daunting (which is why domestic theatre never insists, if an individual prefers to watch). But no-one will criticise or mock – those present are friends after all – and any nervousness simply imparts a new dimension to the character being played. So what was written as bombastic sometimes becomes halting in performance, or noisy becomes quiet: the results can be surprising and magical.

If people come to more than one performance, they can progress from audience to small part, and from small part to bigger role. On the way, they can add something of their own, or try out something different – a costume or prop, and accent or gesture. They can make a strong entry, or a long-drawn-out death. We find they enjoy it!

Together the script, costume, props and audience empathy provide a platform for confidence and enjoyment.

More than this, the very occasion of a performance can be enough to draw out your friends' creativity – they suggest ways to help, bring props, or decorate cakes in the theme of the play. Once given a part, they find resources to mime, perform, ad lib, lead or join in singing. This contribution is creativity discovered 'in the moment' – how to play their part in the company of others. As time goes on, they may choose to apply their creative resources in either familiar or ambitious ways – such as making headgear, finding new words for a well-known song, and writing lines, or eventually whole plays.

All these talents and gifts are brought without expectation or cost – simply to enjoy and remember.

Ellie's story, looking back

I remember attending domestic theatre productions at different people's houses when I was younger, and every year my dad used to throw a party and we would put on a play he had written with Beth. They used to write these plays based on my favourite stories when I was younger, or around things that I was particularly interested in. I especially remember loving the *Little Girl with the Kind Heart* play, where I had to rescue my friend (who was a mouse) from a big box, and the Beatles play where we got to sing and had 'blow-up' guitars. I was always the lead character then, and I felt very special that my dad had written a play for me. I absolutely loved it and I would often invite friends to come stay with me for the weekend of the play so they could join in.

From when I was very young I remember the experience rather than the actual plays – I don't think I could tell you many of the names of the plays that I acted in, or the plotline, but I can remember the experience of going to a domestic theatre production. It was always a big fun party, and I would get to see my friends and eat and then dress up and play. The dressing up was supposed to be part of the production but I mostly remember getting dressed up and messing around! I remember enjoying following some of the plays outside or through the house and getting very excited. It was all very real and dramatic when we were outside or moving around.

I'm pretty sure I told all my friends, 'When you come there will be a big play in the garden and my dad and everyone will be in it and it's really embarrassing, but it's really fun!' I think sometimes people can be a little bit embarrassed doing something a little different, but actually once everyone came, they got involved if they were the more confident type, or else watched if they were more shy. They all had a really good time.

3. Putting on your own production

Organise a party

People love to be invited to a party, especially where there's going to be live entertainment that includes them. We found it worked to discuss our domestic theatre party with our friends and family to find out who was enthusiastic about the idea, in the hope that this would build up the atmosphere of anticipation: that way, guests would come along 'expecting the unexpected.' We allowed time for the extra bit of organising that is involved. We started with people we know reasonably well, and invited them to bring a friend. Sometimes we weighed up numbers of men and women, though people often take roles of the opposite gender.

On the practical side, we suggest you allow between 20 and 45 minutes for the actual performance. In our experience, starting about an hour or so after the start of the party allows everyone to arrive and a sense of expectation to build.

Combining a play and a party adds up to a lot of work, so it makes sense to recruit friends to spread the load. For example, ask your guests to bring food or drink to share.

Invitations

We always put the time the play begins on the invitation: this is to make sure people don't miss out by accident – and you will definitely want them to be on time if they are in the cast. (It may even be wise to let people know that if they haven't arrived by the time on the invitation, you may have to give their favoured part to someone else.) Sometimes we say 'bring a friend' on the invitation, if that's the approach you want to take. Some people like to say on the invitation what time the party will finish, too.

As domestic theatre basically involves inserting a play into a party, it helps to think about whether you want people to enjoy the food before the play or after, and include this on the invitations. If you ask people to arrive in time to eat something before the play, they may be able to relax and enjoy it more.

Other tips for the invitation are to tell people if there's a theme, so they can come in a suitable costume (green for *Under the Greenwood: Robin Hood May Play*, long dresses for Victorian-era women, etc.) and – if you are going to pre-allocate – to ask people to ring up if they want a part.

Numbers

Don't worry too much about numbers – if you have at least 10 people you have got enough to go live. Plays with few characters are easily expandable, for example by adding non-speaking handmaids or extra shepherds, etc. Another idea is to pair people up to play a single part, speaking alternate lines: in *Penelope on Ithaka*, six men played the three suitors to uproarious effect.

When there are more parts than guests, each person can get more than one. This works well – indeed, it is a positive advantage, since with fewer people, everyone can try out more parts and more aspects of themselves.

Filling your living room with people enhances the atmosphere. You will be surprised how many you can fit in. If there are more people than parts, you have many candidates for the parts and the audience.

Making the most of your home

You don't need a large home or room – we have squeezed up to 50 people into a living room measuring 12 feet by 9 feet. This can add to the fun and help people get to know one another. In the summer, go out of doors if possible. In winter, a safe bonfire can provide warmth and light, and add to the atmosphere of the play.

You will need three areas, whatever size space you have:

* A designated space where people can step forward to read their lines, as if a stage.
* Somewhere for food and drink.
* A place to lay out props (and if necessary don costumes).

Living room, kitchen and bedroom work well to fit these requirements. A garden or balcony is a bonus (especially for smokers). It is not absolutely essential to have a space for a stage, since people can read their lines from where they are, especially in a very crowded room. Some scripts have fights and chases, but with a bit of ingenuity these too can be improvised or mimed, if there isn't space to give them free rein.

Preparing the space used for the play

Domestic theatre never uses a proper stage, but it helps to clear a space at one end of your living room. If you have a bare, plain-coloured wall, you will make it easier to focus on the characters and avoid distracting the eye. So you may need to rearrange the furniture a bit. Remember to leave chairs for people who cannot stand. Some people will choose to sit on the floor.

It can add to the atmosphere to decorate the entrance to your home or to the room where the play will take place, e.g. with an ivy wreath or decoration on the lintel. Add mistletoe at Christmas. Get friends to bring small bunches of flowers from their gardens, especially if they will add something to the theme of the play. Old Christmas cards or postcards can provide shapes for room decorations – hearts for Valentines, eggs for Easter, etc.

Some plays call for scenes in different settings, evoked in different areas, lightly decorated according to their theme. In a living room performance of

Demeter and Core, the action moved from the Underworld on the sofa, decked in black plastic, to Demeter's temple on an armchair swathed in red velvet and plastic flowers.

Scripts

Make enough copies for each person with a part to have a script – again, simple but essential. Note that those with small parts will not need the whole script – in fact it is better if only the main characters who are in most of the play have complete scripts. (Otherwise the audience – and the other characters – are tempted to read the scripts instead of directly looking at and enjoying the performance.) Anyone who is hard of hearing should be offered a complete script, to help them follow what's going on.

One of the hardest jobs of preparation is marking up the scripts. Texts can be photocopied easily enough, but it really helps to go over each script with a highlighter pen, marking up every time that particular character speaks, enters, exits or is the subject of another stage direction. This can be quite time-consuming, but it makes it much easier for people to work out when to come in.

We discovered that A5 scripts, if available, are preferable to A4 because they hide much less of a character's face when they are reading out their lines. A double page opening of this book can be copied with care on to A4. If you photocopy scripts from this book, or produce your own scripts on A5, you will have to allow time for the extra work in cutting and stapling the photocopied sheets.

We also give everyone a programme listing the title, characters, setting and audience participation. For example, 'The action takes place in the early 19th century, in the marshes of Kent and in London. The audience hiss and growl as the Kentish mist' (for *Great Expectations*).

In effect, the programme is the same as page 1 of the script. It gives everyone basic information to follow the play, even if they have no prior knowledge of the story.

At the end of the play, ask everyone to give their scripts back so they can be kept for another time.

Giving out parts

Make a list of all the parts and write names down as you allocate them. This may seem obvious but everything can become a bit hectic when you give out parts on the day, and anyway you will need a list if people are going to switch parts around. Sometimes it is fine to earmark some keen friends or family for a particular part, as noted when thinking about invitations. (Agreeing parts beforehand also helps if you want people to devise their own costume.)

Deciding parts on the day is also possible – often it can amount to a version of 'first come, first served', leading to wonderful serendipitous choices and great individual successes. During the casting of *Five Break the Spell*, just as we were saying, 'Now we need a farmer', the front door opened and revealed a bearded, twinkly-eyed neighbour of few words, who instantly accepted the part of Mr Earthy.

Another rule we find useful is that the host should have first pick of the parts, as reward for their hospitality.

Recently we have started assembling everyone, making sure they have sight of a programme or cast list, and inviting them to practice saying the words, 'I can do that part!' Getting everybody to say this in unison, before the casting begins, makes it easier for them to say it when the time comes to claim their part in front of everyone. The host or organiser – in fact it can be anyone – simply reads through the list of characters and one person will be first to say, 'I can do that part!' after their choice is read out. They are then given a script and any props or costume. (Note that this procedure can take a little time when plays have a large number of parts.)

Finally, remember the golden rule that people who really don't want a part in the play can have an equally important role as audience.

Casting as the gentle art of persuasion

Whatever casting method you choose, try to ensure everyone has a part you think they will enjoy. They should 'play themselves in the part'. For example, they may choose to speak in their ordinary voice, or try out an accent – either way brings great results, but leave them to decide.

In general, a word of explanation about the part is all that's needed. For example, you may say to the doctor in a mummers play, 'Your lines sound lunatic, but speak them with the utmost conviction, as he's a sort of witchdoctor'. Your scripts should include only a minimum of stage direction (e.g. 'wailing').

Another rule of thumb is to think in terms of 'bit parts' and 'cameo parts'. So for example if someone is not confident, you can say, 'Don't worry, it's just a bit part, you can manage it easily.' Or if someone wants a large part, but you cannot accommodate them (because all those parts are taken, or because they have arrived late) offer them a 'cameo' role. This will make them feel like a Hollywood star in a small movie, and encourage them to act their two lines with a flourish – much to the appreciation of all.

We have found that casting 'against character' works very well. Everyone benefits if someone shows a less familiar side of themselves – the modest person with the lead role, the good guy cast as the villain. You could offer fighting parts to quieter people to give them a taste of boldness, or seductive parts to someone who wants to try out a bit of sexiness. This is quite different from asking people to do something they don't want to do. Your aim is to notice people's qualities and creativity, and to suggest a role in an encouraging, confident manner.

For years Beth agonized about what to do if two people really wanted the same part. Eventually we realised we could actually have them share the part and let them decide amongst themselves whether to speak in unison or speak alternate lines. We also did this once when we were performing the *Mummers Play for Lammas: Death of the Summer Lord* outdoors on an island in the Thames. There was one person without a part and our friend Rick generously offered to share his part as Friar Tuck. As Friar Tuck is a larger-than-life character this doubling suited the story. They even both fitted into Friar Tuck's large tunic and the rest of us got used to their two heads poking out of the costume. And as the duo were named Rick and Patrick, it seemed meant to be!

How much direction does the play need?

The key things the director or host has to do for the performance itself are:

- Decide when it is time to start, and tell everyone.
- Make sure people get their costumes, props and scripts.
- Run through the audience participation, sound effects and any songs before the play starts.
- Explain to the actors what's required in any fights or more intimate parts such as dancing or smooching, and leave them to work out how best they want to do the scene. (But don't forget to tell them who is supposed to win the fight – it is easy to get carried away!)
- During the performance keep an eye on the script and if necessary remind people when it's their turn to speak.
- At the end, lead applause, curtain calls, cast photos, etc.

Once your guests have their parts, the play does not need direction as such, although people do appreciate encouragement and some prompting. Otherwise our main advice is to remember your own insignificance as director:

- Improvisation is good: ideally, performers should express their own enjoyment and lend something of their own character when they speak the part. Accents, halting delivery, gestures, humour – welcome them all. They will come naturally.
- Never force a role on anyone: offer them the opportunity to take part. You may find two people want to swap: let them. It always works better.
- Remember there are no star parts and no duff parts: all actors contribute to the play, and what seems a few lines on paper can emerge as a great triumph in performance.

We have never found that a play has floundered because people have different ideas about what is best. This is because, first, it's a party, not a competition, and second, when there is a play involved, people become naturally more respectful of a director – that is, you, the host.

Costumes

Costumes are an essential part of a domestic theatre production, but aim to 'keep it simple'. Our watchwords include:

- Don't buy – get donations, or use material people already own to make simple striking transformations. For example, we made a turban out of a silver jumper, and used it for an exotic Turkish Knight.

- Put the word out for plain colours. You can get a lot of mileage out of white petticoats and white sheets, black cloaks and shawls, and red skirts. The eye accepts their transformation into different costumes, and they can be re-used in other productions. For example, a red skirt could do service as a devil's cloak or a dragon's body.

- Get people to bring their own clothes as costumes for their parts, since they will be happy wearing them. For a play with lots of goddesses, we were surprised how many normally denim-clad females have evening dress and finery ideal for goddess gear stashed away in the back of their wardrobes.

- If you love flowers and can string a garland together, a simple ivy garland intertwined with a few flowers makes any woman feel like a goddess.

- Hats are a wonderful shorthand for characterisation. Even without any other costume, a hat can turn a party guest into a performer with an instantly recognisable part, and a character to go with it – soldier, witch, police officer, gentleman, Dame Spring.

Over time, people will offer costumes which can be used and re-used – an old butcher's apron, a waistcoat or jerkin, a spangly top. A black felt hat creates an old man, a straw hat signals a farmer, flowered head-dresses evoke village maidens and their rural charms.

You can make simple costumes yourself, or enlist the help of friends. For example, stick card together and cut it in the old-fashioned shape of an admiral's hat for Nelson's headgear (or Napoleon's, at a pinch). The King of the Underworld in one performance enjoyed his crown so much he wanted to keep it. (He relented when he learned how much effort had been required to make it out of card and gold ribbon.)

If you need to buy, use children's toys or costumes. Brightly coloured plastic crowns can be picked up cheaply. The character of 'Global Capitalism' held up a child's globe as a way of simultaneously communicating the part and lampooning its aspirations.

Props

To mark your activity as a theatre performance, you need props. These explain the action and establish the character. Part of your preparation is to read the play carefully and note what's required. Make your own decisions about what will work best.

The basic requirements are to prepare the props in advance, find a way of storing and carrying them, and make sure the characters are holding them when the performance starts.

As with costumes, it is a positive virtue to make props yourself, although sometimes it is easier to buy them (a plastic sword rather than a couple of bits of wood). Never hire them: apart from the expense, hired costumes feel out of place – too expensive or commercialised. Often a little ingenuity will do the trick. It is amazing what can be made out of cardboard or card: a horse's head, crowns, pirate hats, cut-out flowers.

So: find a bottle for the doctor's medicine, an old book for a character to refer to, some hand-drawn notes or Monopoly money for payment. Buy ribbon to tack together for a knight's rosettes or suffragette ribbons. Use long blue cloth for a river or sea.

Making props can be a great way to prepare, e.g. as an activity for children, or to give a friend a role. We had a team of people cutting and colouring cardboard flames for battle scenes, or the fire in the *Brontë Saga*. Another year a friend scrunched up orange tissue paper as a different way to create the same effect.

In other plays the props are a major part of the excitement and audience participation. Rolled-up socks are ideal for pelting the evil characters, whether the story calls for stones, cannonballs or rotten fruit. This becomes especially popular with children and even teenagers!

The pitfalls: a few words of warning

Candles: use only with extreme caution. They create a wonderful atmosphere but your normal safety precautions may not work with so many people in a small space. We have had flowing medieval costumes smouldering where they have had contact with tea lights marking a path on the ground. Take great care with home-made lanterns. These are best made with a tea light inside a jam jar, blue-tacked to the bottom, with a string handle to hold or suspend from a stick.

Fight scenes: only use plastic swords, never wooden ones, so that nobody gets hurt. For *Under the Greenwood: Robin Hood May Play*, only use cardboard tubes for the staves, never garden canes as these pose a danger to people's eyes.

Storage: you will probably want to store props and costumes for use on another occasion. So remember you must have space for those you decide to keep.

Ask guests to return props and scripts after the play: make a clear announcement at the end of the play to ensure their safe and orderly return for re-use another time.

Photo opportunities: these are great fun but domestic theatre doesn't readily lend itself to video. A theatre performance has a cast photo and a curtain call, and some people have a talent to 'snap' as the performance proceeds. That's probably about right. As we say in Chapter 6, to enjoy domestic theatre as essentially a one-off, coming to life on a single occasion – don't video. (If you ever go semi-public and want to video, see our reports, also in Chapter 6.)

***The final clearing up*:** we found it helped to encourage people to join in with putting away props, scripts, costumes, and washing up. Sometimes it created the space for another party to emerge as the gathering flowed into singing, story-telling or games – as well as saving time and energy at the very end of the party. It is a natural part of the sharing.

Jackie's story

I wasn't sure what I was letting myself in for. It was nice having something to talk about before the play started, instead of standing there clutching your wine glass, desperately thinking of something to say. I was glad to have a non-speaking part, because it was the first time I'd been. (In retrospect, though, I wouldn't have minded having a speaking part.) Anyway, I was the horse in the Halloween play, wearing a friend's mum's costume. There was a kind of safety in the costume. I was quite hidden, but I remember it was very uncomfortable.

After that, in later plays, I didn't have any peripheral parts: it was straight in, with new-found confidence. It doesn't feel silly because everyone else is having the same experience. You can't forget your lines, because you've got the script. And if you come in too early, someone will tell you.

Hats and headgear make a real difference. What I remember about Fair Sabra was that ridiculous black wig. I saw it in a tacky shop for about three pounds. I had always wanted to have hair like that, when I was a child, cut across at the front. I remember quite a serious chap had heaving fits of convulsive laughter when he saw it. He couldn't stop.

I enjoyed playing the pirate Mary Read – she was so unconventional – and the Lady, in the *Candlemas Wooing Play*, when she turns away all the suitors.

Richard's story

I don't like plays where I have a minor role. I like to have a major speaking part. I like the fights too. I always like to win.

My first experience was when we read *Under Milk Wood* by Dylan Thomas. We sat here and read the parts. I found that intimidating – many of the speeches are long, and you feel you have to say them in a Welsh accent. In domestic theatre, the longest speeches are about ten lines and you can say them how you like. But it's still my ambition to put on *Under Milk Wood*!

When I was in high school we used to put on a revue for a couple of years. I helped write it. I remember, before television arrived, we used to go to the neighbours' for an evening's entertainment – this was in 1960s Australia. You'd each do your party piece, read poetry or sing a song.

Props can be quite humorous. They delineate a part. A top hat and a cape for a villain add something. People aren't used to seeing them nowadays and the audience is immediately amused.

4. Finding your own style

Varying the script and experimenting

After you've tried out a few scripts, you may want to adapt the stories and speeches to make them topical, or directly relevant to your circle of friends. Original mummers plays encompassed themes such as wars and political events that were topical then, and performances probably interspersed traditional content with references to local events and characters. So it makes sense to treat these domestic theatre scripts in the same way. There are many straightforward suggestions:

- Mention the venue: just add a simple couplet, such as we did in the Halloween play, when performed in a South London cooperative: 'Of the Bonnington café, I'm the ex-proprietor/Gone aloft to pastures quieter'.

- Incorporate a recent or upcoming event relevant to members of the audience. This could be something as simple as a recent birthday or forthcoming wedding.

- In another Halloween play, we mentioned the death of a child's pet: 'Enter the ghost of the unknown mouse/I died on Thursday in this very house'.

- Add topical references: update recent events, e.g. by varying a couplet to refer to the latest Prime Minister. Alternatively, you can take an ancient character, such as Paddy from Cork in a mummers play, and bring in modern Irish politics (as described below).

- Expand the theme: graveyard epitaphs (based on your own research or local history) can be added into the action of the Halloween play. We recently performed *Votes for Women* in memory of Martin's neighbour Helen Garner who had worked for the Fawcett Society. Martin wrote extra lines into the start of the play.

- Adapt songs: songs fit almost anywhere in domestic theatre. Choose a well-known tune that everyone can identify with (such as 'Ten Green Bottles' or 'My Bonnie Lies Over the Ocean'), and adapt the words to your theme or venue, or write them from scratch. (You will need to give out a song sheet so everyone can join in.)

It works better to write the new material a few days (or hours) before the performance, rather than adding it at the very last minute. That means you can brief the performers and add a note to the scripts in the right place. This is different from pure improvisation – people can and do improvise as they wish during the performance.

Adding topical references

We did the *Easter Pace Egg Play* just after the Birmingham Six had been released in March 1991, and expanded the lines of the Irish character, Paddy from Cork. He originally said:

> *I've a scythe on my back and I come to work hay*
> *I'm a hard-working lad for a pittance of pay.*
> *On St Patrick's Day I had a drop of porter*
> *To tell the truth it was more than I ought to.*

We added:

> *For I raised my glass to the Birmingham Six*
> *Whose lives were ruined by an establishment fix.*
> *And then I had to celebrate some more*
> *When I remembered the release of the Guildford Four.*
> *But the scales of Justice will not be even*
> *Till we've cleared the names of the Maguire Seven.*
> *No wonder we Irish think English judges stink*
> *When we come here just to work and take a drink.*

History records that the convictions of the Maguire Seven were quashed later in 1991.

Moving around your space

In theatre language, moving the action from place to place during the performance – from room to room, outside to the garden, or to different points in the neighbourhood – is called promenade or perambulation. It adds surprise and novelty: the players lead and the audience follow. In practice it is helpful to explain the route in advance and to give a few instructions at the right moment. Do consult with anyone who has difficulties in walking so you can have strategically placed chairs for them if necessary.

Moving from place to place creates a special rhythm for the play, as well as a kind of psychological scene-shifting. You could connect the setting to the action, for example moving from a feast in a dining room to a bedroom for a love scene, to an outdoor space for a contest, and in this way make the most of your home. Our friend Ann de Boursac put on *Sir Gawain and the Green Knight* in her flat, the interior of which was ready and waiting for the play: a round wooden table under a candelabra of candles for King Arthur and his court, a canopied bed for the temptation scenes, and at the front door, a domed portico which was perfect for the Green Chapel.

If you are doing the whole play on the move outdoors, enlist different people to prepare each location. When Beth put on *Demeter and Core* in perambulation around farm buildings at Lower Shaw Farm in Wiltshire, the man playing

Hades transformed the woodshed into the Underworld. The words 'Hades rules OK' are still visible, bearing witness on the woodshed wall. The cast and audience then ran across the cobbled farmyard following Hermes and Core to Demeter's temple (a sumptuously draped climbing frame) in the hay barn. As they arrived a shaft of afternoon sunlight spot-lit Demeter there, enhancing the other-worldly atmosphere.

You can't plan for shafts of sunlight, but when performing outdoors you can use the transition from day into darkness. By starting your play in daylight, you can time it so that you know which scenes will take you into dusk and plan how people will read their lines if night descends (bring a torch!).

Processions

Whereas perambulation is linked to the action of the play, a procession is usually added on at the beginning or end, to announce the play or to involve the community in its celebration. As well as creating a striking impact for onlookers, taking part in a procession in costume provides a powerful experience for the domestic theatre performers. Processions can be indoor or outdoor, daytime or night-time.

For example, a play can start with the arrival of the players in costume, singing as they approach the performance area: try this with the *Easter Pace Egg Play* (run through the song beforehand). Or – even simpler – some plays start with the players outside, knocking on the door to come in. This is the usual beginning for the *Xmas Mummers Play*. It makes a dramatic start to the performance, as the cast file in, introducing themselves and taking the audience straight into the action. And remember, just moving from scene to scene (see 'Moving around your space') can be developed into a procession with torchlight and music.

Alternatively, at the end, everyone involved – players and audience – can leave the venue and parade around the neighbourhood. This is especially effective with torches at night-time. Although there are community theatre companies that specialise in pyrotechnics and night-time extravaganzas, your own 'home made' procession with torches and banners can be just as effective for you, your friends and your neighbourhood.

When we did the *Jack O'Lantern and the Wild Horse* play one Halloween at a community café in Vauxhall, some artists made a giant puppet of Jack O'Lantern. After the play, everyone joined in a procession with drums, carrying candles and flaming torches, singing simple chants round the square, and ceremonially burning the puppet at a bonfire.

Adding music

As the following sections show, music can enhance domestic theatre in lots of ways: processions, individual performances, dance. At the simplest, if you have musical friends with instruments, they can contribute an introductory overture or background music for particular scenes.

At the other extreme, we once did a musical version of the *Xmas Mummers Play* with parts for piano, penny whistle, flute and violin, put together quickly by Luke Riley. There was a musical theme for each character, music for the fight scene and even music for the love scene while George and Fair Sabra performed a poignant dance.

If you have any unused musical instrument in your home, you could dust it down and make it available for the play. You may find that one of your guests knows how to play it and can make music with it to enhance the performance.

Songs do need to have a run-through before the play begins as many people lack confidence in singing in a group. Beth always says 'If you think you can't sing, please sing extra loudly. That way we may get interesting harmonies.' There is often an audible sigh of relief that no-one is going to be criticised for their singing and the result usually pleasantly surpasses expectations. Enthusiasm counts for more than perfection in domestic theatre.

Songs and dance

Some of the play texts have accompanying songs, such as 'We Wish You a Merry Christmas' for the *Xmas Mummers Play*. Don't assume that everyone knows the words: photocopy them, hand them out, and practise the tune with everyone just before the play begins. (Accompanying instruments take the experience to another level, but most songs work very well without.)

Songs that you enjoy can be added more or less where you like. We wrote our own words to the tune of the well-known folksong 'Turali Turali' to sing at the beginning of the *Mummers Play for Lammas: Death of the Summer Lord*.

The music section of your local library may have sources with song words, or you can consult the internet. We have used *Who Really Killed Cock Robin? Nursery rhymes and carols restored to their original meanings* by Norman Iles. An example that we liked is the pagan version of 'The Holly and the Ivy', which we sang in Country and Western style! But there are other traditions which you can draw on: our Karl Marx play ends with 'The Internationale'.

Alternatively you may prefer to write your own words to suit the theme of the play.

If you don't want to go as far as song, you can use simple chants, to enhance the action through a chorus, or to accompany dance. For example, accompanying a circle dance:

The spirit of the flowers has come to me in the form of a beautiful dancing green woman
The spirit of the flowers has come to me in the form of a beautiful dancing green woman
Her eyes fill me with peace, her dance fills me with love.

This chant was adapted from Lisa Thiel's song 'The Spirit of the Plants' (included with permission © 1984 Lisa Thiel).

A simple circle dance wonderfully enhances the experience of a play, and can be added to the action or incorporated at the end. The farandole has everyone in line with arms raised in an open ended circle. Dancers follow the leader, weaving around in step to the music. People in the circle face alternately left and right, and then travel round the circle taking alternate left then right hands.

Jackie: an impromptu song

Dame Spring was very symbolic for me. I remember having a singing lesson when I was about eight, and I was absent-mindedly singing in the corridor. The teacher called out my name, and to my horror made me sing the verses in front of the whole school (or it felt like that. Two or three classes anyway). The song was 'Spring has come and I am glad'. That was the song I sang as Dame Spring: I sang it loud and proud. It was healing that traumatic experience – getting one back on that horrible Mrs F. It wasn't in the script for the play. There was just a pause while someone was getting changed.

Games

Some games and activities are associated with traditional festivals:

- Halloween: apple-bobbing, dressing up in masks.
- Twelfth Night: King of the Bean. (Bake a cake with a bean in it. Whoever gets the bean is king for the night and can give orders to everyone.)
- Easter: Easter bonnet parade, egg decorating and rolling, hunt the egg.
- May: hobby horse processions and races.
- Midsummer: have a party outside by the light of a bonfire.
- Lammas races around the beginning of August (your school sports day: men, women, children, three-legged, egg and spoon).

Other traditional games can be fitted in where you like: pass the parcel, blind man's buff, hunt the thimble, skipping. More activities associated with particular seasons are listed in Chapter 7.

Cabaret slots

You can create a slot in most domestic theatre plays for individuals to add a performance of their own as long as it is related to the theme of the play. For example, for Halloween people can step forward with ghost stories, spooky poems and songs, or simply tell the company about someone close who has died. For Valentines celebrations, people can recite love poems.

A cabaret addition can reveal unsuspected talents and give budding musicians a place to develop their repertoire and confidence. In fact, these additions are usually an unexpected joy – such as a learner playing a tune on the flute – performed amongst friends.

If any of your friends have particular interest and expertise in dance, you can incorporate this in the performance: ask them to bring a music recording and do a dance as part of their performance. A friend who was learning Arabic dance was very pleased to demonstrate it in the part of Fair Sabra.

Children in performances

Children are great assets to domestic theatre: boundlessly enthusiastic, inventive and ready to enter imaginative worlds. But domestic theatre is not children's theatre, and their input is best actively managed.

The key to successfully involving children in performance is your flexibility, but also remember that there can be rivalry about parts. Here a firm negotiating stance is sometimes required: justify your decision as director in terms a child can accept, e.g. the star is the person in whose house the play is being performed. Explain that the other parts are important and that there will be times in the future where they too will have more exciting roles.

Younger children's attention span is shorter than the length of the play, so that they may talk, cry or walk around. We have found that toddlers can become very distressed if they see their parents in costume. George's wooing scene with Fair Sabra was once conducted with his real-life daughter clinging to his legs throughout, saying, 'Daddy, Daddy, don't dance, don't kiss the lady.' We have therefore found it's best to let young children accompany their parent on stage in a more structured way, holding hands or perhaps adding a few lines to explain their presence.

Over seven years old, children's enthusiasms can easily get out of hand, so that their participation is better harnessed, as described below. Lastly, over 14 years old, they tend to become refuseniks in terms of taking part, but may accept a role as photographer, or help with hospitality.

The following are some tips for including children:

- Create a role in advance. Choose a story they identify with, or one of their favourites. Add a non-speaking part for a child to accompany an adult – such as a servant, additional knight or friend.
- Use audience participation, and explain what is required and how important it is.
- Add sound effects: for example, coconut shells can be banged together as horse's hooves.
- Practice their words in advance – especially for young children with bigger parts. They will be used to this in any school productions they have done

and often enjoy learning their lines (whereas domestic theatre works better for adults if they don't have time to study their lines).

- When the children are performing, put adults on stage at the same time: it works better if there is someone who can guide them or explain any word they are not familiar with.

- Remember you can cast children in adult parts. Often this offers an additional dimension – but all the points about careful management apply with even more force.

- Rehearse. A friendly adult – no reason why it has to be a parent – can go over their parts with the children before the play starts. This keeps them occupied and manages potential over-excitement.

- Harness their spontaneity. Children learn rhymes, routines and songs at school or in their other activities, and their ready-made skills and ideas can be slotted into a production, allowing them to show off dance, mime or tricks.

In one domestic theatre event, three young brothers arrived for a performance of *Demeter and Core*. They asked to be the three-headed dog Cerberus at the gates of the Underworld, so we suggested they make up a rhyme to introduce themselves. When the action moved to the Underworld, the brothers chorused this with great aplomb, crouched menacingly under their mum's fur coat:

> *We are the three-headed dog Cerberus*
> *And you won't get further than us.*

More ways to involve children

Children are usually good at making props, such as treasure chests, mobile phones or hats. They also love to give out programmes and are very good at making sure everyone has got one.

A special word is needed about involving children as writers. Most domestic theatre is a sure-fire winner, but – except for the children themselves and their fond parents – a play written by children is not. We have had better results where we slot children's ideas into an adult framework. Plays devised by young children themselves are fun for the performers, but don't often follow the parameters of a domestic theatre performance. However, good ways to involve their ideas are:

- They can contribute to storyboard workshops – suggesting characters and contributing to story-lines.

- Role play – they can act out scenes which adults can adapt and write up later.

- They can offer prompts – what would a particular character say or do in a given situation? If they know the character, children often produce plausible suggestions. Even those who only knew Enid Blyton in passing came up with highly plausible suggestions for what George (of the Famous Five) would say.

We are never sure how much of the play children are taking in, but as shown by Dora's and Ellie's accounts (below), it can prove a magical experience in ways adults would not guess.

Dora's story, aged 10

It's fun. You don't have to be brilliant at acting or anything like that – you don't have to feel pressured into it. My first play was *Under the Greenwood: Robin Hood May Play*. I was one of the dogs. Me and Ellie were the dogs together: we went for Robin Hood's ankles and bit him – we pretended – and made a lot of noise. I enjoyed the bit after the play. We were singing 'Robin Hood' and there were races with two teams.

I did a nativity play at school: I was a silver bell and a snowflake. You don't read from lines in normal plays: I like learning the lines, personally, but having the lines written out is quite good if you can't remember them.

I like having plays outside in the garden and having a fire. In one play we did a rap:

I am the great goddess Inanna
And I like eating bananas
I have them on muesli and also on my sweet
And I also love to have them for my special treat.

I loved being the dragon with my friend Josie. We had this really nice silk and Josie put it on her shoulders and it came down to below her feet, and I put one on too. Josie said the lines. I got on her shoulders and we had the claws and walked around. Then we died. The worst thing was when we had to get up again.

I like making props like the mobile phone and the cigar in the pantomime. We made the cigar really huge: we had some brown paper and stuck some glitter on, then Sue (Josie's mum) said 'I know, we can put talcum powder in it', so we did, and smoke came out.

Ellie: growing up with domestic theatre

My favourite part of the plays was always the props and costumes, finding them, making them and then dressing up in them. I also very much enjoyed making the scripts with my dad when he used to have plays at his house. We would go to the photocopying shop and then cut them into size and put them into packs. I would then highlight everyone's lines for them. I think this appealed to my organised side!

My favourite memory of all is writing my own play. My friend Dora and I wrote a play together about two little mice (I think). It was a Halloween play and we had brilliant props (lots of multi-coloured Halloween sweets) to make potions with. I'm not sure whether this was my favourite because I loved writing and performing the play or because I got to eat lots of sweets which I was never allowed to do. But I was young!

Nowadays people come and say domestic theatre is a really good idea for a party and gets everyone talking and mixing. Although you are performing there really is no pressure as everyone is in the same boat and everyone has scripts to read from. I appreciate it was a great activity to do with a child and really helped me be creative, and hopefully when I have children my dad will help them write and perform a little play with their friends.

5. Devising your own play for domestic theatre

Choose a story that suits you

You may already have a favourite story, or be able to think back to one that caught your imagination in the past. If so, it's a good idea to ask yourself what it is about this story that appeals to you. Often it will have a theme that is significant in your life: perhaps a quest, or a love story, or a narrative that resonates with your cultural identity. Sometimes you will want to write for, or about, someone you know well and care for, such as your child, parent, lover or friend. This is a great idea and a true gift to that person.

Getting in touch with these motives will encourage you, and help channel your – and others' – confidence and energy. This isn't to say that you must psychoanalyse the stories: just give yourself room to enjoy them and to feel passionate about the writing and what you are trying to say.

Here are some examples of themes and stories which inspired our plays:

- *The Little Girl with the Kind Heart* (a Baba Yaga story): children's difficulties with step parents.
- *Great Expectations*: parents who are absent from their children.
- The Brontës: rivalry between sisters, the autocratic father, and the idealised brother.
- *Sir Gawain and the Green Knight*: a quest, and the dangers of seduction.
- *Alice's Adventures in Wonderland*: leaving childhood and entering adolescence.
- Famous Five: challenging gender stereotypes.

In many cases, however, the 'shadow side' of the story will not necessarily be the most important. The story can grow simply from an obvious interest – the character of the local area, local history or a current enthusiasm. Similarly, you may want to give your own 'take' on an eternal theme – for example, war and peace, heroic journeys or separated lovers.

Sometimes the season itself offers a prompt: *Sir Gawain and the Green Knight* begins at Christmas, *Five Break the Spell* is good for the summer holidays, and of course the plays for the festivals are all timed for a specific season of the year. (There is more about this in Chapter 7.) There are other occasions too: in the year 2000 we wrote a play for the end of the 20th century, exploring how Picasso became its greatest artist.

Some stories offer a framework to have fun with your favourite story-lines, characters and events. Pantomimes are an obvious example, where you can bring in satire, character vignettes, bawdy references, and song (not to mention certain obvious kinds of audience participation). We developed a female version of a Christmas mummers play because we got fed up with the constraints of the largely male traditional cast list.

We like to encourage people to be bold and experimental in creating their own domestic theatre plays. We even once wrote a musical about our favourite pop group based on the lyrics of their early songs. Performers were given the choice of either singing or speaking their lines. This was one of our most popular shows and at one performance, not only did everyone sing their lines, but they sang them in the accent of our heroes' native city. Sadly, for copyright reasons, we feel unable to include the text in our A to Z of plays.

Books and plays you could adapt

If you choose a book to adapt, it is helpful if the stories are well known (usually through film adaptations or the school curriculum). Here are some we have not tried yet.

- *Macbeth, Twelfth Night, A Midsummer Night's Dream, Romeo and Juliet* – William Shakespeare
- *A Christmas Carol* – Charles Dickens
- *Pride and Prejudice* – Jane Austen
- *The Canterbury Tales* – Geoffrey Chaucer
- *The Secret Garden* – Frances Hodgson Burnett
- *Tess of the D'Urbervilles, The Mayor of Casterbridge* – Thomas Hardy
- *Cold Comfort Farm* – Stella Gibbons
- *Swallows and Amazons* – Arthur Ransome
- *The Forsyte Saga* – John Galsworthy
- *The Idiot* – Fyodor Dostoevsky

(NB: Famous stories we have adapted are *Hamlet* by Shakespeare and *Great Expectations* by Dickens, *War and Peace* by Tolstoy and the Brontë novels *Jane Eyre* and *Wuthering Heights*. For summaries and scripts, see section 8.)

Make the most of available dramatic forms

Mummers plays have a set formula which you can copy, add to or update. Some other forms suit domestic theatre because they offer a series of tableaux, rather than a dramatic narrative. A play like Samuel Daniel's 17th century masque called *The Vision of the Twelve Goddesses* provides a simple framework for friends to choose their own goddess, and even bring their own costume and write their own lines. Pantomime is expected to include breaks for songs.

These different forms allow you to develop a play to suit the preferences and abilities of your audience. If people like histrionics and hamming it up, a Victorian melodrama may provide a suitable structure. If people like dancing, the courts of kings and queens offer a good setting.

You can also choose your story to fit the number of parts you want. We expected to have a lot of women wanting parts in our first performance of *The Odyssey*, called *Odysseus in Transit*, so we selected the episodes where Odysseus visits females, e.g. Circe, rather than using the famous Cyclops story.

Have fun with the characters

Choose the number of characters to suit your event: most plays can have quite a lot of parts, which means they will include small parts for beginners. You probably will have between 10 and 20 parts.

Remember that domestic theatre benefits from a brisk pace, so your main aim should be to get your characters on and off promptly, whilst making it obvious who they are and what they contribute to the plot.

You can write with particular friends in mind: parts they will enjoy, or that suit them well. Otherwise you want characters to be quite vivid, showcasing one quality: sexiness, mystery, grandeur, etc. This is easier for both performers and audience to grasp.

Don't hesitate to use comic devices, e.g. where one character re-appears, each time with mounting incongruity: in our Brontë play the audience greatly enjoyed the pleading appearances of the curate offering Charlotte marriage every time there was a lull in the action. (Reader, she did marry him in the end.)

Some characters will have the role of summarising the plot or explaining its meaning. Ways to achieve this include prologues, narrators and epilogues to introduce, explain or close the action. In the same way, don't be afraid to use personification, e.g. 'Spirit of the 20th century', 'Global Capitalism', or 'Money'. These are age-old theatrical devices which were made to do a job – i.e. to tell the audience succinctly what is happening and what they need to know.

A similar device is a chorus: this has the added advantage of two or three characters speaking their lines in unison. Not only does this create a powerful effect, but it can be useful to help those who are less confident about speaking their lines, or to include children.

A final tip is to create a scene at the end where everything is resolved and all the characters come back to make a final comment – just like in Shakespeare's comedies or in pantomime, where the main characters all get married at the close.

Practical tips for writing whole plays

Writing a play sounds like a mammoth enterprise, but remember:

- You don't want a performance that lasts too long – 20 minutes is fine for a short traditional play or sketch. Longer than 45 minutes risks losing the audience's attention. The average word-count for our plays is about 3,000 words.
- You don't have to do it all by yourself – ask your friends. You will be surprised by their talent and dedication.
- You are deliberately aiming at something lively and accessible and unpolished – not an intricate masterwork.

We have found some rules of thumb to help us:

- **Time required for writing:** we allow one evening for planning, and three 'script evenings' (preferably spread over a few weeks) for putting together what has been written in between. We have found that is sufficient to break the back of the writing. On top, allow time for typing up and for any final editing you want to do.
- **Boil the story down to its essentials.** This is the most important piece of advice. It is very easy to let your enthusiasm for your story lead to over-elaboration. Avoid going down that route – it leads to a longer play with more to do, and probably more difficult for the audience to follow.
- List six things that happen – any more than that and it is too complicated.
- Decide your storyboard first: a list of characters, their main role or motivation, and the key events in the play. (This is the first evening of planning.)
- Produce a 'treatment': this is the summary of scenes and characters, where you can list who comes on, summarise the essence of what they have to say, and be clear when they leave the stage. You may find it helpful to think in terms of 'acts', as in conventional drama.
- Make sure characters are introduced. If necessary they can do this themselves – 'In comes I ...' – or otherwise another character has to talk about them, so the audience can work out their identity.
- Don't make the speeches too long. Four lines are fine for most speeches: rarely should you need as many as ten lines.
- Write a draft: if you have a treatment based on your original storyboard, you should be able to write short speeches for each character. Then in one of your writing evenings you can read through the speeches, adjust the actions, check there is no duplication, and go through speech by speech until you are done.
- You may prefer to divide up the scenes between writers, and go away

and come together later – or else exchange chunks of text by email, before getting together for a script evening.

- Check the stage directions. It is surprisingly easy to forget who is on stage at a given time. The clarity of your stage directions is essential to make the play work for people who have only just seen the script.

Co-writing

Beth's viewpoint

Sometimes Martin writes most of the play and sometimes I do. Quite often I have started the play and Martin makes some additions to the structure. Later on I am only dimly aware of the exact point where the baton was passed.

We may work on a play concurrently. With *War and Peace* I wrote some lines and Martin gave them to different characters! He did 'A Boy's Story' version of it for his summer garden party. Then I added more lines for Madame Tolstoy as I was so impressed that she copied out the whole of the novel of War and Peace seven times by hand. I thought she probably had her favourite bits and scenes she did not care for at all. I put on *War and Peace: Madame Tolstoy's Version* in the autumn and winter. I wouldn't claim that my version is better, in fact it probably added complications fitting in new lines, but we include the expanded version in our A to Z of plays.

I think of Martin as sometimes more experimental than me. For example he wrote *Sir Gawain and the Green Knight* shifting between rhyming couplets and alliterative verse. I could never have done that. Having a co-writer is like painting the walls of a room with someone else. You turn round and they have made so much progress while you weren't looking! Martin also slips in impossible stage directions like 'Audience release doves' at the end of *It's Picasso!* So we asked the audience to imagine it. Actually, we saw in the photographs afterwards that a couple of people had (unnoticed by us) drawn doves on the back of the programmes and were waving them at the end of the play. I really like the audience taking the initiative.

I like to give myself lots of time to work on creating a play and am not as good as Martin is at finishing off in a rush. Sometimes I start a play and reach a block, or else run out of steam about two thirds of the way through. I wrote the first part of *Votes for Women* and then Martin finished it off the day before his summer party. When I got to the party, the scripts were still being collated so I didn't know that he had inserted the Derby Day race where Emily Wilding Davison gets mown down by the King's horse. I was upset when this scene appeared in the play because I had not known to bring the relevant props of horse's heads on sticks. But in the event we introduced it as a 'dumb show' and it worked fine for the audience to imagine the horses and the terrible climax. In subsequent performances (now using the horse-head props), this always proves a popular scene.

I think that having a co-writer makes me much more ambitious than if I was just writing it myself. I know that if I get stuck, then Martin will finish it off. I would never have attempted *The Odyssey* on my own.

Martin's viewpoint

I used to think that creativity was inherent and individual. Now I know that someone else's views are an essential stimulus. Beth and I don't have just one pattern as co-writers, but I always know she will see the big picture and get to the heart of a story's psychological truth. 'It's all about failed parents!' she exclaimed, on re-reading *Great Expectations* (like Dickens's own father, she might have added). Despite Pip, Estella, Magwitch, the Pockets and a host of children and parents, I had never noticed this theme. Once we have agreed on what our play should be about, I like to knit together the entrances and exits, and give each character enough lines to help the overall balance.

Sometimes one of us writes 99% of a play, in terms of lines generated, and sometimes it's the other way round. But they are all shared enterprises. I always write as though Beth is in the room, even if I am sitting alone with a notebook and a glass of wine. And because I like to leave most things till the deadline, it is a great comfort to know that between us we will complete the play, no matter what.

For me, the key part of co-writing is that the other person is never wrong, and my ideas – no matter how dearly held – are never better than Beth's. We just work things out, confident we will have a finished play and enjoy the result.

Fitting the play to the party-goers

When Beth organised her first pantomime, she was so scared of not pulling it off that she decided to ask everyone to tell her what part they had always dreamed of playing in a pantomime. That way participants would either have a main part, or else play the role they had always wanted. She managed to incorporate everyone into *Hansel and Gretel*, except for one man, who had insisted he wanted to be a teapot. In the end he was Hansel and Gretel's father, and therefore had a main part. But afterwards he commented that he really would have preferred to be a teapot. The moral is: if that's what someone wants, write a part for a teapot into your pantomime.

Subsequently, for an ecological version of *Sleeping Beauty*, entitled 'Sleeping Bratty', Beth did incorporate everyone's preferred roles, using twelve good fairies – Feminist Fairy, Cat Burglar Fairy, Genie Fairy, etc. Each fairy composed their own four lines about what they would wish the new baby.

Doing the research

It is not always necessary to do background reading, but it helps to anchor you in the original facts or story – and therefore to provide a firmer foundation for your imagination. It can also add to your enjoyment if you think of it as a small research project: not only do you re-read famous texts, but you have the scope to read more generously around the subject, and explore its byways, using biography, anecdote, interpretation, and conjecture. This provides rich material for your story and helps communicate your message to the audience. Researching *Ravers and Stunners*, we discovered from the biographies that Ned Burne-Jones used to bombard William Morris and their other friends with apples from the apple loft at the Red House in Kent. This proved a popular piece of audience participation in the play (with rolled up socks replacing apples). It is possible to visit the Red House and imagine the Pre-Raphaelite larks.

One enjoyable way of researching is to read an author's entire oeuvre, and then produce a composite story for your play. This is what we did for *Five Break the Spell* from Enid Blyton stories and it could also work for Biggles (the flying hero from W. E. Johns' books for boys). If you have less time and want to adapt a novel, listening to an abridged audio book is a useful tip.

Using rhyming couplets

We always use rhyming couplets because writing realistic speech is much harder, both to write and to speak. Performers feel more nervous about how to say it – it feels more like 'acting'.

You may think that you can't write poetry, but elegant and accomplished verse is the last thing that is required for domestic theatre. Taking it too seriously is the very thing that will get in the way of your natural inventiveness and your sense of fun with words. Be instinctive and use your natural powers of word association. We have found that most of our friends can knock together a few lines with gusto and raw energy, with a little encouragement and when the occasion requires it. Here are some tips:

- Go for a strong bouncy rhythm.
- A basic rhyming couplet is fine for most plays – sometimes original source material will use other verse forms which you can adapt or copy (for example, alliterative verse in *Sir Gawain and the Green Knight*).
- Don't be afraid of obvious rhymes – their very predictability is an asset – but try to avoid re-using the same ones.
- Avoid rhymes that don't fit the sense, where a word appears only because of its sound, without any relevance to the action or what the speaker is saying.
- If you can't think of a rhyme for a particular word, think of a different way of saying what you want, using a different word.

- Don't get stuck: give yourself a time-limit to find a rhyme, before switching to a new word or new angle of approach. For example, allow ten seconds as your routine to find a rhyme, with another ten seconds to search your mind if it doesn't come straight away. That way you never spend more than half a minute getting a rhyming couplet (and habit will soon reduce the time).

- Work fast and don't worry too much. The result will be entertaining and will get the message over. If you have the leisure, you can go back and tinker a bit to make improvements.

- Rhyming dictionaries are quite slow to use and few houses have them on their bookshelves, so don't use them (apart perhaps from finding rhymes for one or two important words). Stick to your own knowledge and invention.

- Sometimes you can deviate from rhyme for dramatic effect – where the action calls for a particularly important speech, or where a particular character fits with another type of verse.

Finding a rhyme

Suppose you want to find a rhyme for *murder*. One way is to run through the alphabet in your mind, finding *girder* and *purdah*. Does any rhyming word link in with your story? Can you make it amusing? If nothing fits – and on the face of it, it seems unlikely anything will – try *killing*. This has many more options (willing, billing, filling, etc). Or stick with murder if it's essential but use it in the middle of the line, and try again for a fitting end-rhyme. Don't be afraid to think laterally: e.g. death, coffin, dispatch, shoot, poison, gallows, manslaughter.

Audience participation

Audience participation is one of the most enjoyable parts of a domestic theatre production. It celebrates the communal – it is not about making people do things they don't want to, or standing out in front of everybody else. Let your imagination loose. Ideas will come that will suggest how to act out the most unlikely stage directions.

How do you get the audience to enact the battle of Guernica as we did in our play *It's Picasso!*? Our solution did require some preparation: we copied out sections of Picasso's painting of 'Guernica' onto large pieces of paper for audience members to wave at the given moment. Meanwhile, others imitated the sounds of bombs and sirens.

Writing *Five Break the Spell* we were struck by how often tunnels appear in Enid Blyton's adventures. We included some scenes at either end of a tunnel, which the audience created by lining up with joined hands to make an arch with a partner. The children enjoyed running in and out and it involved nearly the entire audience in the play.

One of our most frequent uses of audience participation is to ask the audience to make the sound effects – this is much better than using recorded sounds. Whether it is the builders' noise in *Kapital Marx: Karl Marx in Maitland Park*, or moorland storms in the *Brontë Saga*, enough people always join in to make it work.

Helping out your student friends

You don't always have to write your own play – sometimes there is one that is ready-made, where you take an existing script and turn the occasion into domestic theatre. If a friend is studying a play for a course, help them to use domestic theatre to bring it to life even if the text may be highly traditional and old-fashioned. Apply the principles of organising a party, providing hospitality, casting and costumes to what would otherwise be a dry read-through: it's a lot more fun. Friends completely unfamiliar with, say, Alan Bennett or Caryl Churchill will bring their own personalities to the cast, providing a memorable evening and some unexpected interpretations.

One friend was pursuing a course in Drama and Irish Studies, so we adapted the long 18th century poem *The Midnight Court* by Brian Merriman into a play, using the experience gained in domestic theatre.

And it doesn't have to be a full-length play: share the reading of a long poem and make a sound recording. Your friend can play it while doing household chores. It's more fun than simply listening to your own voice. Children will enjoy joining in too.

Penny's story of writing the panto

One of the greatest pleasures of this Yuletide holiday season just past has been taking part in writing and performing a pantomime – 'domestic-theatre-style'. So what was in it for me? The first was the socialising. The writing process was collective. The idea of doing a panto came from Gill and Tosh, after my birthday production of *Demeter and Core*. I soon realised this would mean writing a script, and after various conversations with Beth and Martin, I rather liked the idea. I organised a group visit to a pantomime put on by our local church – we could do better than that!

Over a meal we roughed out a few characters and storylines, and assigned a scene each to the various authors. During the next few weeks it came together, with Beth cheering from the sidelines and reminding me of the importance of deadlines. Script conferences all involved eating meals in company – civilised adult food, civilised adult company. The final details of plot and character were agreed on Tuesday evening, I typed up the final version of the text on Wednesday, my friend Gill photocopied it on Thursday, and the performance took place at Gill and Tosh's house on Saturday evening. It was a great success! Once again many magical things happened, and Gill's mother said it was the best birthday she has ever had. (A reference to her, inserted into the text at the last moment, caused her particular delight. She rang Gill three times in the next few days to tell her so!)

As a single parent and self-employed, I was living a socially isolated life and particularly missed having people other than children to talk to over meals. I really enjoyed doing something in a group that was neither work nor politics, but play. I enjoyed the liveliness of it all – all the possible storylines and bits of business that had to be woven together.

The second aspect that I really enjoyed was the sense of power in writing a play. You can decide not just on characters and storylines but outcomes. You can have the Queen Mother sack the corrupt timeservers, retired generals and such from the NHS Trust Board and turn it into a people's collective. You can make wicked, wide-boy builders repent, and have a cat implementing an equal opportunities policy. You can have a love triangle of harmony, not rivalry. And it is all possible because it's a pantomime and only for fun. Doing it for fun frees the imagination. By imagining new possibilities, however unlikely, and presenting them, in pantomime form, we empower ourselves and make a very small move towards making the world more how we would like it to be.

A third and more personal joy for me has been reclaiming my capacity to write, and to write rhyming couplets. And to be frivolous!

6. Going semi-public

Choose your event carefully

After you have put on plays in your home, at the homes of friends and even of friends of friends, you may wish to venture into a more public arena. We have found that people respond enthusiastically to domestic theatre, so that they often suggest it for more formally organised events and in other settings.

Whereas we believe domestic theatre is suitable for anyone's home, we have found that 'going public' is better for those who are more adventurous. It requires someone who will be the focal point on the day, and who is willing to stand up and lead.

Even then, it is better to think of it as 'going semi-public'. In public venues, not everyone has come with the expectation of a shared theatrical event, let alone with the implicit acceptance of being willing to take part or be an audience member. Furthermore, the range of settings is very varied. So it requires a bit more energy and purpose to carry it off.

However, domestic theatre works brilliantly as an addition to a gathering where there is a shared purpose and a core group willing to take part, such as festivals and organisations like Growing Old Disgracefully. It also contributes to memorable evenings in cafés or restaurants, as an extension of feasting, or even to community protests.

For example, in 1997 a friend of ours adapted *Sir Gawain and the Green Knight* for the Newbury bypass road protesters with all sorts of references to bailiffs, cherry-pickers, etc. We heard that it received a warm reception when it was performed at the road protest camp itself.

Practical arrangements

The most important practical consideration is the space in which the play will be performed. If possible, visit the venue in advance to see the building and performance area yourself. At all costs refuse a stage or traditional seating in rows.

The best arrangement is to have a circle of chairs. This way it will be easier to get volunteers for the play and everybody there will feel part of the action whether they have a speaking part or not. A raised stage and rows of chairs cut performers off from listeners. Also avoid rooms with high ceilings, since people's voices will not carry so well. Nevertheless, several performances have taken place outdoors. Here the obvious practical advice is to make sure the audience will be as close to the players as possible – after all, they are an essential part of it! That way they will at least be able to hear.

Otherwise there is a straightforward checklist:

- Discuss terms. On principle, we don't charge for putting on domestic theatre plays but if a restaurant invites you, you may be able to get free meals for some friends as well as yourself. With clubs and festivals, ask for free entry for several friends as well so that you have a support crew.
- Check what time the play is scheduled to go on.
- Check if the organisers are going to decorate the performance area or otherwise create a congenial atmosphere for you.
- Make arrangements for someone to bring the scripts and props, and collect them up again afterwards.
- On the day, get there early.

Examples from experience

Over the years Beth has put on domestic theatre plays in a range of venues. She describes her experiences below. Judge for yourself if any of them are suitable for you and your friends.

Community café

The Bonnington Square Community Cafe in Vauxhall has put on several domestic theatre events over the years, mainly through the connection with my sister, Kath, a stained glass artist who used to live in the square. Kath arranged with her talented and artistic neighbours to put on plays and decorate the stage area, sometimes as part of their local festival. As people know each other and are co-operatively-minded, it is easy to find people to take part in the plays, and add flourishes of their own, even cabaret or a procession.

Similar community cafés with strong local roots would provide an excellent venue for domestic theatre performances – ideal, because of their cheap and nourishing food.

Weekend activity centres

There are quite a few weekend activity centres around the country. The one I know best is Lower Shaw Farm near Swindon, Wiltshire, which organises low-cost weekend events and week-long events in the school summer holidays. This was the first place that I ventured to do domestic theatre outside the home. Luckily the residents already had a dressing-up box of costumes and were keen to join in themselves. They gave me a free hand to experiment and as a result I learnt a lot from doing plays there. I remember *Under the Greenwood: Robin Hood May Play* on the lawn (where my mother played one of Friar Tuck's dogs) and a Women's Weekend where everyone dressed up as goddesses for Samuel Daniel's *The Vision of the Twelve Goddesses*. I also had the advantage that I had been to Lower Shaw Farm previously for many other events so I knew many of the visitors there. My familiarity and the enthusiasm of the Lower Shaw residents were key factors in the success of domestic theatre plays there.

Restaurant

One time I was invited to put on the *Easter Pace Egg Play* in a small French restaurant,'Le Bon Temps Rouler' in South London. I managed to negotiate some favourable terms. I would be getting six free meals for friends who were to join in the play and also the two waiters would take part. This meant that two thirds of the casting was accounted for and I would only need to persuade four diners to join in the play. The proprietress made a poster to advertise the play and concocted magnificent Easter bonnets out of paper plates, yoghurt pots and tissue paper for all the diners.

I was nervous about finding the rest of the cast from the unsuspecting diners. I spotted one man who looked perfect for St George, so I went to chat with him and his wife. I first persuaded his wife to have a small part as a village maiden, and that led to him agreeing to have a go as St George. I then looked around for a doctor. There happened to be a table of medical students from Kings College celebrating someone's birthday. One of the students looked ideal for the part. Having got him to agree to be the doctor, he then encouraged the 'birthday girl' to be the second of the village maidens. And so the play went on: the waiters had made their own costumes and were the stars. The regular customers were amazed to see them dressed up, everyone played their part and all the diners joined in the song. Sadly, the proprietress retired shortly afterwards, otherwise we might have gone there again.

Expeditions

We also did the *Easter Pace Egg Play* in the middle of the Kentish countryside at the Norman church at Dode. Six of us took a rucksack of costumes, scripts and props on the train to the nearest station at Stone Street and then walked along paths through fields to the church. There we met up with about fifty others who had gone there by car.

Luckily it was a sunny day and we did the play just outside the church. When you are asking for volunteers for the play from a big crowd, you have to become a bit of a 'showman'. It's like, 'Roll up, roll up, who wants to be the Prince of Paradise today?' It did not matter that there were many more people than parts available because the play was followed by other activities. People joined in a conga led by a woman with a large dragon mask as we snaked around the church. Then we had egg-rolling in which we hurled decorated hard-boiled eggs down the steep slope behind the church and ran down after them. People had brought food to share: the feast was laid out in the church, lit by flaming torches with straw on the stone flags as in Norman times. At the end of the day our sturdy band gathered the props and costumes back into the rucksack and set off back across the fields to the railway station. It was unforgettable.

Festivals

Domestic theatre works best where it is the main focus of a gathering just as it is when you put on a party in your home. It can be quite a challenge to do it at a festival where there are lots of different workshops, talks etc. going on.

Festival organisers have a different agenda from you. They may well want you to put on a play, but they may not come up with the support they promise. One 'Day of the Dead' festival I took part in gave me lots of problems. I had agreed to put on the Graveyard scene from *Jack O'Lantern and the Wild Horse*. There were so many activities going on at once that it was difficult to gather people together to cast the play. The organiser had promised that the stewards could take part, but the stewards told me that they had been specifically instructed that they couldn't. Then the organiser suddenly decided to bring forward the time of the performance without informing me. I wanted to do the play in the friendly church hall with a captive audience of market stalls but the organiser insisted that the play be performed in the church in front of the altar (which was very intimidating) because that was 'where the media were'. I did manage to cast all the parts and everyone was delightful in the play but it made me wary of festivals.

Institutions

Recently an academic suggested that I organise a performance of *Kapital Marx: Karl Marx in Maitland Park* in the politics department of a university. The day before, the academic dropped out and in fact nobody came to the play from the politics department, even though it was right there under a portrait of Karl Marx in their foyer. Luckily, academics and students came from other departments and I brought friends with me, making ten of us altogether. When you have a lot fewer people than parts, it is essential to present this in a positive light as the opportunity for individuals to play multiple roles.

Certainly the play was performed with great gusto despite everyone (except Karl Marx) having to keep switching parts. However, it left me wondering whether the fun of domestic theatre fits in with the university ethos.

Libraries and community centres

Recently, I have been invited to put on our plays in local libraries. The most successful was under the auspices of the Friends of the library concerned. This meant that they already had a committed group who were used to attending the monthly event, would take care of advertising the play and would be welcoming to whoever turned up to join in.

The play was the same one about Karl Marx. There was an interesting mix of professional actresses (who conveyed clearly the meaning of every line) and non-professionals who added freshness and individuality. A local Tory councillor, who unexpectedly volunteered to be Global Capitalism, played it with such panache and conviction that this was reported in the local paper.

A community centre may also have a committed group who organise and attend events with local relevance. There is something extra special when you re-enact historical events on the very spot where they took place and we found this when, together with the residents, we put on a performance of *The Building of the St Pancras Almshouses, 1850–1863* in their own communal hall.

Avoid video

Someone you know will probably have a camcorder. However, we have found that most people want to join in and share the experience, rather than record it. But if there is someone whose favourite position is behind a camera, there is no harm in letting them film for their own use, so long as it is unobtrusive and everyone agrees. Playing it back may add to a sociable evening later.

Nonetheless, it cannot be denied that people tend to be more self conscious in front of a camera, and find it harder to relax. And it may also be that people are happy to put on a silly costume at a social event, but don't want their work colleagues to see it on screen later. So on balance, we feel that video is less desirable than still photography.

Even so, amongst your friends you may have a film-maker who can arrange access to decent equipment and who can edit footage into a lively film. They need to be good at capturing the spontaneity and excitement of the event. You don't want to end up repeating scenes to please the cameraman. If you do video, we recommend you cover the whole process, from guests arriving, to scenes at the party, to giving out parts, and then the play and the departures at the end. This gives a much better feel of the event.

You also need to ask, who is the wider audience for whom the film is being made? If it is people connected to the film-maker and nothing to do with you, there is little point in agreeing. And if you are going to invite friends round to view it, would you not be better putting on another play?

I have made a film as part of a community festival, where the film-maker covered several events as well as the domestic theatre performance in the community centre. It was played back some months later as the finale of the festival. But this required a package of external funding and lots of grass-roots organisation.

7. The perennial themes

This chapter contains more information to help you make a choice of play, and plan your domestic theatre event. The first section, on festivals, suggests domestic theatre plays and other activities suitable for each season, whilst the next section gives some background on the tradition of 'mumming', or mummers plays, which inspires the performance style. The final sections give some of our experience in writing and performing plays based on history, and on favourite stories from literature.

Festivals and the seasons

The Festival calendar

Winter begins

Halloween 31 October
Winter Solstice 21/22 December
Christmas Eve 24 December
Christmas Day   25 December
New Year's Eve 31 December
New Year's Day 1 January
Twelfth Night 5 January

Spring begins

Candlemas Eve 1 February
Valentines Day 14 February
Spring Equinox 20/21 March
Easter (variable)

Summer begins

May Eve 30 April
May Day 1 May
Summer Solstice 22 June
Midsummer's Eve 23 June
Midsummer's Day 24 June

Autumn begins

Lammastide 31 July–13 August
Autumn Equinox 23 September

No-one knows the exact origins of our seasonal festivals but they are clearly linked to the farming year. Before electric or gas lamps were invented, people were keenly aware of the length of daylight. So the longest night (the Winter Solstice on 21/22 December), the longest day (22 June, Summer Solstice) and the points where night and day were of equal length (the Equinoxes on

43

20/21 March and 23 September) marked four quarters of the annual cycle. The cross-quarter days in between mark the beginning of each season: Winter begins at Halloween, Spring at Candlemas Eve, Summer at May Eve and Autumn at Lammas.

In past centuries when people lived in small villages, they were forced to co-operate for their own survival. The work couldn't be done without people pulling together and then, after the work, there was play. The seasonal festivals originally ensured that the necessary agricultural tasks were carried out by the due date. But over the years they each evolved a different theme which taken together are a way of helping us deal with the various stages of life from birth to youth to maturity to death. Drama and ritual play a crucial part in transmitting these themes. Some of these folk plays (or mummers plays) have survived and our versions of them are included in our A to Z of scripts.

Halloween 31 October

Plays: *Jack O'Lantern and Wild Horse; Brontë Saga; Hamletta.*

Seasonal celebrations: dressing up as ghosts and monsters, scary stories, fortune-telling, bonfires.

This was traditionally the time when the flocks were brought back from the summer pastures and those animals which could not be fed during the winter would be killed and smoked or cooked over bonfires. In England, though not in Scotland or Ireland, the Halloween bonfire has transferred to Guy Fawkes Night on 5 November, although in recent years Halloween has been making a comeback in the UK due to American influence.

Our Halloween play *Jack O'Lantern and the Wild Horse* (based on traditional Souling Plays) is chock-full of ghosts, but you could make up your own. It is the festival of death so is an appropriate time to write your will, remember loved ones who have died, and prepare for the harsh days of winter ahead.

Winter Solstice 21/22 December and Twelve Days of Christmas

Plays: *Xmas Mummers Play; Sir Gawain and the Green Knight; Yuletide Women's Mummers Play.*

Seasonal celebrations: charades, feasting, pantomime, nativity play.

This is midwinter. The drama of the shortest day is re-enacted in the *Xmas Mummers Play* in which St George (representing Day) defeats the Turkish Knight (as in 'Night'). We breathe a sigh of relief that the days will get longer from now on and know that Spring is on the way. It is the season of rest and recuperation, feasting and keeping warm, the slack time of the agricultural year. The excessive present-giving is a recent innovation: before the 20th century the emphasis was on eating well. The Twelve Days of Christmas traditionally provided a gathering crescendo of games, songs, plays, and forfeits, culminating in Twelfth Night excesses and entertainments.

Candlemas Eve 1 February – Valentines Day 14 February

Plays: *Candlemas Wooing Play; Ravers and Stunners.*

Seasonal celebrations: Lighting of candles, festival of conception, spring cleaning, Valentines, love songs, romances.

In previous centuries when people only had candles to light their way through darkness, they had to eke them out frugally through the winter. So when February came, they celebrated the start of Spring with a blaze of candlelight. This is when ewes come into milk before lambing. It is a shame that Candlemas is one of the least known festivals. Being the festival for conception, it can be a focus for women who want to conceive.

After Candlemas, there is traditionally a fortnight of annual spring cleaning. Symbolically, this can clear a space for what we want new in our lives, whether a child, a relationship, a new job or a home. The spring cleaning ends with the boisterous celebrations of Valentine's Day. The *Candlemas Wooing Play* (though in past centuries performed by ploughboys in early January) is very appropriate for Valentines as it is about 'Who does a woman want?'

Spring Equinox 20/21 March and Easter

Plays: *Easter Pace Egg Play; Great Expectations.*

Seasonal celebrations: Easter egg hunts and egg-rolling, Easter bonnets, walking the maze, pilgrimages.

Easter Sunday is fixed on the Sunday following the full moon after the Spring Equinox. The season for sowing seeds. Eggs are hatched and young animals are born. Easter eggs symbolise the seed. At Avebury in Wiltshire, children roll decorated hard-boiled eggs down the slopes of the ditches around the prehistoric standing stones. In the *Easter Pace Egg Play* St George and his adversary, the Prince of Paradise, fight but are interrupted and so are left in equipoise – just as Day and Night are briefly balanced. Walking the maze was a former Easter custom, perhaps symbolising that our path through the year will not be a straight line, but full of twists and turns. Easter bonnets come from the need of gardeners and farmers to have a new hat in Spring to protect them from sun and rain.

May Eve 30 April and May Day 1 May

Plays: *Under the Greenwood: Robin Hood May Play.*

Seasonal celebrations: dawn processions, maypole dancing, May garlands.

All round England Morris men and women get up before sunrise on 1 May to dance in the dawn in order to welcome the summer. This was traditionally the big party night before the shepherds left to take the flocks off to their summer pastures. *Under the Greenwood: Robin Hood May Play* has bawdy undertones as befits the festival for sexual frolics. Any unpartnered lads and maidens went off to partner up in the greenwoods on May Eve and eventually came back with the dawn, bearing a stolen tree trunk for a maypole and flowers for May garlands. There are a number of May Day celebrations around England such as the Hobby Horse processions in Padstow, Cornwall and in Minehead, Somerset and the Jack-in-the-Green processions in Hastings, Sussex and in Rochester, Kent.

Summer Solstice 22 June, Midsummer Eve 23 June and Midsummer's Day 24 June

Plays: *Five Break the Spell; Odysseus in Transit.*

Seasonal celebrations: Midsummer Eve bonfires, camping, walking, expeditions.

22 June marks the Summer Solstice, the longest day. This is an ideal time to go on holiday as the days feel twice as long and camping and walking are a pleasure. In Cornwall, Ireland and much of southern Europe, bonfires are lit for the night of 23 June, St John's Eve. In northern Europe, this is the season of strawberries and other fruits and flowers. We have often performed a 17th century masque, *The Vision of the Twelve Goddesses* by Samuel Daniel, and sometimes have improvised our own version.

Lammastide 31 July – 13 August

Plays: *Mummers Play for Lammas: Death of the Summer Lord; Nicolette and Aucassin; Queen's Champion.*

Seasonal celebrations: summer fair, sports day, large family gatherings.

The first two weeks of August are when most people like to be away on holiday, little knowing that they are celebrating the forgotten festival of Lammas. This was the 'gathering of the clan', a cross between our village fair and the school sports day. In the farming year, it celebrates the beginning of the corn harvest. The Lammas play *Death of the Summer Lord* has been lost since the start of the 17th century, so we wrote our own text for the title. Its theme is the son (the Turkish Knight) overcoming the father (St George) which betokens that the days are once more shortening as Autumn begins.

Autumn Equinox 23 September

Plays: *Demeter and Core; Penelope on Ithaka.*

Seasonal celebrations: harvest festivals.

At the Autumn Equinox day and night are once again of equal length. There are harvest festivals at church. In Ancient Greece, the story of Demeter and Core, in which the daughter separates from the mother, was enacted on this day as part of the Eleusinian Mysteries. They were the destination for the thousands of people who made the ritual procession from Athens to Eleusis. After the material harvest, we may look to our spiritual needs, and reflect on the experiences we have gained during the spring and summer.

And so that completes the circle, for the next festival is Halloween again, the festival of death, at which, at the time of fallen leaves, we can look at what we have lost or fear losing.

Mummers plays

Domestic theatre draws strongly on the traditions of mummers plays. Performing one of these plays makes a great domestic theatre event.

The plays are now little known in the UK outside enthusiasts for folk customs, or the specific localities where performances survive. So what are they? From the 17th to the end of the 19th century, local people, generally in elaborate costume – which in some places originally included black face – acted out traditional stories, such as St George, Father Christmas or Robin Hood (in the 'hero plays') accompanied by a range of devils, doctors and everyman characters. They feature highly schematic plots, nonsense rhymes and a mixture of bawdy, insult and conflict. The plays are specific to seasons and particular places, although they share common themes such as combat and wooing. Some share the same characters, such as St George, Jack or the Doctor. They have local names such as 'soulers' in Cheshire or 'ploughjacks' in Lincolnshire. There are also Scottish and Irish versions.

The typical plot is described in *England in Particular* by Sue King and Angela Clifford of the environmental charity Common Ground:

'Two or more characters such as St George, the hero, and Bold Slasher/ Turkish Knight, the villain, start the dialogue with boastful taunts that result in a fight. One of the two is killed or badly wounded, and is then lamented by one of the other characters. A doctor is then called for; he claims he can cure everything, ...and miraculously revives him.'

In fact, you do not have to look far to find out about mummers plays. Many people know them through Thomas Hardy's description in *The Return of the Native* where in Chapter Five of Book Two, Mrs Yeobright holds a party for her returning son, Clem. This description, and the rehearsal in Chapter Four, show the established part of mummers plays in community life (albeit with rehearsals, unlike our vision of domestic theatre).

For educational purposes mummers plays have sometimes been performed as part of the programmes of the National Gallery or Shakespeare's Globe in London, using recreations of traditional costumes. In Philadelphia, USA there is a Mummers Museum and an annual parade on New Year's Day, drawing on traditions originating in 19th century European immigrant communities, and later blended with an African-American heritage. The emphasis is on elaborate costumes and the parade is now televised, but the event still features community participation by local New Year's Associations.

The learned literature on mummers or mumming or folk plays (including regional versions) can be discovered through the Vaughan Williams Library at Cecil Sharp House (the headquarters of the English Folk Dance and Song Society) in London. In some parts of the country, mummers plays have been revived, for example at Antrobus in Cheshire, and Marshfield in Gloucestershire. In Sussex, a Christmas mummers play based on a local original script is performed round local pubs each year by the World Famous Ashdown Mummers, whose members started in a morris side. Some elements of mummers plays have become traditional folk customs. For example the procession, dancing and combat seen in these plays also feature in the Abbots Bromley Horn Dance in Staffordshire.

As described in the section on Festivals, a mummers play performed for domestic theatre allows you to act out eternal themes of light and dark, night and day, life and death – seen in the swordfight between the forces of light (symbolised by St George) and the forces of darkness (the Turkish Knight). However, in mummers plays, the losers are not permanently killed – they are revived to come again next year.

Their subjects are issues which concern everybody, though they may not be spoken of: fertility, hunger, danger of death from war or hardship. And if these specific threats are less real in 21st century Britain than in previous centuries, the language and drama of mummers plays still put us in touch with their eternal themes. As with seasonal celebrations, to which they are closely related, they help us deal with the stages of our lives, from birth through youth and maturity to death.

The plays are also subversive – like some other ceremonies they included role reversal, where the commoners or poor people act out (or mock) the behaviour of their 'betters', and make fake obeisance. The plays were performed in the presence of social superiors and the original function of costumes or black face was to act as a symbolic disguise – not a true disguise, but a device, since the players' identities were known. (In *The Return of the Native*, the heroine, Eustacia Vye, attempts disguise in the part of the Turkish Knight.) In some areas the characters used to wear their jackets inside out. The plays gave licence to demand money from the audience, as well as symbolically binding an interdependent community to the success of the crop.

Mummers plays provide a model for the style of performance of domestic theatre. The action is simple, the lines are declaimed, the aim is amusement and involvement (perhaps scandal), rather than conventional drama. Improvisation and local character are encouraged. Mummers plays are very portable, designed to be repeated in different locations on the same day, and could also be put on in people's homes (as in Thomas Hardy's novel). Like today's domestic theatre, they used public spaces known to the community – so that the site was part of the tradition.

There are important differences. Modern revivals are performed in pubs and a collection is taken, which brings them outside the strict ambit of domestic theatre. They offer a different kind of fun and revelry, whose aims are essentially public – to re-create folk customs, rather than to bring to life a new, immediate and temporary community in your own living room.

We found the excellent booklet, *Eight Mummers Plays* by Alex Helm very helpful in writing this section.

History plays

Examples of plays written for domestic theatre: *Ravers and Stunners; Votes for Women; Kapital Marx: Karl Marx in Maitland Park; The Building of the St Pancras Almshouses, 1850–1863*.

Domestic theatre brings history to life: from the history on your doorstep, to great episodes which forged our destiny, to colourful characters of the past. Turning the past into dramatic form allows you to draw out interesting themes for today, or shine a light on facts or events which are little known.

Involving the audience is especially important in plays about historical events. It stops them thinking they are watching a worthy history lesson and instead they can imagine they are actually involved in the events.

Start with an approach that interests you. But remember, you don't want to end up with a dry parade of facts. Bring the story to life through characters, and root the play in what's important to your own life, including your curiosity about your own local area.

Are you going to have a comedy or a tragedy? *Ravers and Stunners* came out as a comic tragedy about ambition, creativity and love affairs, drawn from the lives of the Pre-Raphaelite artists. *Votes for Women* inspired because of its serious and passionate tone about the suffragettes and liberty.

The first step in writing a history play for domestic theatre is to narrow your story down into a manageable drama. For example, you need not feel obliged to cover the whole of your subject's life as this may prove unwieldy. For *Kapital Marx* about the life of Karl Marx we selected the years 1850 (when he was living in Soho) to 1870 (when he had published the first volume of *Das Kapital,* his most famous book). Marx and his family were tremendous letter-writers so there was a wealth of primary material which we could distil down into the play.

Next, decide which characters you are going to focus on, and which dramatic events to include. In *Ravers and Stunners,* we put in Ned Burne-Jones's apple fight but did not have room at all for his wife and family. In *Kapital Marx in Maitland Park* we made the most of the drinking and spying in London, with a relatively small part for Engels.

Similarly in the *The Building of the St Pancras Almshouses, 1850–1863* we included the court scenes so we could dramatise greed, displacement of communities, and speculation over the acquisition of the land. Most people can identify with these themes today!

Another opportunity is writing for an anniversary: there may be a centenary or other anniversary coming up for your subject. We wrote *Votes for Women* for the 100th anniversary of the founding of the Women's Social and Political Union in 1903 which coincided with the 75th anniversary of women getting the vote in Britain. We were determined to publicise the poignant stories and courage of the suffragettes which is why this play has such a large cast. When we put on *Votes for Women* again, seven years later, we found it was powerful enough to stand alone, without being hooked onto an anniversary.

History plays also allow you to make the most of local connections and of your friends' family links with great events. We even wrote two versions of Act 2, Scene 3 in *Votes for Women*, one for the South of England (set in Pinner) and one for the North (set in Oldham). The Pinner version featured artist Jane Terrero and her friend Edith Heal, who was the grandmother of our friend Christianne. At one performance at a club which met in a Victorian pub near the site of the headquarters of the Women's Social and Political Union, Christianne played her grandmother Edith Heal – even wearing her grandmother's clothes. Beth introduced the performance by evoking those brave suffragettes who would have passed by in the street outside but of course would not, in those days, have entered the male-only pub.

When the play was performed in Manchester, the production used the Oldham version which replaced Edith Heal and Jane Terrero with Annie and Jessica Kenney, two suffragette leaders who had been brought up in Oldham. During researches in the Women's Library, Beth had seen a list of delegates to a suffragette conference from all over England, Wales and Scotland. Using this, wherever our *Votes for Women* play may be performed, people can put in the names of local women suffragettes into Act 2, Scene 3 so that the audience and participants feel a local connection.

Lastly, finding out about your local history enhances your walk down the street. We have used history to bring our local area to life. Passing the St Pancras Almshouses, and seeing the names of Dr Fraser and the Reverend Thomas Dale engraved on the wall, we know more about who they are. Other people become interested too. Although there's no blue plaque on the house in Kentish Town where Karl Marx and his family moved in 1856, those who have taken part in our domestic theatre play make the connection when they pass through Grafton Terrace.

Practical tips

Research: If you decide to write an historical play, this could entail doing quite a lot of research. There is no need to be daunted as it can become an enjoyable quest and there are resources to help you. These are:

- Local libraries for biographies and background histories of the period chosen.

- Specialist libraries in London: ones that Beth has used are the Vaughan Williams Library, at the English Folk Dance and Song Society, the Marx Memorial Library in Clerkenwell, the Royal Institute of British Architecture in Portland Place, and the Women's Library in Whitechapel.

- Museums: you can make an appointment to go 'behind the scenes' to see original material.

- Local history archives: here you can examine old maps, old newspapers, census records, etc.

- It may be possible to visit the former homes of your chosen subject if these are now open to the public.

Although it may be possible to do a lot of the research by surfing the net, we think nothing beats going to the actual location. There are a number of places around London with connections to the Pre-Raphaelite story, including Hampstead Heath, the Working Mens College (now subtitled the College for Women and Men) and the Red House in Bexley.

Research pays dividends, and can add to your ideas in surprising ways. When adapting John Boyd Hyland's *Ladies' Mumming Play* (as the *Yuletide Women's Mummers Play*), we discovered that Daniel Defoe's *General History of Pyrates* was full of gripping detail about the pirates Mary Read and Ann Bonney, so we put it all in the play. They really did get pregnant, sail with Captain Rackham and terrorise other pirates.

If someone asks you to write a play: We don't charge for putting on performances of domestic theatre. This is on principle as we wish to empower people to participate and then to consider putting on their own plays. Therefore if somebody asks you to write a play for them think carefully about what would be a fair exchange.

When Beth agreed to write *The Building of the St Pancras Almshouses, 1850– 1863,* she arranged to be paid in hot lunches in cafés of her choice (receipts submitted and a limit of £10 per lunch). This was marvellous for Beth as she gets very hungry doing research!

Classic books and stories

Myths and epics

Examples of plays for domestic theatre: *Demeter and Core; Odysseus in Transit; Penelope on Ithaka; Sir Gawain and the Green Knight; Under the Greenwood: Robin Hood May Play.*

Myths and legends have been told and re-told for centuries because they are multi-layered, entertaining and speak to our deepest fears and longings. They are great fun to adapt and when you re-enact a myth, you'll be carrying on a great story-telling tradition. People quickly enter into the vivid emotions of the myth and can create a compelling performance right there in your living room. Several stories involve epic voyages (such as *The Odyssey*) and their wide sweep makes a pleasing contrast with a confined domestic space.

Reviving earlier versions: There are children's versions and there are grown-up versions of the well-known myths. However, it is worth hunting up a fuller version because it will have more details with which to dramatise the story. The children's version of *Demeter and Core* that we heard at school did not include the maid Iambe telling Demeter a rude joke or the old nurse-maid Baubo lifting her skirts to Demeter to make her laugh (this can be done by having Baubo's back to the audience). Nor did the Robin Hood stories usually include a coarse and lusty Friar Tuck dancing with Maid Marian.

Yet these comic moments fit right into the dramas that distil the big emotions steering us through betrayal, loss, the power of maternal instinct, anger or retribution. At the end we are left with a feeling of calm that passions have been resolved in a manner which we can accept.

Selecting your themes: When Beth walked into a university library and asked for a copy of *The Odyssey*, she was shown a row of huge bound volumes. *The Odyssey* is very long so we decided that we would not do all of it at once. We called the first half *Odysseus in Transit* because Odysseus seemed to be endlessly delaying his return home.

The next year we wrote the second half of *The Odyssey* and called it *Penelope on Ithaka* as it opens with Penelope having adapted to life without Odysseus. Coincidentally, the writer Margaret Atwood had just published her book *The Penelopiad* about the very same topic so we gave her a cameo role (and sent the play to her publishers). In the latter half of *Penelope on Ithaka*, Odysseus returns and there is the bloodbath of the suitors and the maids. This is a very brutal ending to the play but we felt we had to trust the myth and did not try to 'happify' it.

Making the most of your location: It's amazing how easily myths can be adapted to be put on in different locations. We've put on *Sir Gawain and the Green Knight* in one room or (as described in the section on moving around your space in Chapter 4) going from room to room, or between outside and inside a house. Another time, the party host had arranged for feasting and musical entertainment between acts.

Usually our plays are entirely in rhyming couplets, but Martin wrote this one with the nobles and court speaking in rhyming couplets and the Green Knight and Chorus speaking in alliterative verse. The original medieval text was in alliterative verse and we wanted to show the clash of cultures between the Arthurian court and the older culture represented by the Green Knight. Certainly, when the Green Knight speaks he has an air of coming from some faraway era. We have never had any problems with people speaking or understanding the alliterative lines.

Art and literature

Plays for domestic theatre: *Brontë Saga; War and Peace: Madame Tolstoy's Version; It's Picasso!; Great Expectations; Ravers and Stunners.*

We choose literary classics because the stories are well known. This is another feature of the 'shared experience' of a domestic theatre event. What's more, since we choose the stories we like, we enjoy researching and writing them. They enable us to explore perennial themes of war, history, art and family in an accessible way. Our adaptations allow us to contrast our own, contemporary 'take' with what we understand the authors wanted to say. And because most people are familiar with at least the main characters or outline of the story, there is room for light-hearted treatment and shared humour.

When we do a play derived from literature, we often put the authors in as well. Our *Brontë Saga* included the Brontë family as well as their created heroes and heroines.

We found that we could include the themes of classic art by dramatising the lives of great artists, as with *It's Picasso!* and the Pre-Raphaelites in *Ravers and Stunners*. Here the audience generally know the artworks a bit, but are less informed about the lives.

To remain plausible, you need to be accurate about historical events but you can adapt the order in which they happen. For example, in *It's Picasso!* we have time going backwards as this suits our approach, gradually revealing the sources which made Picasso so famous.

Satires and spoofs

Plays for domestic theatre: *Hamletta; Nicolette and Aucassin; Zenda: the Prisoner of Sibling Rivalry*

Larger than life characters and outrageous rhymes are natural tools for satires and spoofs, so domestic theatre works very well in this way. Some of our adaptations of classics have been in this vein. There is not much new that anyone can say about Shakespeare's *Hamlet* so we added a feminist half-sister in our adaptation. *Nicolette and Aucassin* is itself a medieval satire on chivalric stories, so the work was done for us.

In many stories it is relatively easy to satirise political life. Prime ministers or presidents can be introduced as themselves, or as versions of story characters – Tweedleblair and Tweedlebrown in *Alice Through the One Way Mirror*, for example. This play also introduced Sigmund Freud to comment on Lewis Carroll's own character.

The summer of 2011 was the first chance to deal with the previous year's Labour Party's leadership election result, in the context of Coalition politics and media tycoons. We adapted the 19th century novel *The Prisoner of Zenda* as a way of fitting in topical references, as described in Chapter 5.

We have also found that domestic theatre can draw fruitfully on the recognised pantomime format, with its subversive comment and audience participation. A group of friends who worked in the health services concocted a 'Dick and the Whittington' pantomime about the tribulations of the local hospital. (See Penny's story at end of Chapter 5.) Martin found that the same approach worked well in works pantomimes or Christmas revues, where everyone is geared up for do-it-yourself sketches, even if they have never heard of domestic theatre.

Children's stories

Plays for domestic theatre: *Queen's Champion; Little Girl with the Kind Heart; Five Break the Spell; Alice through the One Way Mirror.*

As we said in Chapter 4, we find that domestic theatre works well if it mixes adults and children, rather than aiming solely at the children. But there are well-known children's stories, and there is a child inside every adult. Beth's sister wanted a birthday play about a TV serial her family had enjoyed as children, to be enacted by them 40 years later, so we produced the swashbuckling *Queen's Champion*. Similarly we found the Baba Yaga story (*Little Girl with the Kind Heart*) worked very well in domestic theatre. Adults were only too pleased to enter into the spirit of the performance, because it was a favourite of Martin's daughter Ellie, then aged about seven. The result was an unforgettable cameo by a retired couple as squeaky gates.

Finally, children's stories can be retold with an adult perspective, as with the Famous Five demanding to be set free from their stereotypes in *Five Break the Spell*. In fact, the plays adapted from children's stories are amongst the most satisfying because they make the greatest imaginative demands on the audience – a nursery loom going 'clickety-clack', a house on hen's legs, or the castles, tunnels and caves of adventure yarns.

8. Scripts to get started

Introductory note

We have included these plays for you to use in domestic theatre productions. The remainder of the book comprises an A to Z of plays, followed by notes on sources and further reading.

You are welcome to photocopy and perform them in your home or for community events. However, we do not give permission for professional theatre performance or broadcast or for the plays to be used in any setting where profit is made. Please contact the authors through the publishers if you wish to use the plays in such ways.

When using our plays for your own private and community events, we would be very happy if you acknowledge *The Domestic Theatre Handbook* as the source.

Please take all reasonable health and safety precautions when putting on plays in your own home or elsewhere, for example in fights and combat scenes. The plays are performed at your own risk, and the authors take no responsibility for any accidents which occur during or arise out of the performance of these plays.

Finally we hope you enjoy your domestic theatre events. Good luck!

About the plays: an A to Z

In order to help you choose which play to use, we give a short summary of each one.

Alice through the One Way Mirror

A contemporary take on Lewis Carroll's famous 'Alice' stories.

Brontë Saga

The family life of the famous sisters with scenes from *Jane Eyre* and *Wuthering Heights.*

Candlemas Wooing Play

Adapted from the Lincolnshire ploughboys wooing play, traditionally performed on the Monday following Twelfth Night, when the ploughboys went back to work.

Demeter and Core

From the Greek *Homeric Hymn to Demeter.* The tale of Demeter's mythic search for her daughter Core (Persephone) was re-enacted during the Eleusinian Mysteries.

Easter Pace Egg Play
Performed at Easter in the North of England. In this version Nelson watches the fight between St George (representing Day) and the Prince of Paradise (Night).

Five Break the Spell
A pastiche of children's stories from the 1950s, involving a villain, secret tunnels and a captive author. Suitable for children and adults who remember being children.

Great Expectations
From Charles Dickens' 1861 novel. The play allows the audience to vote between the happy and sad endings for Pip and Estella, and is especially suitable for election years.

Hamletta
An invented version of Shakespeare's play restoring Hamlet's forgotten half-sister, who brings common sense to the wounded and warring males.

It's Picasso!
The life of Picasso, Spanish-born painter (1881–1973), who in this play epitomises the spirit of the 20th century.

Jack O'Lantern and the Wild Horse
Adapted from the Cheshire Antrobus Souling Play, this is a spooky one for Halloween.

Kapital Marx: Karl Marx in Maitland Park
Marx lived in Kentish Town from 1856 until his death. This play is based on research into the period and brings to life his family, friends, foes and political ideas.

Little Girl with the Kind Heart
Especially suitable for children, this is based on one of the many retellings of the Russian Baba Yaga folk tales.

Mummers Play for Lammas: Death of the Summer Lord
Inspired by a report of a libel case brought by the Earl of Lincoln in 1601, after local May revellers went too far with their 'Lord of Misrule'.

Nicolette and Aucassin
A re-telling of a 13th century French medieval tale which pokes fun at the excesses of the courtly and chivalric romances of the time.

Odysseus in Transit
From *The Odyssey* by Homer (approximately 8th century BC), the play re-enacts the hero's encounters with the Lotus Eaters, Circe, Sirens, Scylla, Charybdis, and Calypso.

Penelope on Ithaka
In *The Odyssey*, Penelope spent the nineteen years of her husband's absence weeping, weaving and rejecting suitors. Here she stars in her own version of events.

Queen's Champion
A play in seven adventures, based on the 1950s BBC TV drama for children and subsequent novel by Shaun Sutton. Action and intrigue set in the time of Elizabeth I.

Ravers and Stunners
A dramatic account of the art, lives and loves of the Pre-Raphaelite painters in the Victorian era.

Sir Gawain and the Green Knight
Based on a 13th century poem, the play follows the magical tests faced by Sir Gawain, from the court of King Arthur to his final encounter with the mysterious Green Knight.

The Building of the St Pancras Almshouses, 1850–1863
Based on local research, this play tells a tale of worthies and benefactors, noisy builders, set-backs, struggles and finally success in providing local homes which still stand today.

Under the Greenwood: Robin Hood May Play
Devised from fragments of early Robin Hood plays performed at May time. Plenty of duels and traditional mayhem.

Votes for Women
The struggles of the suffragettes told through the lives of the Pankhurst family and fellow protesters, featuring political conflict and militant action.

War and Peace: Madame Tolstoy's version
The great novel is re-enacted in scenes from ballroom and battlefield, set against the dramas in the author's own life and marriage.

Xmas Mummers Play
Inspired by the many traditional Christmas mummers plays. This version follows custom by including mainly male characters.

Yuletide Women's Mummers Play
Adapted from a 20th century mummers play. The followers of the Witch of Winter include Pope Joan and the pirate, Mary Read.

Zenda: the Prisoner of Sibling Rivalry
In a topical spoof from 2011, Daviband is kidnapped on his way to the leadership and his younger brother Ediband steps in. Cue deeds of derring-do and romance, until the prisoner of Zenda is freed.

ALICE THROUGH THE ONE WAY MIRROR

Adapted from Lewis Carroll

CAST

Lewis Carroll/Dodo
Alice
Prologue
Queen Victoria *(chorus)*
Sigmund Freud *(chorus)*
Feminist *(chorus)*
White Rabbit
Walrus
Mock Turtle

Cheshire Cat
Mad Hatter
March Hare
Dormouse
Tweedleblair
Tweedlebrown
White Knight on horse
Red Queen

The audience shout their opinions on therapy and take part in the caucus race which is organised by Lewis Carroll (who is also the Dodo).

Enter Lewis Carroll/Dodo with Alice and Prologue with chorus (Queen Victoria, Sigmund Freud and Feminist) hidden behind blanket upstage.

Lewis Carroll *(waving goodbye to Alice)* B-b-bye Alice, home to b-b-bed
　　　　　Rest your b-b-beautiful sleepy head.
　　　　　Tomorrow you won't have far to search
　　　　　You'll find me in the cloisters of Christ Church.

Alice waves, then sits to sleep. Carroll/Dodo exits.

Prologue　　　Once a famous literary relic
　　　　　Was created by a stuttering cleric.
　　　　　He was a wonderful story teller
　　　　　And became a Victorian best-seller.
　　　　　His book gives our adventure in Wonderland
　　　　　But some say it should be banned
　　　　　For though the book became a common metaphor
　　　　　It's not necessarily one we're much better for.

　　　　　To understand Lewis Carroll's dream
　　　　　I think we need a reflecting team
　　　　　For the non-systemic, that's a kind of chorus
　　　　　To comment on the action for us.

Chorus lower blanket.

Queen Victoria, Sigmund Freud and Feminist *(together)*
     We are the reflecting team
     We watch the play behind the screen
     And take care to observe the entire system –
     We see meanings where others missed 'em.

Queen Victoria I'm quite amused as I'm your Queen Victoria
     I think it's just a harmless phantasmagoria.
     My values include full grown men
     Making friends with little children.

Feminist   I think there's nothing sicker
     Than this crazy mixed up vicar.
     Remember how we saw his character lapse
     When he handed in his photo snaps.

Sigmund Freud I'm Sigmund Freud. A case like Alice's
     Will certainly benefit from psychoanalysis.
     Hear my view. That man's stammer
     Was surely caused by the loss of his mamma.

Prologue   Our heroine is stirring from her sleep
     Let's sit back and take a peep.

Exeunt Prologue and chorus.

Alice   I'm aged seven, going on twelve
     Into our subconscious it's time to delve.
     So now I'll leave childhood's pure garden
     And let adventures my spirit harden.

Enter White Rabbit.

White Rabbit I'm late, I'm late, I'm in a state
     I've got a very important date.
     The Queen will chop off my head
     Oh! How I wish I'd stayed in bed.
     While my worries chase tomorrow
     I'll disappear down this rabbit burrow.

White Rabbit disappears through hole (i.e. exits).

Alice   How strange. I'd like to quiz that rabbit
     If I get the chance, I'll grab it.
(picks up bottle) Look! Here's a magic drink!
     I wonder if it makes me shrink?

Alice drinks and exits down rabbit hole. Enter Dodo.

Dodo   Now this is the secret of a caucus race:
Everyone starts in a different place,
Then they run round very fast
Until they stop and no-one's last.

Dodo organises audience in caucus race (i.e. running round in circles).
Enter Alice.

Alice   I don't think very much of your wheezes
Especially when organised by an extinct species.

Dodo   Pay attention girl, I implore you.
An eminent dodo can never bore you.
If you can't understand a simple rule
You must be some kind of silly fool.
And remember, just because I'm a dodo
Doesn't mean I swoop on girls like Quasimodo.

Alice   What would my teacher say – or my cat –
If I had the nerve to speak like that?

Enter White Rabbit.

White Rabbit   Oh fur and whiskers, I'm in a fluster
This'll take all the courage I can muster!
If I don't come when she calls me
Something terrible will befall me.

Exit White Rabbit.

Dodo   Before you follow him far and near
Let me warn you about what we fear:
Roving around this childhood park
Is a Jabberwock, a monster dark.
Instead, I'll direct you to two aquatic creatures
Who have some remarkable adult features.

Exit Dodo.

Alice *(crying)*   I'm just an innocent little girl.
All this nonsense puts me in a whirl.

Alice spins round. Enter Walrus and Mock Turtle.

Walrus *(to audience)* I am the Walrus, that's what I do,
Watch out, girls, I'm after you.

Mock Turtle   My history is very grievous
I doubt anyone will ever believe us.
In fact I feel somewhat tearful.

Walrus *(to Mock Turtle)* Let's give this little girl an earful.

Mock Turtle   Once I was a real turtle, a real man
Now I'm just a fake amphibian.

Walrus   He's the picture of adult folly
He's so very, very melancholy.

Alice   Tell me why you're upset
Is it childhood you regret?

Mock Turtle   I went to school in a marine academy.
It was hard to learn under the sea.
We had drawling, stretching and fainting in coils
And lots more never-ending toils.

Alice   Oh Mock Turtle do stop crying please!
I don't remember those in my GCSEs.

Walrus   Girl! Pay attention!
Or I'll put you in detention.

Alice   I'm a girl; I have my rights
I don't have to stay if you're not polite.

Enter White Rabbit.

White Rabbit   Oh no! Oh no! I'm really busy
I've got myself in quite a tizzy.
(sees Alice)   I say, you there, Mary Ann:
Will you fashion me a glove and a fan?
I'll need them when I see the queen.
She'll be the highlight of your dream.
But enough of this idle talk:
Eat this mushroom on its stalk.

White Rabbit gives Alice mushroom then exits.

Alice   'Eat me', 'drink me' or a magic mushroom
Those are the things to lift my gloom.
But as to sense, I'm at sixes and sevens.
Now, who's materialising in the heavens?

Enter Cheshire Cat, above.

Cheshire Cat   Alice there's no need to panic
I'm your counsellor (psychodynamic).

Alice   Is it true that your kind guides me?
Dear cat, please come and walk beside me.

Cheshire Cat	Your destination I must know Before I tell you the way to go.
Alice	The Queen's the one I've heard about But everyone's mad and there's no way out.
Cheshire Cat	You'll see the queen at the trial. Meanwhile admire my grinning therapeutic style. So turn left for March Hare, right for Mad Hatter I'd say they're both good for a natter.
Alice	Your grin is wide, your speech is knowing. Will your therapy help me while I'm growing? Audience, please help me guess: Is it No or is it Yes?

Audience cry out their opinions.

Cheshire Cat	Although my manner's quiet and soggy I'm a very powerful moggy. I smile and smile, and can unsheathe Some nasty claws and very sharp teeth. That's all. Time's up! I'm fading like a ghost Just at the moment when you need me most.
Alice	You counsellors are all the same Our problems are just your game.

*Exit Cheshire Cat. Enter Mad Hatter, Dormouse and March Hare
carrying tea table.*

Alice	It's time to pursue my mystery quest But watching adults, I'm not impressed. *(approaches tea table)* I hope those in charge of this nice spread Turn out to be somewhat better bred.
Mad Hatter	No room! No room! All places taken! Two adults and a dormouse who'll never waken.
Alice	This looks like an empty chair I think I'll sit down right there.

Alice sits down.

March Hare	Now, girl, we don't suffer fools We're the ones who make the rules.
Mad Hatter	D'you mind! There exists a certain etiquette I'm afraid you just haven't got it yet.
March Hare	That chair is reserved For some one much more deserved.

	We talk in riddles and can be quite rude When we're in that kind of mood.
Dormouse	Who's this? I'll have a peep Then go gently back to sleep.
Alice	This all seems mighty queer I think everyone's gone mad round here.
Mad Hatter	You can't spend your life in a daze Try to learn our adult ways.
Dormouse	I echo what's just been said Then I lay down my sleepy head.
March Hare	This dormouse is a boring old duffer.
Mad Hatter	Just watch while I make her suffer. I know just the thing to rouse her Get some hot tea and douse her.

Mad Hatter pours tea on dormouse.

Alice	Why should I learn your mad ways? They're the opposite of childhood days.
March Hare	I don't think you'd be so cocky If you met the Jabberwocky. Oh, look at all this clutter I'll just lubricate my watch with butter.

Exeunt Mad Hatter, March Hare and Dormouse. Enter Cheshire Cat.

Alice	I've been brought up to be kind and gentle Why has all the world gone mental?
Cheshire Cat	Now don't get in a flap I'll show you a pair who like a scrap. See Tweedleblair and Tweedlebrown Fight over the New Labour crown.

Exit Cheshire Cat. Enter Tweedleblair and Tweedlebrown.

Tweedleblair	As PM I'm much better. *You* must make do with the Exchequer.
Tweedlebrown	We were Labour brothers in arms 'Till you dished me with no qualms.
Tweedleblair	As party leader, I've got the lot. Who wants to vote for a Tweedle-Scot?
Tweedlebrown	I'm behind our success: you can't dodge it. With my budgets I can bodge it.

Tweedleblair   I say that's all baloney –
You know I'm the people's Tony.

Alice   Will you two stop this quibbling!
You're just like me and my own true sibling.

Tweedlebrown   We'll have to have a battle
To see who'll swing the victory rattle.

Tweedleblair   Now Tweedlebrown I'm ready for a fight
I'm the champion of the right.

They fight.

Alice   I wish a monstrous crow would fly down
And take both Tweedleblair and Tweedlebrown.
Audience, you have to imagine that, of course.
Now exit Tweedles. Enter Knight on horse.

Exeunt Tweedleblair and Tweedlebrown. Enter White Knight on horse.

White Knight   In comes I, a White Knight,
Not exactly looking for a fight.
In fact I'm a martyr to my neuroses
I take them in bigger and bigger doses.

White Knight falls off horse. Exit horse.

Alice   Excuse me sir, if I may be so humble
Is it lack of practice that makes you tumble?

White Knight   I understand your girlish outlook
But I've practised and read the best book.
I trundle round in my sweet dream
Always an eccentric to the furthest extreme.

Alice   Please explain why you're tarrying.
What's the funny thing you're carrying?

White Knight   This contraption is a box-cum-umbrella
To keep my clothes dry – quite a smart fella!

Alice   But there's no use carrying it around
Because all your clothes will fall to the ground.

Exit White Knight, muttering in a bewildered manner.

Alice   While I'm a model of childish deportment
These adults are such a disappointment.
They seem to think anything odd is OK.
Now what have we here? A game of croquet.

Enter Queen with mallets.

Queen	Audience, put on your playing-card suits
	Hurry up! Obey me – I'm a bossy boots.
	My courtiers give me all their power:
	How gratifying to see them cower.
(organises croquet game)	It's my party so I make the rules.
	I don't care if everyone feels like fools;
	With flamingo mallets and a hedgehog ball
	I'll soon drive my guests right up the wall.
	One mistake and it's 'Off with your head!'
	It's no use grovelling and going red.

Enter White Rabbit.

White Rabbit	Pay attention to my rallying call:
	Come to the courthouse one and all.
	The trial is just about to start
	You are summoned to play your part.

Queen	Let the trial begin. Start with the jury –
	They'll be the first to feel my fury.
	Sentence first, verdict last:
	That'll make the trial go fast.

| Alice | Your majesty I don't want to displease ya |
| | But I don't think that's the right procedure. |

Queen	Nonsense! I punish them before they do wrong
	So they're in a state all day long.
	First, hear the jury confess their faults:
	I think they're all a load of dolts.

Enter Walrus.

| Walrus | I really regret my adult need |
| | To subject little oysters to my greed. |

Exit Walrus. Enter Mock Turtle.

| Mock Turtle | I'm overcome with an indefinable sorrow. |
| | I doubt things'll get better tomorrow. |

Exit Mock Turtle. Enter White Knight.

| White Knight | I'm full of inventions, that's my quirk |
| | Trouble is, none of them seem to work. |

Exit White Knight. Enter Mad Hatter, March Hare and Dormouse.

| Queen | Speak! Whether you're nervous or not. |
| | Else I'll execute you on the spot. |

Mad Hatter, March Hare *(together)*

> We are much too frightened to speak,
> So come on dormouse: give a squeak.

Dormouse
> Squeak, squeak, squeak!

Alice
> Queen, your forcefulness made them flustered,
> I don't call this natural justice.

Queen
> The sentence must match the crime
> But first admire this trick of time:
> Even before the wicked deed's committed,
> I know the punishment that is fitted.
> Now Alice you face the charge
> Of suddenly becoming much too large.
> You've changed your size all day long –
> In fact you're accused of just being WRONG.

Enter Prologue and chorus (Queen Victoria, Sigmund Freud and Feminist).

Prologue
> You might be surprised at what comes next
> We stop the action and reflect.

Sigmund Freud
> The charges in this trial are dud
> The real question is: who's stolen childhood?

Feminist
> We've seen role model after role model
> Be more like Gazza than Glen Hoddle.

Sigmund Freud
> When children became pubescent
> Carroll couldn't face them as adolescent.

Prologue
> Let's ask Alice what she thinks
> She might make some helpful links.

Alice
> Adults insist on rules *they* flout:
> I was never so ordered about.
> The world isn't at all like we were told
> It's a madhouse when you get old.

Feminist
> You find adults grumpy and cruel
> And they treat everyone like a fool.

Queen Victoria
> Childhood should be pure and not corrupt.

Feminist
> Perhaps the change to adult is too abrupt.

Prologue
> Between child and adult let's create
> A brand-new adolescent state.
> A kind of teenage buffer zone
> Where they can practice follies of their own,

A place where youth's banners are unfurled
Against the entire adult world.

Alice   I have to say I'm beginning to doubt
Whether all this therapy will help me out.
I vote we give up these dramatic parts
And have some real-life cakes and tarts.

THE END

BRONTË SAGA

CAST

Mrs Gaskell, biographer
and novelist *(with handbag)*
Elizabeth Brontë (Brontë Spirit)
Maria Brontë (Brontë Spirit)
Patrick Brontë, father
Charlotte Brontë
Emily Brontë
Anne Brontë
Curate
Branwell Brontë
Ned Ludd

Methodist
Spectre of Disease
Jane Eyre
Adele, a child
Rochester
Mrs Rochester *(with flaming torch)*
Cathy
Nellie Dean
Heathcliff
Linton
Heathcliff's dogs *(bark and snap)*

Host *and* Guest *for alternative ending, if desired*

Audience participate by waving paper flames (in Jane Eyre) and (in Wuthering Heights) making eery moorland voices:

> Cathy, come to your moorland home
> Where your spirit can freely roam.

SCENE 1
Brontë family values

Enter Mrs Gaskell.

Mrs Gaskell   I'm Mrs Gaskell, literary investigator
And I'll start the play as your narrator.
Novels and biography are my bag –
I'm a sort of 19th century Melvyn Bragg.
I'm researching three heroines of cult fiction
They'll be famous, that's my prediction.
But first hang on to your wits:
Here come the ghostly Brontë spirits.

Enter Brontë Spirits.

Brontë spirits *(in unison)*
We are the Brontë spirits, Elizabeth and Maria
We met our death when we moved from here.

Dead Elizabeth   We went to a school for clergy daughters
Needlework, classics and French they taught us.

Dead Maria	In that poor cold place, the best Dad could afford,
	We gave up our lives for the Lord.

Exeunt Brontë spirits. Enter Patrick.

Patrick	Patrick Brontë, a poor son of the Irish soil
	I made good through years of toil
	Rising from Irish hut to Cambridge college
	To become a man of classical knowledge.
	I took my vows and joined the church
	But now God's left me in the lurch.
Mrs Gaskell	I'm sorry to bother you, vicar
	But please can you tell your story quicker?
Patrick	Alas! My life was hit by great calamity
	Which took me to the edge of sanity.
	First my wife died, then two daughters.
	I try to bear it like God taught us.
	Now I'm left a single dad
	Full of woes and very sad.
	Parent of four bright kids
	But if I die, they're on the skids.

Enter Charlotte, Emily and Anne.

Charlotte	I'm Charlotte the go-getter
	So do what I say – to the letter.
	After a smattering of education
	I've got ideas above my station.
	Now I think it would be very cool
	If we three girls set up a school.
Emily	I'm Emily and from my earliest youth
	I've been odd, and a bit aloof.
	If you make me do what I don't like
	I'll jolly well go on hunger strike.
Anne	I'm Anne, the one who gets forgotten.
	Sisters, your ideas are pretty rotten
	I wish you'd all stop messing
	And get on with some governessing.
Patrick	What you girls need is lots of learning
	That's the way to get you earning.

Enter Curate.

Curate	Excuse me. Is anyone about?
	Marriage to a curate is a good way out.

> If you want a quiet life
> One of you can be my wife.

Daughters *(together)* Get out, you whipper-snapper
You'll never be as good as papa.

Daughters (Charlotte, Emily and Anne) chase curate away.

Anne   Even if we haven't got a mother
At least we've got a Brontë brother.

Enter Branwell.

Branwell   I'm Branwell, one action-packed Irish gallant
A true artist – yes, I've got talent.
I mix it with the local toughs
I'm expert with the fisticuffs.
And if I don't make it as a fighter
I'll still become a famous writer.

Enter Ned Ludd and Methodist.

Ned Ludd   I'm Ned Ludd, king of the weavers
We'll smash the looms, you've got to believe us.

Methodist   We Methodists reject your snobbish creeds
They just don't answer to our needs.

Patrick   How dare you have the effrontery
To criticise Church and country?

Branwell   It's alright, Daddy
He'll regret it if he calls me Paddy!

Ned Ludd   Watch it, you Irish nouveau riche
Feel the power that we unleash.

Branwell and Ned Ludd fight but neither wins.

Exeunt Branwell, Ned Ludd and Methodist. Enter Spectre of Disease.

Spectre   I'm the Spectre of Disease
of Disease   I'll bring the poor to their knees.
Close the graveyard, get clean water
Or I'll carry off another daughter.

Exit Spectre of Disease.

Patrick   I must work around the clock
To minister to my troublesome flock.
Each Sunday I teach the mill hands,
Bury the dead and call the banns.

But please don't think I'm a fuddy-duddy
When I now disappear to my study.

Exit Patrick.

SCENE 2
The fictions come to life

Charlotte, Emily and Anne remain on stage.

Charlotte	Our financial prospects are quite dismal. Life as a governess is too abysmal. While Branwell rants and rages, We'll write our Brontë pages. Let's embark on a literary career So our fame spreads far and near.
Anne	Yes, let's write about being private tutors Winning the hearts of well-heeled suitors Or orphan children who are depressed But suddenly receive a surprise bequest.
Emily	Forget that stuff about a virtuous wife All I care about is inner strife. I'm driven on by hunger's fury There's the lifeblood of my story.
Charlotte	Hear my idea: let's see which sibling Turns out the best at juvenile scribbling. I'll start: first see the tale I spin About a governess heroine.

Exeunt Charlotte, Emily and Anne. Enter Mrs Gaskell and Brontë Spirits.

Mrs Gaskell	See them throw off spinsters' shackles Admire how their imagination crackles. But before they tell their stories for us Let's hear again from the Brontë chorus.
Brontë Spirits	Let the spirit of this place Bring you to a state of grace Rise above your humble station Girls, let rip your imagination.

Exeunt Mrs Gaskell and Brontë Spirits. Enter Jane Eyre.

Jane Eyre	I'm Jane Eyre, I'm sad and motherless I make my living as a governess

79

I rule my life by one word: virtue
Stick to what's right – that can't hurt you.

Enter Adele.

Adele
I'm Adele, Miss Eyre's French pupil
I run about and can't sit still.
I'm an only child and I'd like to say
Why aren't there more children in this play?

Jane
Our plots are so very complicated
That children's parts must be truncated.
So run along now and write your own
That way you'll never be alone.

Exit Adele.

Jane
But right now I'm in a funk
My new boss is a sexy hunk.
And even though I find him dishy
Something round here is pretty fishy.

Enter Rochester.

Rochester
I've set aside my inner pain
And fallen for my virtuous Jane.

Rochester and Jane smooch.

Rochester
(aside)
Alas, marriage can't be automatic
I've a secret, locked in the attic.
Still, I'll try to trick her:
(to Jane)
Jane, when you're back, we'll see the vicar.

Exit Jane. Enter Mrs Rochester.

Mrs Rochester
Imperialist looter of the Jamaican isle
You've locked me in your stately pile.
First I was your teenage bride
Now I'm only fit to hide.
I'm confined to a secret place
A lifelong object of disgrace.

Rochester
Oh, no! It's my legal wife.
Get away, blight of my life.

Mrs Rochester

(waves torch)
If you try and wed Jane Eyre
I'll rend her veil and tear her hair.
I swear by this flaming brand
Husband – you'll lose your hand.

Exit Mrs Rochester. Enter Jane.

Rochester	Jane, I know this sounds awful But our wedding can't be lawful. But please accept my ardent passion And live with me, after a fashion.
Jane	Rochester, I thought our love was true No, I won't subordinate myself to you. Stop! I've said enough. Now I'm leaving in a huff.

Exit Jane. Enter Mrs Rochester.

Mrs Rochester	Now audience let tongues of flame Consume the proud Rochester name.

Audience wave flames.

Mrs Rochester	Note that he gets purification by fire. Whereas I am sentenced to a funeral pyre. He'll rescue me but as he tries I'll perish and he'll lose his eyes.

Mrs Rochester chases Mr Rochester through audience; she dies in the flames, he is burnt and scarred.

Rochester	I once was cruel and overweening Now I've been taught life's true meaning.

Enter Jane, taking Rochester by the hand.

Jane	Passion's now a burnt-out shell But reader, I married him, what the hell. Rochester, as you've purged your pride I'll spend my life by your side, And you might like to know Now you're blind, I'll run the show.

Exeunt Jane and Rochester. Enter Emily.

Emily	Can this be a best-selling novel? I think it's a load of drivel. It's all virtue and correct behaviour La-di-da, the heroine gets her saviour. In *my* heroes, passion seethes and rages Unrequited down the ages, So through my novel I can come closer To the state of anorexia nervosa. Here they are – they'll scare you stiff: Bring on Cathy! Enter Heathcliff.

Exit Emily. Enter Cathy, Heathcliff and Mrs Gaskell.

Mrs Gaskell	Audience, you get to make the moorland sounds And make them as scary as Heathcliff's hounds.
Audience *(wailing)*	Cathy, come to your moorland home Where your spirit can freely roam.

Exit Mrs Gaskell.

Cathy	Now Heathcliff, be a sweet Just prostrate yourself at my feet. Don't look so cross and surly Just because I've treated you unfairly.

Enter Nellie Dean.

Nellie Dean	I'm the housekeeper, Nellie Dean I'm as plump as she is lean. I'm the keeper of secrets and storyteller So, Cathy, just forget that fella.
Heathcliff	I'm an evil brooding presence But I've fallen for your effervescence.
Cathy	Heathcliff! I'm vain and wanton I love you but I'll marry Linton.
Heathcliff	For these real or imagined slights I'll take control of Wuthering Heights. And yes by crikey Make it home to my warring psyche. Where are my hounds, the dogs of hell?

Enter Heathcliff's dogs.

Heathcliff *(to dogs)*

When Linton comes, chase him across the fell.

Enter Linton.

Linton	Make way for me, Linton, the local toff If Heathcliff's Irish stout, I'm the froth.

Dogs bark and snap at Linton's heels.

Linton	Cathy, this is no place for your beauty, Come and live somewhere snooty. Though I stand for what you love to despise Marry me, Cathy and I'll open your eyes.
Cathy	Oh what lovely words you've uttered. I know which side my bread is buttered.

> All right, Linton, let's get wed
> I'll live with you until I'm dead.

Cathy takes Linton's arm.

| Heathcliff | Spurn me and you spurn yourself
I'll return a man of wealth. |

Exeunt Heathcliff and dogs.

| Cathy | Oh Nellie, I dropped a clanger
When I left behind my doppelganger.
I've gone and married a stuffed shirt
Now Heathcliff's really very hurt. |
| Nellie Dean | No, I think you've got some brains
To end up mistress of Thrushcross Grange.
But now let's advance some years
To see this story end in tears. |

Enter Heathcliff.

| Heathcliff | I'm now the owner of Wuthering Heights
All right Linton, want a fight? |
| Linton | You disgrace a gentleman's suit –
You're nothing more than a low-born brute. |

Heathcliff and Linton fight. Linton is vanquished. Exit Linton.

Cathy	Heathcliff, we're a pair. Yes, I'm capricious But you are well and truly vicious.
Heathcliff	Cathy, don't be my cause of sorrow I love you like there's no tomorrow.
Cathy	Nellie, I pine for moors and cliff edges And Heathcliff's childhood pledges. Can you hear those moorland sounds I hear them calling all around.

Audience call to Cathy.

| Audience | Cathy, come to your moorland home
Where your spirit can freely roam. |
| Cathy | I miss Wuthering Heights and even the dogs.
Oh Nellie, I'm going to pop my clogs. |

Cathy dies. Exeunt Nellie and Cathy who is dead.

| Heathcliff | My love is such a driving hunger
It only lives in rain and thunder. |

My spirit lies in earthly passion
Born of years of dark repression.
Now you've gone, I'll rant and rave
Cathy, I'll love you beyond the grave.

Enter Branwell.

Branwell   What my sisters tell as fiction
I enjoy as real-life action.
Since I can't join their writing club
Come on, Heathcliff, let's go down the pub.

Exeunt Branwell and Heathcliff. Enter Anne, Charlotte and Emily.

Anne   Honest, I've written two very good books
About girls with rather ordinary looks.
There's governesses and great houses
Remote settings and cruel spouses.
It's all wonderfully dramatic
And like your books, very cinematic.

Charlotte   Yes, I wish I could introduce us
To a couple of film producers.
Anne, dear, I daresay your books are good
But they're just not right for Hollywood.
So, perhaps the way to fame
Is publication under a false name.
It'll create a sense of mystery
And start the myth of Brontë history.

Enter Curate.

Curate   Ladies, I'm your father's curate and I suggest
You marry me and forget the rest.
You could do worse than give your life
To God's will as a clergy wife.

Anne, Charlotte,   Get lost! Now our fame is soaring
and Emily   We find you much too boring.

Exit Curate.

SCENE 3

The tragic ending

Enter Spectre of Disease and Brontë Spirits.

Spectre   Howarth is a cess-pit of diseases
of Disease   Which keeps the poor on their knees-es
And now it's my turn to claim
The bearers of the Brontë name.

Brontë Spirits	One by one we'll reclaim our sisters
	Their poor health can't resist us.
	But first let's see poor Branwell
	Drink his way to hell.

Brontë Spirits withdraw aside. Enter Patrick.

| Patrick | As my ageing eyesight fails |
| | I fear Branwell's gone off the rails. |

Enter Branwell with Heathcliff.

| Branwell | Fame? I've had not so much as a ripple. |
| | So now, I think I'll take a tipple. |

Branwell drinks.

| Heathcliff | I smell disappointment on your breath |
| | Go on, boy – drink yourself to death. |

Exeunt Heathcliff and Branwell to join Brontë Spirits.

Enter Charlotte, Emily and Anne.

Emily	I've put all my pent-up fury
	Into one amazing story
	Now with consumption I'll fade away
	Alas! this is my dying day.

Emily dies and joins Brontë Spirits.

| Anne | I was always the girl with gumption |
| | Now I too must die of consumption. |

Anne dies and joins Brontë Spirits.

| Patrick | My grief is dreadful and unsurpassed |
| | Please let this bereavement be my last. |

Charlotte	Emily's dead and can't be deader
	So I put her second novel in the shredder.
	Alas I'm just so upset
	I think I'll have to write *Villette*.
	Now I think I'll have to marry
	Any old Tom, Dick or Harry.

Enter Curate.

Curate	My income is at your disposal
	If you accept my marriage proposal.
	Although you are too big for your boots,
	I'll remind you of your Irish roots.

Charlotte	Dad, I'm going to marry the curate I'm thirty-six, there's nothing for it.
Patrick	Nonsense, you're too old to wed Stay at home and look after Dad.
Charlotte	Oh curate dear, I'm pegging out That's my career up the spout. Of the sisters, only I stayed the course Now I'll join them without remorse.

Charlotte dies and joins Brontë Spirits, escorted by Curate, who exits.

Enter Mrs Gaskell with handbag.

Mrs Gaskell	Here's a rich biographic brew I think I'm on to something new. Now I can weave the Brontë spell Around the tale of parsonage hell. The moors will make it atmospheric And the blame must fall on this mad cleric.
Patrick	Six children have pre-deceased me Oh God, now I ask you to release me.
Mrs Gaskell	For their troubles there's one person to blame Patrick Brontë is the name. *(hits him with handbag)* You're a terrible father and this is why: You sent your daughters away to die. You housed the others in a dreadful museum Where no-one ever came to see 'em. While you ignored their lonely plight They spoke out for women's rights. You could have done a whole lot more To help the Irish and the poor. At least in this state of desolation There remains one lasting consolation: They've left their literary hoard To help the English Tourist Board.
Patrick	Biography isn't the art of slagging Please, Mrs Gaskell, stop that handbagging.
Brontë Spirits	There we leave Patrick in dismay As we reach the end of our play.

(Alternative ending from here if required)

Audience, thank you for taking part
We hope it's left you in good heart,
And may comedy and tragedy
Fuel your appetite for cakes and tea.

THE END

Alternative ending (if required)

Enter Host and Guest.

Host   Audience don't you think it such a shame
      That Mrs Gaskell gives Patrick all the blame?
      All these deaths are heart-rending
      Our play has such a sad ending.

Guest   They wrote, they suffered, then they died
      Our story is a look at the dark side.
      It's an emotional opera – like Rigoletto
      So we'll comfort ourselves with tea and gateaux.

Host   Perhaps it's not as bad as it looks
      As the Brontës live on through their books.

Guest   So let's thank the actors, our dear friends
      You'll be glad to know this is

THE END

CANDLEMAS WOOING PLAY

CAST

Tess, Village Maiden
Eustacia, Village Maiden
Dame Spring
Fool
Sergeant
Lady

Farming Man
Lawyer
Dame Jane
Eezum Squeezum
Doctor Potion

Enter Village Maidens, Eustacia and Tess.

| Eustacia | In come we, two maidens bold and gay |
| | I'm Eustacia, she's Tess; listen to what we say. |

| Tess | At Candlemas we make cradles of hay |
| | To welcome the Goddess Brid that day. |

| Eustacia | And we throw out the old garlands and greenery |
| | To clear the mess and improve the scenery. |

| Tess | Now come all ye women who wish to give birth |
| | For Dame Spring will soon be treading the earth. |

| Eustacia | If you want to hear the patter of tiny feet |
| | Now is the time your man for to meet. |

| Tess | We herald the Mistress of the Vernal Rites, |
| | Of the Cuckoo's song and the shorter nights. |

| Eustacia | She'll encourage you to have a seasonal fling |
| | So prepare to let rip, here comes Dame Spring. |

Village maidens dance off. Enter Dame Spring.

Dame Spring	I am Dame Spring to welcome you
	Who've come here on Candlemas Day.
	We all desire your favour
	For to see our Wooing Play.
	It hails from Lincolnshire
	It's meaning I can't say
	But you'll see all the men are dunces
	And the women get their way.

Fool enters.

| Fool | In comes I, bold Tom |
| | I'm as bold as a lion (well, not really) |

I'm like a pair of old bellows
All full of holes
Or an old iron stiddy
With not many coals.
Okum, Spokum, France and Spain
In comes our Sergeant all the same.

Sergeant enters.

Sergeant | In comes I, the recruiting Sergeant
I've arrived in here just now.
I've orders from the Queen to enlist all fellows
That follow horse, cart or plough.
For the war we've a mandate from the electors
So get lost all you conscientious objectors!

Lady enters.

Lady | In comes I, the Lady bright and gay
With misfortunes despite my sweet charms
For I'm so scornful, I've been drawn away
Out of my true love's arms.
He swore if I didn't wed him
As you shall understand
He'd enlist to be a soldier
And go to some foreign land.
So my love enlisted and joined the volunteers
But I don't mean to sigh for him
I'll have him for to know
I'll get another sweetheart
And with him I will go.

Sergeant | Now madam I desire to know if I'm the man
To please your fancy, I'll do the best I can.
I'll give you gold and silver
All brought from India's shore,
And I'll forever love you
Pray what can I do more?

Lady | What care I for your gold and silver?
What care I for your house or land?
What care I for your rings or diamonds?
All I want is a handsome man.

Fool takes Lady by the arm and dances.

Fool | A handsome man will not maintain you
For his beauty will decay

The finest flower that grows in summer
In the winter fades away.

Farming Man enters.

Farming Man   Here comes I, the Farming Man
Upon my principle for to stand.
I've come to woo this lady fair
To gain her love is all my care.
I may look like a country oaf
But for your oven I'm a harvest loaf.
Underneath my rustic fashions
You'll get to know my earthy passions.

Lady   To gain my love this will not do
You speak too clownish for to woo.
Therefore out of my sight be gone
A witty man or I'll have none.

Exit Farming Man. Enter Lawyer.

Lawyer   With fine words as smooth as silk
Marital breakdowns I do milk.
I earn my living at the Inns of Court
Where I'm easily sold and bought.
You can meet me in the lover's bower,
My rates are only £90 an hour.
A man of wit I am the best
So choose me from above the rest.

Lady   A lawyer I suppose you be
You plead your cause so wittily
But by-the-by I'll tell you plain,
You plead a cause that's all in vain.
(indicates the Fool) Give me that man with the ragged pants
I'm sure he knows what a woman wants.

Lady goes towards the Fool.

Fool   Well met, sweet lady, well overtaken.

Lady   You are kindly welcome, sir, to me.

Fool   I'll wipe my eyes and I'll look again!
Methinks sweet lady, I now thee see.

Lady   What hast thou to pleasure me?

Fool *(makes lewd gesture)*
Why this, my dear, I will give thee
And all I have, it shall be thine.

Lady	Kind sir, I thank you heartily.
Sergeant	Stand back, stand back thou silly swain! This girl will go with none but me!
Fool	I will not.
Sergeant	Stand back or I will cleave thy brain.
Lady	Yes, sir, but you are not in the right Stand back and do not counsel me For I love a lad who will make me laugh In a secret place, to pleasure me.

Exit Sergeant.

Fool	Good wench! Do you love me pretty fair maiden? You do? (Oh blimey!) Whenst to be our wedding day? Let it be tomorrow.
(to audience)	I'm going to ask all you stick-me-jacks To me and me lady's wedding And what you like best You must bring with you. Me and me lady will have a barley chaff dumpling Buttered with wool and a gallon of ropey ale with it.

Fool pauses and shuffles round with a stick.

Fool	Only wait a short while and Perhaps old Dame Jane Crane will be here.

Dame Jane enters with a doll.

Dame Jane	In comes I, old Dame Jane With a neck as long as a crane. Once I was a blooming maid Until innocently I was laid Dib dab over the meadow Now I'm a downright old widow.

Dame Jane hands the Fool a doll.

Dame Jane	Tommy it's a long time since I saw you But now I've caught thee. All my joy is ended Since you stopped calling on me. Tommy take your bastard – look at its chin.
Fool *(protests)*	Does it look like me?

Dame Jane	Its nose, its eyes are as much like yours As ever it could have been.
Fool	Who sent you here with it?
Dame Jane	The overseer of the parish said I was to bring it To the biggest fool I could find So I thought I'd bring it to you.

Dame Jane hits the Fool on the leg.

Fool	That's my leg you old faggit! Well I'll make a note to thank you. Only wait a short time for old Eezum Squeezum.

Eezum Squeezum enters with a big club.

Eezum Squeezum	In comes I old Eezum Squeezum On me back I carry a beezum And in my hand a whip leather frying pan. Is there anyone here who can me stand!
Dame Jane	Yes, I can, for my head is made of iron And my body is made of steel My hands and shins are knuckle bone And you can't make me feel.
Eezum Squeezum	If your head is made of iron And your body's made of steel Your hands and shins are knuckle bone I can make you feel. I'll slish you and slash you as small as a fly And send you to Jamaica to make mince-pies.

He hits her with the club and Dame Jane falls down.

Fool	Oh Eezum Squeezum, what hast thou done? Thou's killed old Jane and her only son. Five pounds for a doctor.
Eezum Squeezum	Ten pounds to stop away.
Fool	Fifteen pounds if he comes at once.

Enter Doctor Potion.

Doctor	In comes I, Doctor Potion (I'm very good at self-promotion).
Fool	What diseases can you cure?

Doctor	Hipsy, pipsy, palsy, gout Pains within and pains without, I can draw a leg and set a tooth And almost restore the dead to life forsooth.
Fool	Very clever, doctor. Try your experimenting on this old girl.
Doctor	So I will. I'll feel the old girl's pulse. This old lady's not dead. She wants a little of my wiff waff Rubbing round her tiff taff. This old lady's not dead, only in a trance Come on, rise up, old girl, and let's have a dance.

Dame Jane rises up and dances a turn with the Doctor.

Fool	Our play is nearly over And the lady is my lover The girls all used to say me nay But my lady will comfort me night and day.

Fool and Lady go out arm in arm. Dame Spring steps forth.

Dame Spring	We've done all our spring cleaning And applied the psychic Hoover While the fields are greening We're off to seek a sprightly lover. This is the time to clear the clutter And to tidy up your life For love to set your heart a-flutter And forget all pain and strife. It's time to let your lust burst out And find a mate without a doubt. Though winter's not yet over, Spring is on the way, And soon we'll be celebrating St Valentines day.

THE END

Note

This play is adapted for Candlemas (2 February) from the 'Ploughboys Wooing Play' from Jerusalem in Lincolnshire. It was traditionally performed on Plough Monday, the Monday following 12th Night (5th/6th January), when the ploughboys went back to work.

DEMETER AND CORE

Based on the 'Homeric Hymn to Demeter'

CAST

Iris, messenger goddess	Hecate, older goddess
Zeus, Ruler of the Heavens	Calladice
Hades, Ruler of the Underworld	Sisters of Calladice *(non-speaking)*
Core, daughter of Zeus and Demeter	Iambe, maid
Calypso, friend of Core	Metanira, Queen of Eleusis
Other friends *(non-speaking)*	Baubo, old nurse
Helios, Sun God	Hermes, messenger god
Demeter, Corn Goddess	Rhea, mother of Demeter

Handmaiden *(non-speaking)*

Goddesses:

Aphrodite	Artemis
Athena	Tethys
Hera	Hestia

The audience hold flowers for Core and her friends to pick.

PROLOGUE
On Mount Olympus

Iris enters.

Iris   Here comes I, Iris, to tell you a story
The tragic tale of Demeter and Core.
I tell of Demeter with the beautiful hair
And Core her daughter praised for her feet so fair –
Of a mother raging wild when Hades stole her child
While Zeus Lord of the Sky turned a blind eye.

Exit Iris. Enter Zeus and Hades.

Zeus   I, Zeus, greet my brother Hades, welcome be.
What brings you this morning to call on me?

Hades Hail, Zeus, Lord of the Sky
I ask a favour which in your power may lie.

Zeus   Yes?

Hades I want your child Core as wife and Queen
As she's the loveliest maiden I have ever seen.

Zeus   It's tricky as her mother, our sister won't agree.
      But it's the only favour you ever asked of me.
      It puts me in a sticky position:
      If I consent to grant your petition
      I'll have to suffer Demeter's wrath for evermore
      Because of what you're asking for.
      Seize her while I'm busy if you wish to gain your ends.
      Go now while she's playing with her friends.

      They're picking flowers in a meadow, Enna by name,
      And I'll go to the temple so I won't get the blame.

Exeunt Zeus and Hades.

SCENE 1

Flower meadow at Enna in Sicily

Enter Core, Calypso and friends.

Core   How peaceful is this valley with flowers round our feet
      Let's pick some for my mother – they smell so sweet.

Calypso   Core, see the dark clouds passing across the sun
      Are they some ill omen to spoil our fun?

Core   Nonsense! Calypso, nothing can spoil today
      See the roses, violets and crocuses so gay.

*Core and friends gather flowers from the audience. Then exeunt Calypso
and friends.*

Core   Here's irises and hyacinth our senses to entrance
      And a narcissus so fragrant it makes the sky dance.

Core reaches out to pluck it. A loud noise is heard.

Core   The earth is opening – a great chasm I see.
      And who's this in a gold chariot? Father, help me!

Hades enters and seizes Core, who now cries out for her mother.

Exeunt Hades and Core, struggling. Enter Iris.

Iris   Though Core resisted, it was all in vain.
      Could she ever hope to see her mother again?
      Her call rang through the mountains up into the sky
      Fearfully her mother heard echoes of her cry.

Exit Iris.

SCENE 2
Visit to Helios

Demeter enters beating her breast and crying 'Core'.

Demeter	I seek by day, I search by night Since my Core vanished from sight. I comb the rocks, I scan the seas I follow birds and ask the bees. But not a single trace is left I'm filled with grief, my heart's bereft.

Enter Hecate.

Hecate	I, Hecate, greet thee Demeter in your distress, I saw not who carried away Core under duress But I heard Core's cry and I knew it wasn't right So I've come to offer help in your dreadful plight.
Demeter	We'll go immediately to call On Helios, the Sun God who sees all.

Enter Helios, the Sun God.

Demeter	Sun, treat me with honour, if ever I pleased you With what I say or what I do. That girl I bore, that innocent flower so fair, I heard her crying in the empty air. You who look down with your sunbeam rays, Did you see who it was who took her away?
Helios	Demeter, bringer of seasons and daughter of Rhea I have to tell you what you won't like to hear: I respect you greatly and honour your grief But Zeus is the culprit and Hades the thief.

Demeter weeps.

Helios	Now stop your weeping and don't be so sore He's not unworthy as son-in-law. He's the Ruler of Many in the land down below He's your own blood, your brother, as you know.

Exit Helios.

Demeter	My own brothers have me betrayed They stole my child, an innocent maid. I curse the Gods because of Hades' lust Henceforth all will turn to dust.

Demeter wanders off crying for Core. Exit Hecate.

SCENE 3

The well at Eleusis

Demeter sits by the well in disguise. Enter Calladice and her sisters.

Calladice	Welcome, old woman, who waits at the well
	You are alone, what tale can you tell?
	Come to our city, our women will welcome you
	We would befriend you with what we say and do.
Demeter	My name is Doso, I just came from Crete
	My heart is sore with travelling and with grief
	I was abducted by pirates, we sailed for many a day
	But when they came to port and feasted, I ran away.
	I crossed bare country, walking through the dark.
	Dear girls, to whose house may I go to find work?
Calladice	Mother, let me and my sisters help you with this.
	I am Calladice, daughter of Celeus of Eleusis
	Our mother Metanira would be honoured if you
	Would come to our place, so this we beg of you.
	We need a nurse for a young son Demophoon,
	He is much loved and you could care for him.

Exeunt all: Calladice and sisters lead Demeter to the palace.

SCENE 4

The palace at Eleusis

Demeter is sad and cast down at the loss of her daughter. Lame Iambe guides her to a stool with a silver cloth. Baubo the old nurse attends.

Iambe	I want to cheer this woman up a bit –
	Shall I tell her a joke or a naughty limerick?
	I'm embarrassed so I'll whisper it in her ear
	As I don't want the audience to hear.

Iambe whispers in Demeter's ear. Demeter remains stony-faced.

Iambe	My best joke failed, she didn't even snicker
(to Baubo)	So Baubo, lift your skirt as you've no knickers!

Baubo the old nurse lifts up her skirt to Demeter and this makes her laugh. Enter Metanira, carrying baby Demophoon (a doll).

Metanira	Dear woman, will you takes a cup of sweetest wine?
Demeter	Wine may not pass my lips but please mix for me
	Some water mixed with pennyroyal and barley.

Metanira gives her this which Demeter takes as a rite.

Metanira   Gracious lady, you have a royal bearing
So I give you little Demophoon, into your caring.
Take care of this child for whom I prayed so hard
And you will certainly receive a just reward.

Demeter   Woman, may the gods bring you all the best.
I will gladly take care of your son as you request.
He'll not suffer from a nurse's ignorance
For I am the mistress of the magic of plants.

Exeunt Demeter and everyone.

SCENE 5
The Palace of Eleusis some time later

Enter Iris.

Iris   And so Demeter brought up Demophoon so fine
She anointed him with ambrosia as if he were divine
She breathed on him sweetly with an adoring gaze
But secretly at night she held him in the blaze
Of the fire so he would never die
Until one night his mother did them espy.

Exit Iris. Enter Metanira, running.

Metanira   My baby, the stranger hides you in the flames
(screaming)   And makes me weak and brings me bitter pain.

Demeter storms in, throwing the baby to the ground.

Demeter   Stupid woman, you didn't know the luck you had
I was doing good and you thought that it was bad.
I would have made your child immortal
But now he's back to being mere mortal.
Yet since he slept in my arms relaxed and unbuttoned,
When he comes to his prime, he won't be forgotten
Because the sons of Eleusis will start to do battle
And will carry on killing and dying like cattle.

Metanira sobs.

Demeter   I am Demeter, the bringer of blessings,
Have the people build me a huge temple
With a resplendent altar at the acropolis
On the hill above the Callichoros
And I myself will inaugurate the mysteries
To teach you how to piously do the ceremonies.

Demeter throws off her disguise and is revealed in majesty. Metanira swoons.

Calladice and sisters rush in to look after her and the baby. Enter Iris.

Iris

At dawn Metanira told all to her husband Celeus
Who called an assembly of the people of Eleusis.
He ordered them to build a sumptuous shrine
For Demeter the mother goddess divine.
So there in the temple Demeter stayed
And great lamentation for her daughter made.

In this terrible year no harvest came
As the cattle pulled their bent ploughs in vain.
For Demeter in her anger hid the seed
And brought to the earth great times of need.

Exit Iris.

SCENE 6
Demeter's temple

Demeter is robed in black. Handmaiden brings in Iris.

Iris

Demeter, father Zeus whose knowledge is endless
Calls upon you to come back to Olympus.
Come on don't let the word of Zeus go unheeded
For now some compromise is needed.

Demeter is unmoved. Goddesses go up in turn to plead with her. Each is brought in by the Handmaiden.

Aphrodite

I come, Aphrodite with my scarf of amity
To plead that you restore the earth's fertility.

Athena

I am Athena with my shining shield
To beg you fair Demeter to bring the harvest yield.

Hera

I come, imperial Hera, with my sceptre of command
To ask that you end the famine on the land.

Artemis

I come, Artemis the Hunter, from the forests deep
To beg you to wake the fields from their sleep.

Tethys

I come, Tethys, with my trident bold
To plead that you let the earth with fruits unfold.

Hestia

I come, Hestia, goddess of the hearth
To plead with you to restore seasons to the earth.

Demeter

I would not ever again set foot on Olympus
However much you plead and fuss
Nor would I restore harvests to the human race
Until I see my daughter's lovely face.

Exeunt all.

SCENE 7

On Mount Olympus

Enter Hermes and Zeus.

Hermes
    Demeter won't listen when she's made up her mind
    The earth will go to ruin and wipe out all mankind.

Zeus
    Demeter is so stubborn! To do her will I'm bound
    She won't let the grass grow till Core is found.
    We need to set her daughter before Demeter's eyes
    So go persuade Hades to yield to a mother's cries.

Exeunt Hermes and Zeus.

SCENE 8

In the Underworld

Hades and Core (as Queen Persephone) sit together on a couch.

Hades
    Cheer up dearest, why are your eyes so red?
    You've lots of subjects though all of them are dead!

Core
    I shan't cheer up! I want you to let me go
    I don't mind visiting but I miss my mum you know!

Enter Hermes.

Hermes
    Hades, King of the Dead
    Zeus ordered me to bring back Queen Persephone
    Who is Demeter's daughter Core
    So that her mother, seeing her with her own eyes
    Would stop her terrible wrath against the gods.
    For she may wipe out the race of man on earth
    Concealing all their seeds in the ground
    So the gods no longer receive their sacrifices.

    She's got a terrible anger,
    And she doesn't mix with the gods,
    But she sits far away from them
    Inside the perfumed temple at Eleusis.

Hades
    My dear, you may go to your mother in her black veil
    Think kindly of me, no need to weep or wail.
    As a husband I am not unworthy of you
    As I am the brother of your father Zeus.
    When you are here, you will reign over everyone
    You will have the greatest honour under the sun.
    There will be eternal punishment for those who
    Do not fulfill the proper ceremonies for you.

Core rejoices and jumps up quickly with joy.

Hades slips a pomegranate seed in a glass of wine and gets Core to drink it. As he does, he speaks aside to the audience.

Hades   Mum's the word!

Exeunt Hermes with Core. Exit Hades.

SCENE 9
Temple to Demeter at Eleusis

Demeter and Core are reunited.

Demeter   First thing, please straightaway assure me
That you ate nothing down there, dearest Core.
For if you did not eat in the Underworld
You'll remain here with me, my darling girl.

Core   Well, mother, when helpful Hermes, the messenger
Was sent by Zeus to collect me from the Underworld
I immediately jumped for joy and didn't pay any heed
When Hades made me eat a pomegranate seed.
How he came and seized me – with connivance by Zeus,
And carried me into the earth, I will tell you.
We were all of us in a lovely meadow at Enna
With Electra, Ianthe, Fair Calypso and Urania,
Cutting lovely flowers: iris, rosebuds and lilies
And a gorgeous narcissus which I was about to seize –
When the earth opened and the dark Lord
Grabbed me and carried me off in his gold chariot.
Terrified, I cried aloud. I tell you all this
Though it still causes me great distress.

They embrace. Hecate enters and hugs Core. Enter Rhea, mother of Demeter.

Rhea   Come here, my daughter. Zeus with his deep voice
Calls you to come up to the race of gods
And he offers to give you whatever honours
You want among the gods who live forever.
He consents that your daughter spend a third part
Of the year in the mist darkness as Queen Persephone
And the other two parts with you and the other gods.
But come now my child and obey him!

Don't be too angry with Zeus in his dark clouds
And make the crops productive now for humans.

Demeter   Forthwith shall I bring in a harvest from the lands
And weigh the whole earth down with flowers.
I will teach the kings who administer the law
The ministry of my rites. And I shall reveal to them
The mysteries of the worship of the corn
That in silence is the seed of wisdom born.

Demeter showers the audience with flowers.

THE END

Note

This story is taken from the *Homeric Hymn to Demeter* from the 8th or 7th cenury BC. The tale of Demeter's frantic search for her daughter Core was re-enacted (possibly on the Autumn Equinox itself) during the Eleusinian Mysteries. These were ten days (15th–24th September) of rituals and offerings which gave comfort to generations of initiates between the late 15th century BC and 400 AD when the sanctuary at Eleusis was destroyed by the Goths.

EASTER PACE EGG PLAY

CAST

Lou, handmaid to Dame Spring	Doctor Brown
Sue, handmaid to Dame Spring	Tosspot
Dame Spring	Lord Nelson
King George	Dirty Bet
Prince of Paradise (also called Bold Slasher)	Soldier
Molly Masket	Paddy from Cork

Audience participate by joining in the Pace Egg Song.

All sing

> Come search up your money,
> Be jubilant and free,
> And give us your pace egg
> For Easter Monday.
>
> Go down to your cellars
> And see what you'll find
> If your barrels be empty
> I hope you'll provide;
>
> I hope you'll provide
> Sweet eggs and strong beer,
> And we'll come no more to you
> Until the next year.

Enter Lou and Sue, handmaidens to Dame Spring.

Lou

> Welcome good people, we bring a tale of yore,
> I'm Lou and she's Sue; we've never acted before.

Sue

> We're Dame Spring's maids with our Easter bonnets,
> We hope you lads will write us merry sonnets.

Lou

> In case you don't, try this surprise
> We'll now splash water in your eyes.

Lou and Sue flick water at the audience.

Sue

> Here's water for your home and for your land,
> And water for your health, it's better than sand.

Lou

> Don't shriek and cry and run away;
> For we bring good luck on pace-egging day.

Sue	Now we've done our best, we can do no more, So step in Dame Spring, come in at the door.

Enter Dame Spring.

Dame Spring	I am Dame Spring to bring our merry rhyme For pray you remember it's pace-egging time. At Easter we have lots of fun There's much more to it than the hot cross bun.
Lou	There's flicking water, skipping on the hill To make sure the crops germinate well.
Sue	With the eggs we couldn't eat in Lenten-tide We do egg rolling and egg hunting outside. The egg is the symbol of the seed you know When the cosmic egg breaks, the corn will grow.
Lou	We symbolise the serpent by walking the maze Where the mystery's revealed in many ways.
Dame Spring	As days grow long and nights grow short Between rivals there's a battle to be fought. King George, radiant symbol of the light, Must fight a dark and doughty knight. If you don't believe a word I say Step in King George and clear the way.

Exeunt Dame Spring, Lou and Sue. Enter King George.

King George	In steps I, King George, a champion bold With my sword I won three crowns of gold.

Enter Prince of Paradise.

Prince of Paradise	In steps I, Prince of Paradise, black Morocco King My sword is ready and my bridle bells ring. I'm brave, lads, and that's what makes me good; Watch out, George, I'll spill your precious blood.
King George	If thou be made of Jinnu's race I'll make blood sprinkle down thy face. If thou be made of noble blood I'll make it run like Noah's flood.
Prince of Paradise	Black as I am, and black I be Lately come from Afrikee, Africa's my dwelling-place And now I'll fight thee face to face.

They fight and the Prince of Paradise falls. Enter Molly Masket.

Molly Masket	Oh George, oh George, what hast thou done? Thou's gone and slain my only son! My only son, my only heir, Canst thou not see him bleeding there?
George	He asked me to fight, and why should I deny? I cut his body up and made his buttons fly. I've heard of doctors far and near I've heard of one in Spain I'm sure if he was here he'd bring That dead man to life again.

George takes out his purse.

I'll give, 5, 10, 15, 25 pounds for a doctor
Is there not one to be had?

Enter Doctor Brown.

Doctor Brown	Yes, in steps I, old Jackie Brown The best old doctor in this town.
King George	What can you cure?
Doctor Brown	Ipsy-pipsy, palsy and the gout The plague within and the plague without. If there's nineteen devils in that man I'm sure to drive one-and-twenty out.
King George	Go to and drive them out!

Doctor Brown *(taking out his watch)*

Here I lay down my gold watch
Points to half past one hundred and forty four
I have also a little bottle in my inside

(checking all his pockets) Outside, right-side, left-side, waistcoat pocket
Which my granny gave me three days after she died,
Saying 'Take this, it'll bring any dead man to life'.

Molly Masket	Please bring my dead son to life again! Oh, a mother's life is full of pain!

Doctor gives the Prince a dose.

Doctor Brown	Here, Jack, take a drop of this bottle Let it run down thy throttle Rise up, Bold Slasher, and fight again.

Molly Masket raises a leg of the dead man.

Molly Masket	As green as grass and as cold as brass This man's never stirred a limb yet, doctor.

Doctor Brown   Perhaps my wife's given me the wrong bottle.

Molly Masket   Thou's a limestone!

Doctor Brown *(produces another bottle)* Then perhaps it's my mistake.
        Here Jack, take a drop of this nip-nap
        Let it run down thy thip-thap
        Rise up, Bold Slasher and fight again.

Prince of Paradise rises.

Prince   Oh! My back!
of Paradise

Doctor Brown   What's amiss with thy back?

Prince   My back is bound, my sword is sound
of Paradise   I'll have King George another round.

George   Step forward, Bold Slasher, for another battle
        Draw thy sword, let's see your mettle.

They fight again briefly. Enter Tosspot and Dame Spring.

Tosspot *(shouting)* Stop, stop these swords without delay
        And fight again another day.

King George and the Prince of Paradise shake hands.

King George   That's it, our equinoctial fight is done.
        The battle's neither lost nor won.

Prince   Light and dark remain in equipoise
of Paradise   Thanks to Tosspot and all his noise!

Dame Spring   So the fight is stopped by old Tosspot you see
        A jolly old fellow in every degree.
        He wears a top hat and he wears a pigtail
        And all his delight is drinking mulled ale.

Tosspot   Here I am, an old coffee grinder
        I've lost my wife and I cannot find her.
        If any of you see her, you must send her back
        She's got two broken legs and a hump on her back.
        Although I am ragged and not so well dressed
        I can kiss bonny lasses as well as the rest.

Dame Spring   In his dress, he's a shambles
        And in his speech he don't half ramble!
        Mr Tosspot, here's Molly to meet you, you see
        She's a jolly old lass as ever you see.

Molly Masket	You may be a tosspot but you're not my pot of gold
	For you chase all the lasses or so I've been told.
	For I've gold and I've silver and copper in store
	And by coming pace-egging I hope to get more.
	So the next to come in is Lord Nelson, you see
	With a bunch of blue ribbons right down to his knee.

Enter Lord Nelson.

Lord Nelson	The medals on my chest like silver are shiney
	To show all the battles I won on the briney
	(Trafalgar, Battle of the Nile, and there were more
	But at my age it is hard to keep score.)
	We national heroes are not always solemn
	You can't be when pigeons mess on your column.
	So the next to come in is our dear Dirty Bet
	Who keeps losing her drawers so her petticoat's wet.

Enter Dirty Bet.

Dirty Bet	I'm fresh from the country, old London to view
	And I'll join in pace-egging with this jolly crew.
	I've got a basket for my eggs, a pocket for my brass
	And two bonny lips as I'm a bonny lass.
	If there's anyone as wants to kiss me
	They better be sharp before they miss me.

Enter Soldier.

Soldier	I'm the next to come in, a soldier you see
	I've fought against the French in a far country.
	I've a sword by my side wherever I go
	To teach all the young lasses so and so.
	I think that Bet's offering more than kisses
	I say, she looks a lot keener than my missus.

Soldier kisses Dirty Bet.

| Dirty Bet | So the next to come in is poor Paddy from Cork |
| | He hails from Old Ireland and comes to seek work. |

Enter Paddy.

Paddy	I've a scythe on my back and I come to work hay
	I'm a hard-working lad for a pittance of pay.
	On St Patrick's Day I had a drop of the porter
	To tell you the truth it was more than I ought
	And when I've got money by might and by main
	Well then I'll be off to old Erin again.

Dirty Bet   Our play is now ended so we'll sing our song
It's got a jolly tune and it's not too long.

All *(sing)*   These times they are hard and the money is scant
But one pace egg of yours is all that we want;
And if you will grant us this little small thing
We'll all charm our voices and merry we'll sing.

Come search up your money
And see that it's right;
If you give nowt, we'll take nowt.
Farewell and goodnight!

THE END

Note

The Pace Egg Play is found in the North of England. The word 'Pace' means Easter, when the play was performed. There are recent revivals, for example in Heptonstall, West Yorkshire. In this version Admiral Lord Nelson (1758–1805) is one of the 'pace eggers' who witness the fight between St George (representing Day) and the Prince of Paradise (who is Night). The tune of the 'Pace Egg Song' is available via the Internet or can be improvised.

FIVE BREAK THE SPELL

CAST

Aunt Fanny

Uncle Quentin

Julian

Dick

Anne

George, a girl

Timmy, the dog

Neil, a lost boy

Mr Earthy

Mrs Earthy

Baron Bramshill

Lady Writer

PC Fortescue

Audience participate by forming two lines and joining hands across to make a tunnel in the chase scene.

PROLOGUE
At home

Enter Aunt Fanny and Uncle Quentin.

Aunt Fanny   Well, Quentin, the children are off on holiday.
Were we right to let them have their way?
And go off camping on that farm
Without parents to keep them from harm?
I worry they'll meet someone shifty
Even though it's only 1950.

Quentin   Dear Fanny, don't bother me with silly cares.
I've far more pressing government affairs.
If the children get into a scrape,
I'm sure they'll manage to escape.

Fanny   Quentin, you're in a fearful mood.
I only hope I gave them enough food.

Exeunt Uncle Quentin and Aunt Fanny.

SCENE 1
At the campsite

Enter Julian and Dick from a tent marked 'Boys'.

Julian   Dick, what a spiffing campsite –
Next to a farmhouse, it's just right.
Now we've finished our unpacking
We can start some serious snacking.

| Dick | Yes, Julian, there are sandwiches and ham
Followed by cake with strawberry jam. |

Enter Anne and George with Timmy the dog from a tent marked 'Girls'.

| Anne | We'll drink water from a bubbling spring.
On holiday we won't worry about a thing.
George, after eating we'll wash the dishes.
We girls must do all the boys' wishes. |

| George | No, Anne, I'm not doing such a girlish task.
Why should we do what the boys ask?
I'd rather spend time with my dog Timmy –
He's a brave dog, not a silly ninny. |

| Timmy | I'm George's dog, I take her orders.
It's my job to see off marauders.
Whenever there is harm around
You can rely on this sharp-eared hound. |

| Anne | On this holiday, I shan't do anything exciting.
I find adventures much too nail-biting. |

| George | With excitement, all the world's our stage.
Otherwise, life's dull as the printed page. |

| Julian | Yes, adventures make us come alive.
That's why we're called the 'Famous Five'. |

| Dick | Well, I've brought some field glasses.
I'll look through them to see what passes.
And when we've finished bird-spotting,
We can see if there's any plotting. |

George takes the binoculars.

| George | Look, there's an interesting old place.
Wait! In the window – I saw a face! |

Julian takes the binoculars.

| Julian | It's a ruined mill, quite alone.
The country round is overgrown.
There's no-one there, just a flapping curtain.
You're a girl, George, you can't be certain. |

Enter Neil.

| Neil | Hello chaps, have you come to stay?
Would you mind very much if I join your play? |

| Dick *(aside)* | Who's joining us at this pleasant spot?
He strikes me as a bit of a swot, |

	And acts as if he's in a daze.
	I think he's used to city ways.
Neil	My name is Neil and I'm new to the country.
	I'm staying at the farm with my aunty.
	It is a bit of a bummer,
	But my parents have left me for the summer.
Julian	You're quite welcome to join us, Neil.
	Don't mind the dog – Timmy, heel.

Timmy sniffs round Neil, then licks his hand.

Anne	Timmy's given him a lick –
	Don't worry, he's going to click.
Neil	I'm interested in local history.
	Round here, there's a bit of mystery.
	Some stories of a talented lady,
	Taken away by someone shady.
George	Do you know anything about that old mill?
	Tell us about it if you will.
Neil	I read about it in a weighty tome.
	It used to be part of a stately home.
	All the ways to it are hidden.
	It's private property: entry forbidden.
George *(aside)*	Best not tell him what we saw:
	He still might turn out a bit of a bore.
Julian	Let's go to the farmhouse to find someone to quiz.
	At the same time, we'll get some lemon fizz.

Exeunt all to the farmhouse.

SCENE 2
At the farmhouse, and later in the bushes

Mr and Mrs Earthy are in the farmhouse. Enter Julian, Dick, Ann, George, Timmy and Neil.

Mrs Earthy	I'm Mrs Earthy, you must be friends of Neil
	Come in and have an enormous meal.
	Or at least a drink of lemonade.
(gives the children	You'll like it – it's real home-made.
lemonade)	While you children enjoy a burp
	I'll give the dog a bowl to slurp.

Mrs Earthy gives Timmy water.

Mrs Earthy	Now this is my husband, Mr Earthy He's decent, strong and worthy. You'll find he doesn't say much – He simply lacks the social touch. He works all day in the fields And comes home late to eat his meals.
Dick	We want to ask about the old ruin, And find out what people there are doing.
Mrs Earthy	The old mill isn't worth a visit. There's lots round here: you won't miss it.
Mr Earthy	That place isn't farmed. It's full of weeds. Folk talks about wicked deeds.
Mrs Earthy	Husband, I'm sure you're right. Why one midsummer night, I thought I heard some gentle clicks – My imagination must have been playing tricks. Well, children, off you go to play – Not to the mill; some other way. And remember what I've said – Don't let wild ideas go to your head.
Anne	We'll do just as you've asked us, And spend our time in country pastures.

Exeunt Mr and Mrs Earthy.

Dick	I think there's something fishy here. We've heard strange tales of yesteryear. Seen a ruined mill and overgrown land. A face at the window and people banned.
Neil	What a pity we can't explore. For my studies, I'd like to find out more.
George	I vote that we stay up late And leave our tents to investigate.
Anne	Please don't let's spoil our holiday bliss – Adventures are one thing I'd rather miss.
Julian	I say we can go to the boundary fence – That won't affect our innocence.
Dick	Look, here comes a stranger. I'm afraid he may spell danger.

Enter Baron Bramshill.

Baron	I'm Lord of the Manor, most superior.
	I'm Baron Bramshill. There's nothing queer here.
	I'm a publisher like Faber and Fabers –
	I don't care about my rural neighbours.
	They're just a bunch of peasants.
	I warn you I can be most unpleasant
	If I see you spying with field-glasses –
	And I'm also beastly to trespassers.
	So remember children: stop prowling.
(to George)	And you: stop that dog growling.
	Now then, all of you be off.
	Don't mess with me, the local toff.

Exit Baron Bramshill.

Dick	Well, that's the end of our exploring.
	I fear the holiday will turn out boring.
Anne	Let's forget about wicked crimes.
	Neil, you can tell us about old times.
Neil	That Baron Bramshill – there's little known
	About the history of his family home.
Julian	I've had enough of this scary talk.
	Let's go and find somewhere else to walk.
	Over there looks like an interesting patch.
	Just where Timmy's having a scratch.
Timmy	Audience, off your backsides, up you get.
	This is where you become the set.
	Listen to me, I'm the canine boss
	Form two facing lines and join hands across.

Audience form two lines and join hands across, creating a tunnel entrance.

George	Oh Timmy, what have you found?
	Life's so much better when you're around.
	Now I see the meaning of his canine message:
	Timmy's found a secret passage.
Anne	Do you think it will lead into the estate
	Of the man who's filled with hate?
Julian	If so, it may mean we'll get some stick
	Which means it's a job for me and Dick.
George	It always has to be you and Dick –
	I have to say it makes me sick.

	I'm jolly fed up with your attitude. Boys aren't better. It's a platitude.
Dick	Gender equality is George's fad So when we exclude her, she goes mad.
Julian	George, you'll have a valued role Guarding the entrance to this secret hole. I'd like to ask you how you'd feel Staying here with Anne and Neil.
Neil	Can't I join you on your dare? Why must I stay here – it's not fair.
Anne	If you went, your aunty would be cross. Do what Julian says – he's the boss.
Julian	We'll go into this rocky chamber To find out if there's any danger.

Julian and Dick go down the tunnel.

George	Those two boys get on my wick. I'm going to follow Julian and Dick. Timmy you can be my guard If you see a villain, bite him hard.

George and Timmy go down the tunnel but do not catch up.

Anne	Oh Neil, I do hope they'll be all right. Those dark tunnels give me a fright.
Neil	I always get a rotten deal. It must be because my name is Neil.

SCENE 3

Through the tunnel

At the other end of the tunnel. Julian and Dick are hiding in the mouth of the tunnel. The Lady Writer is chained to her typewriter.

Julian	I hear voices. Let's hide behind this rock, And watch a minute while we take stock.
Lady Writer	Fifty years I've spent in captivity, Compelled each day to creativity, Forced by the baron's evil looks To slave away at children's books. I turn out a stream of psychodrama To corrode the public's moral armour.

Enter Baron.

Baron	Come on woman, you must grovel.
	Churn out one more children's novel:
	I don't care if it's ideological trash –
	All I want is lots more cash.

Baron

Come on woman, you must grovel.
Churn out one more children's novel:
I don't care if it's ideological trash –
All I want is lots more cash.

Lady writer

Cruel man! What a horrible task.
Artistic freedom is all I ask.

Baron *(sees Julian and Dick)* Wait a moment! What's that noise?
I've discovered those two boys.
Scoundrels! What are you doing here
After I warned you not to interfere.

Baron catches Julian and Dick and ties them up.

Baron

You've led me a merry dance.
Now you'll be my captive audience.

Dick

Oh no, we're tied up with rope.
We can't escape. We haven't a hope.

Baron

There may be more where these came from.
I'm off down the tunnel for another one.

Baron enters tunnel and approaches George. Before he reaches her, she speaks.

George

Timmy you've pricked your ears right up.
I do believe you've picked my fears up.

(sees Baron)

On no, it's the wicked lord,
Come to tie us up with cord.
Quick, Timmy, go back to Anne.
She'll get help if she can.

Baron captures George. Timmy goes back to the opening of the tunnel.

Baron

Now then you interfering boy
Come with me, don't be coy.

George

I'm as good as any lad.
I say, let me go, you cad.

Baron takes George to the mill end of the tunnel. The action shifts to the other end.

Anne

Oh no, Timmy's come back without George.
Something's happened in that gorge.

Neil

Do you think they're in trouble?
Let's go down, at the double.

Anne	No. I think my idea's the tops.
	Let's run to the farm and call the cops.

Exeunt Neil, Anne and Timmy. The action shifts to the mill.

Baron	Alright, audience, you've done your bit.
	Go and find somewhere to sit.

SCENE 4
At the mill

Julian, Dick and George are tied up. The Baron has power over Lady Writer.

Baron	Now I've got you in my power,
	A captive audience in my tower,
	Re-united with your creator.
	Let's find out if you hate her.
Julian	Baron, I say you're very wicked.
	Let us go. It's not cricket.
George	I find this very shocking.

There is a knocking at the door.

George	But wait a minute, who's that knocking?

Enter Mr & Mrs Earthy, Neil, Anne, Timmy and PC Fortescue. They remain outside the mill.

PC Fortescue	Open up! Police force to the rescue.
	My name is PC Fortescue.
	Don't let the rhyme offend you –
	I'm here to apprehend you.
Mrs Earthy	Now's the time that good faces evil
	At the Baron's home, the devil.
	He'll claim he's got nothing to hide,
	But I bet the children are inside.
Anne	We want to be re-united with the famous three.
	Hurry so we can set them free.
Neil	From now on I'll stay in the background.
	I'll watch and won't make any sound.

The rescuers enter.

Baron	Zounds, the game is truly up.
	I'm caught out by a growing pup.

PC Fortescue	The law will claim full redress.
	Baron, I insist – you must confess.
Baron	It's true. I'm guilty of a serious crime.
	This old lady's had a miserable time.
	I kidnapped her at a tender age
	And made her write page after page.
	While she produced the books in haste,
	I manipulated public taste.
	I trapped those children in a world of fiction.
	But she made them utter such dreadful diction.
Lady Writer	Yes, I know my work is not very right on.
	But I'll now reveal that I'm Enid Blyton.
	I was forced to do all that typewriting.
	But I do regret the stereotyping.
Anne	Until now I was always meek and mild.
	From here on in, I'm going wild.
Julian	I really think I came off worst.
	It's hard work always being first.
Dick	I'm actually quite a sensitive soul.
	You gave me the opposite role.
George	I never had adventures as of right.
	Thanks to you, it was one big fight.
Timmy	I was always on my best behaviour
	To be the children's doggy saviour.
Lady Writer	Well children, you've done very well.
	This time you've managed to break the spell.
	And now you've earned your release,
	You can live your lives in peace.
PC Fortescue	I've telephoned to Kirrin Bay
	George's parents are on the way.
	So now go to the railway station
	To begin your parents' education.
	Fanny and Quentin will meet you there.
	Your adventure's given them quite a scare.

EPILOGUE

Enter Aunt Fanny and Uncle Quentin.

Fanny

We've seen the error of our ways,
Neglecting our children for days and days.
From now on we'll be more responsible,
Thanks to the warning of the constable.

Quentin

I promise my affairs won't be in such a whirl
That I forget if George is a boy or a girl.
And the minute we get home,
I'll give Timmy a juicy bone.
So all our mistakes were in a good cause.
Now we give way to your applause.

THE END

GREAT EXPECTATIONS

A tale of many parents and few children,
adapted from the novel by Charles Dickens

CAST

Politics, a prologue
Parenthood, another prologue
Pip, the hero
Joe Gargery, a blacksmith
Mrs Joe, Pip's sister
Magwitch
Compeyson, a villain
Sergeant-at-Arms
Miss Havisham, a rich old lady
Estella, her adopted daughter

Herbert Pocket, friend of Pip
Mrs Pocket
Jane Pocket
Pocket children
Nursemaid *(non-speaking)*
Jaggers, a lawyer
Wemmick, clerk to Jaggers
The Aged, parent to Wemmick
Bentley Drummle, a dandy
The Judge

A teller is needed to count the votes.

The action takes place in the early 19th century, in the marshes of Kent and in London.

The audience hiss and growl as the Kentish mist, and join hands to make the river Thames. They shout the cries of London, nod at the Aged, and vote at the end.

The Pocket children 'tumble up' when they go near Mrs Pocket.

PROLOGUE

Enter Politics and Parenthood, with Pip and Joe.

Politics	I'm Politics. As prologue, I set the scene And tell you what the play might mean: Just now, election fever grips all nations: But what happened to our great expectations? We're fed up with spin and cant – We need a play with a political slant.
(indicates Pip)	The hero's Pip, on whose youthful zest Our hopes for a new beginning rest.
	Will he find triumph or despair? Or worse, end up like Tony Blair? Will he lead us to perdition Or be the star of a coalition?

Parenthood	I'm Parenthood. I see meaning closer to home
	In the family life that each has known.
	You'll see this play's about Mums and Dads,
	And how their absence affects growing lads.
(indicates Joe)	Joe Gargery is kind to a poor orphan –
	He's not a symbol for the working man.
	He found goodness through life's travails –
	Nothing to do with political wiles.
	So let's forget about Panorama:
	Sit back and enjoy the psychodrama.
Politics	Your psychobabble's got me in a rage.
	I'm right! So let's clear the stage.
	At the end, the audience can decide
	Which of us is taking them for a ride.
Parenthood	But first, audience, play the weather: mist.
	So let's hear you hiss and hiss.
	Remember: it's frightening. Let's see a scowl.
	And for sound, I suggest a growl.

Audience hiss and growl.

Politics	First we meet Pip on his own
	Sitting sadly by his parents' gravestone.
	Two men have escaped from a prison ship:
	Through the mist, one appears and frightens Pip.

Exeunt Politics, Parenthood and Joe. Pip sits by the gravestone.

Pip	My innocent but heavy heart
	Gets the play off to its start.
	A better future is what I crave
	As I sit alone by the family grave.

Enter Magwitch who grabs Pip.

Magwitch	Gotcha! Now you little whelp
	I'll kill you if you don't get help.
	I've escaped from a prison hell.
	What's your name? Where do you dwell?
Pip	Pip, sir. My parents lie under this stone.
	I live with my sister at the blacksmith's home.
Magwitch	You may be frightened by our sudden tryst –
	But at least I'm not a terrorist –
	Just a man with a desperate past.
	Now: get me food. Do it secret. Do it fast.

	Bring a file. Don't stand and quiver. Do as I ask, or I'll eat your liver.
Pip	How I wish I had a father! I'd best go home and raid the larder.

Exit Pip.

| Magwitch | Here in this vile landscape
Another convict has escaped:
Compeyson – one evil dude
With whom I've got a lifelong feud. |

Enter Pip with food, drink and file.

Pip	Here's what you want. While you gorge, I'll get back to the blacksmith's forge.
Magwitch	Thankee, Pip. You've been true. I'll remember this whatever I do.
Pip	On the way I saw a man who looked queer. I must go: soldiers are drawing near!

Exit Pip. Enter Compeyson.

| Compeyson | I'm shifty and I'm on the run.
I'm the villain, Compeyson.
In the past, my double-dealing tongue
Has done Magwitch grievous wrong. |

Magwitch *(sees Compeyson)* I don't want any more of your stories.
You've done more harm than all the Tories.
There's nothing worse than one who grasses
Especially to us under-classes.
Fight! You're so posh and prim
I'll tear you limb from limb.

Magwitch and Compeyson fight. Enter Sergeant-at-Arms.

| Sergeant | In comes the Law. Now you two roughs
Put an end to these fisticuffs. |

Sergeant separates Magwitch and Compeyson.

Sergeant *(to Compeyson)* *(to Magwitch)*	Now you'll see the error of your ways Year after year, you'll suffer endless days. Magwitch, escaping was a serious blunder You'll spend the rest of your life down under.
Magwitch	I couldn't give a Castlemaine 4X It can't be worse than those prison wrecks.

Enter Pip. Exeunt Magwitch, Compeyson and Sergeant-at-Arms.

Pip	This experience of childhood trauma
	Could turn out a character-former.
	It could even teach me the knack
	Of difficult decisions about Iraq.

Enter Joe and Mrs Joe.

Joe	I symbolise the honest labour movement
	Dedicated to work and self improvement.
	I'm a strong man whose power is dormant.
	Sadly, the missus makes my life a torment.

Mrs Joe	Husband, you're just plain daft.
	I'm the one who has to graft.
	I've no time for men who are mushy.
	You'll get nowhere if you're not pushy.
	And Pip, I'll see your hide is tanned.
(clips Pip)	I'm the one who brought you up by hand.

Joe	Pip, when your sister's temper sparks
	Just think of the future and say, what larks!

Mrs Joe *(to Pip)*	Brother, Miss Havisham has sent for you.
	I don't know what you're meant to do.
	In a great house she lives by herself;
	Tales are told of fabulous wealth.
	If you turn out to be her cup of tea
	She'll make you rich or give you property.

Exeunt Joe and Mrs Joe. Pip goes to Miss Havisham's.

Pip	I'm just happy to go somewhere new.
	It's better than being beaten black and blue.

Enter Miss Havisham.

Miss Havisham	I lived a quiet and sheltered life
	Until a man asked me to be his wife.
	I was jilted on my wedding day
	And left with a terrible price to pay.
	Since then my passion has been burning:
	This is one lady that's not for turning.
	Since I was cut off in my bridal bloom
	I've shut out light, and live in gloom.
	I fill my days with bitter hate
	And wish all men an evil fate.

> I never see a single visitor
> Except my ward and my solicitor.
> Yes, I'm finished with all women and men.
> I loathe you audience! Now Pip come in.

Pip   Miss Havisham, I'll treat you plain and fair
               I've not come to be your heir.

Miss Havisham Pip, you seem a decent sort of boy.
               But I'll make you my unwitting toy.

Miss Havisham takes Pip's shoulder. They walk together.

Miss Havisham Now let my restless spirit walk.
               Go with my ward Estella for a talk.

Enter Estella.

Estella   Pip, you're a mucky pup.
               It must be hard work growing up.
               Now I'll add my withering scorn –
               You'll wish that you had never been born.

Miss Havisham She's the brightest star in the firmament.
               You'll love her, Pip – it'll be permanent.

Pip   I can see that psychologically
               She's an orphan, just like me.
               Yet I love her amazing beauty –
               And all the more, since she's so snooty.

Estella   Alright Pip, you may kiss me.

Estella offers Pip her hand – he kisses it.

Estella   Now I'm going, just to make you miss me.

Exeunt Estella and Miss Havisham.

Pip   Now I've seen higher things
               My social aspirations have taken wings.
               I rue the day I was born humble
               Alas! All hopes of love must crumble.

Enter Politics and Parenthood.

Politics   Now audience, does this bygone wizened crone
               Remind you of a politician close to home?
               A party revolt ended her reign –
               Watch out Prime Minister, it could happen again!

Parenthood	I admire your satirical bite
	But this old lady's no Thatcherite.
	And, please, it simply isn't fair
	To draw comparison with Tony Blair,
	Or the travails of Gordon Brown,
	Or even Liberals who want to bring the PM down.
	She's twisted, but of kindness there's a tiny modicum…
Politics	You're right – she's more like Anne Widdecombe.

Exeunt Politics and Parenthood. Enter Miss Havisham.

Miss Havisham	Years have passed and Pip is still smitten
	With Estella, my adopted sex kitten.
	Now Pip, thanks for all the visits you have made.
	As reward, I'll bind you to a trade.
	Fetch your sister and your guardian
	The blacksmith's an honest working man.

Enter Joe and Mrs Joe.

Miss Havisham	Pip will be your apprentice. I'll pay a premium.
(to Joe)	Go on blacksmith, name your sum.
Joe	There's no need for money, I meantersay
	Well, Miss, it would have happened anyway.

Miss Havisham *(giving Joe money)*

	Take this!
(to Pip)	Gargery is your master now.
	Expect no more from this old cow.

Exit Miss Havisham.

Mrs Joe *(scolding Pip and Joe)*

	Gargery! You're a bumbling lout.
	It's *my* persistence has brought this about.
	I've lived my life on a pittance –
	Now hand over that remittance.

Mrs Joe takes money from Joe. Enter Jaggers.

Jaggers	In comes I from the Inns of Court
	Trials of felons are my sport.
	Beware all you rogues and blaggers
	Pay due respect to the name of Jaggers.
	I'm a sort of legal giant
	Miss Havisham is my client.
	But there's one reason I've made this trip –
	That's to find a boy named Pip.

Pip	I'm Pip, sir, and this is Joe Gargery.
	He's like a step-father to me.
Jaggers	Well, Pip, you've got great wealth to come,
	But your patron insists on keeping mum.
	You must never ask the source of your wealth:
	Leave the mystery person to announce themself.
	Believe me, it's no exaggeration
	To say you've got great expectations!
	There's more news on top of this:
	You're to be educated in the metropolis.
	Joe Gargery, Mrs Joe – what do you say?
	Will you stand in this boy's way?
Joe	Which I meantersay, Pip, what's good for you…
	As long as you remain honest and true.
Mrs Joe	I'll bet the benefactor is Miss Havisham.
	She's got riches – she's bound to lavish 'em.
	But now I must leave this stage –
	Carried off by a sub-plot, never more to rampage.

Exit Mrs Joe.

Jaggers	Pip, as you embark upon your dreams
	You'll find London a city of extremes.
	Rich, poor and the criminal crowd:
	Hear their babble and their cries out loud.

Audience *(making the cries of London)*
> 'Any old iron'
> 'Have you any pots and pans?'
> 'Got a new motor?'
> 'Vote for Ken'
> 'Vote Boris'
> 'Mind the Gap'
> 'Buy the Big Issue'
> 'Roll up for the Olympics'.

Jaggers	But you must disregard these squeals
	And aim for a life that's more genteel.
	Here's the man to guide you through this epidemic:
	He's level-headed, he's my clerk Wemmick.

Exit Jaggers. Enter Wemmick.

Wemmick *(gives Pip money and papers)*
> You'll want money. Take this docket.
> Your room mate will be Herbert Pocket.

Mr Pip, your great expectations
Are bound to bring so many temptations.
Living in the suburb of Walworth
I symbolize the domestic hearth.
You can see me as the middle class vote
On which new Labour once did dote.

Enter Herbert.

Herbert   I'm Herbert Pocket who will take you to parties –
We'll be men about town, a couple of smarties.
You're going to study with my Dad
And meet my mother who's slightly mad.

Enter Mrs Pocket (reading a book).

Mrs Pocket   I'm Mrs Pocket with a cameo role
I've got lots of children or so I'm told.
I just ignore them as I'm so well-bred;
The nursemaid sees they're watered and fed.

Enter Pocket children and nursemaid.

Pocket children We Pocket children, when we come near mother
We tumble up and fall down on each other.

Children run to Mrs Pocket and fall up and down.

Jane Pocket *(holding a large doll)*
I'm Jane Pocket, mother's sensible daughter
I often save the baby from fire and water.
Of health and safety our mother's reckless
I must take charge because she's feckless.

Mrs Pocket   Jane, you naughty girl to interfere
Nursemaid, take the children out of here.

Exeunt Jane Pocket, children and nursemaid, followed by Mrs Pocket.

Herbert   Now, Pip we must meet Mr Bentley Drummle
He's a trendy chap, a right Beau Brummel.

Enter Bentley Drummle.

Bentley   I'm one of your social set – a real fop.
Drummle   I've got money, but not much up top.

Herbert   Now Pip, here's news to knock you down:
I've heard Estella's come to town.

Enter Estella.

Estella	Now that I've arrived in London
	The male sex here is wholly undone.
	I have my orders from Miss Havisham:
	Estella, she said, spurn 'em and ravish 'em!

Pip	Estella, you know how I feel:
	Let me love you now I'm genteel.
	Surely the meaning of my good fortune
	Is that we'll be together one day soon.

Estella	Pip, I despise your adoration.
	My pleasure's in your frustration.
	Men can't resist my jewels and beauty:
	To me they're only sexual booty.
	Bentley Drummle is cruel and stupid.
	So I'll choose him to be my cupid.

| Bentley Drummle | Sorry, blacksmith's boy |
| | I'll take Estella for my toy. |

Exeunt Bentley Drummle and Estella. Enter Joe.

| Herbert | Pip, here's a new delight |
| | Joe Gargery's come in sight. |

Exit Herbert.

| Pip | I love him but he's an embarrassment |
| | I can do without this social harassment. |

| Joe | I thought I'd visit you in the Smoke |
| | But I feel out of place. It's no joke. |

| Pip | I don't mind that you're uncouth |
| | You can't help it – that's the truth. |

Joe	Alas, the honest boy who started out
	Has now forgotten what it's all about.
	Well, sir, you've left me smarting.
	But life is made of oh-so-many partings.

Exit Joe.

Pip	Now I'm beginning to have regrets –
	Despised in love and full of debts.
	London snobbery makes me sick
	I'll seek out sanity in Mr Wemmick.
	He'll help me when I'm down –
	Although he couldn't help Gordon Brown.

Enter Wemmick.

Wemmick	There's one sure way to know where you stand:
	It's portable property, cash in hand.
	Away from the office, at home at Walworth
	Come and see my true worth.

Enter the Aged.

Wemmick	Pip, there's one way to know who you are
	It's to show respect to one's aged Pa.
Aged	My son John honours me the most
	Even though I'm deaf as a post.
Wemmick	Look he's as snug as a pea in a pod
	Make him happy, give him a nod.

Pip and Aged nod.

Wemmick	Audience, show respect to parenthood
	Give him a nod and do it good.

Audience and Aged nod. Exeunt Wemmick and Aged.

Pip	This vigorous head shaking
	Has left my emotions quaking.
	I realise I've turned from the path of virtue
	And done things I shouldn't ought to.

Enter Magwitch.

Magwitch	Pip, I'm the one who gave the dosh
	To get you learning and make you posh.
	Remember me from the swamp?
	You thought I was only an old tramp.
	When I was banished to Van Diemen's Land
	I made a fortune and became quite grand.
	So thank me for being your patron
	And turning you from orphan to gentleman.
Pip	Oh no! This is a social disgrace
	I'll never be able to show my face.
	I thought I was intended for Estella.
	Instead, I owe it all to this old fella.
Herbert	For a returned transport, one thing follows:
	Recapture is sure to mean the gallows.
Magwitch	I've nothing to fear
	No-one knows I'm here.
Herbert	Our fear for your safety is over-riding
	You must live abroad: till then, go into hiding.

Pip	What he's done, he did for me
	The least I can do is help him flee.
(to Magwitch)	Magwitch, at first you made me recoil.
	But from now on, I'll be loyal.

Exeunt Herbert and Magwitch.

Pip	My world has completely fallen apart
	Miss Havisham caused my broken heart.

Enter Miss Havisham.

Miss Havisham	Forgive me, Pip, for what I've done.
	Yes, I was the one who led you on.
	Now my mind is quite de-railed.
	Everything I've done has failed.
	Nothing now can get any worse.
	They'll have to take me out in a hearse.
Pip	Miss Havisham, please don't feel remorse:
	Events have only run their course.
Miss Havisham *(aside to audience)*	
	By the way, the suitor who led me on
	Was known by the name of Compeyson.
Pip	Even though things have turned out a mess
	As you die, please accept my forgiveness.
Miss Havisham	My virtuous love became twisted
	I bet you wish I'd never existed.

Miss Havisham dies. Enter Compeyson upstage.

Compeyson	Crimes come back to exact their price
	And here I am, full of vice.
	Living among the underclass,
	Someone is always sure to grass.
	I've heard Magwitch is returned, and rich.
	Watch out! I'm the one to snitch.

Exit Compeyson. Enter Herbert, Magwitch and Wemmick.

Herbert	Magwitch, now's the time to make a dash.
	Don't forget to take your hard-earned cash.
	Let's climb aboard a river boat.
	The chase will happen when we're afloat.
Wemmick *(to Pip)*	As you help him to his liberty
	Keep an eye on his portable property.

Exit Wemmick.

Pip   Our flight is accompanied by trepidation
And needs some audience participation.
Join hands to make the river sides
And wave your hands to make the tides.
The waters are choppy, the sky is grey
Will I help Magwitch get away?
When anyone mentions the morning mist
Don't forget to growl and hiss.

Enter Compeyson with Sergeant-at-Arms.

Compeyson   Look there in the morning mist!

Audience growl and hiss.

Compeyson   That's the man on the wanted list.
Let's end his criminal pranks
As we chase between the river banks.

Pip   Once more fate has sent us reeling:
It's Compeyson with his double-dealing.

Sergeant   You have with you a returned transport.
It's my job now to take him to court.

Sergeant and Compeyson chase Pip and Magwitch round audience.

Magwitch   Villain! Don't try to save your skin.
Now at last I'm going to do you in.

Magwitch and Compeyson fight. Compeyson dies. Magwitch is mortally hurt.
He drops his wallet. Sergeant-at-Arms arrests Magwitch.

Magwitch   I'm injured, but Compeyson is no more
And I've been taken by the law.
Even though I dropped my stash
I don't regret our little bash.

Pip   Though your portable property's in the drink,
I'll stay loyal while you're in the clink.
So audience, take your seats once more.
Here comes the Judge to pronounce the law.

Enter Judge.

Judge   Your good conduct counts for nought.
I pass the sentence of this court.
For anyone returning from the penal colony
Death is the punishment for your felony.
I say liberals are all cowards.
That's why they call me Michael Howard.

Yes, I've shown liberals' ideas the door
That's why they call me Jack Straw.
In fact, such nonsense is redundant
Whatever Home Secretary is incumbent.

Exit Judge.

| Pip | I'm afraid the end of this whole caboose |
| | Will come with the hangman's noose. |

| Magwitch | Thanks to my injury, I'm very weak. |
| | I'm getting so ill I can hardly speak. |

| Pip | Now I've got forgiveness into my thick head |
| | I'll sit here quietly by your sickbed. |

Magwitch	Pip, you've always been good and never lied.
	Now you sit gently by my side.
	Thank you for remaining loyal
	While I shuffle off this mortal coil.

Magwitch dies.

Pip	He lived through struggles and deprivation
	May the Lord grant him salvation.
	I'll leave the country, but before my separation
	There's one more piece of reparation.

Enter Joe.

Pip	Joe, I was selfish and forgot my roots.
	In fact, I got too big for my boots.
	Let me be once again your old friend Pip.
	Forget about parallels with the Labour leadership.
	All I want is to end this business
	And have some sign of your forgiveness.

Joe	I'll forgive unkind remarks.
	I always say, Pip, what larks!
	Betwixt such two as us, ever friends –
	That's the way our play must end.

Exit Joe. Enter Politics and Parenthood.

| Politics | Experience tempered wild ambition: |
| | That's how elections are lost and won. |

Parenthood	You're wrong about the ballot box
	Life's one long school of hard knocks.
	At the end, love's at stake:
	One human choice, two hearts' ache.

Politics	And now we've reached the epilogue. Imagine time's wheels have turned, cog by cog. Look: in the ruins of Miss Havisham's old home Two lovers meet, all alone.
Pip	I've been abroad for many years. Life has been a vale of tears. I'll just re-visit the scene of my infant cares – I say, who's that wandering there?

Enter Estella.

Estella	Drummle's dead and I'm a widow. Hello Pip, how are you kiddo? Now you're finished as a toff Can we pick up where we left off?
Parenthood	Is this the story of a broken heart? Now they're together, must they part?
Politics	One way to cut through sentimental knots Is to decide it by the ballot box. At least, a show of hands will be enough – We won't bother with that postal stuff. So audience use your programmes to vote On whether Pip has missed the boat.
Parenthood	All those who want the lovers re-united?

Audience vote.

Politics	All those who believe their cause is blighted?

Audience vote. Teller counts votes and declares 're-united' or 'blighted'.

Politics	Pip and Estella, I do beseech Let us hear your closing speech.

HAPPY ENDING
(or go to 'Sad ending')

Pip	Suffering's taught me to be wise At long last I've earned my prize. I loved you once and I love you still. It's decided by the democratic will. Now I'll find the guts at the very least To bring peace back to the Middle East.

Estella   Let's make up for our earlier wrong
And forge a love that's brave and strong.
Together we'll enjoy many a day
And bring a happy ending to this play.

THE END

or SAD ENDING

Pip   I betrayed the labour movement
And now endure this sad denouement.
After all our times of trouble
The electorate's gone and burst my bubble.
I'll be hounded out of town
And be replaced by Gordon Brown
Who in turn will meet his fate
At the hands of the electorate.

Estella   Everything has turned out wrong
I've paid the price for being headstrong.
Forget all past mystery.
Our love has vanished into history.
Forever optimism and love will remain a dream…
Now let's be consoled by strawberries and cream.

THE END

Note

Adapted from the novel by Charles Dickens, first published in 1861. Dickens changed his original ending (where Pip, the central character, goes his separate way from Estella, whom he loves) to one where they are re-united.

HAMLETTA

Or What your parents don't tell you,
adapted from 'Hamlet' by William Shakespeare

CAST

Prologue
Hamlet
Horatio, friend of Hamlet
Rosencrantz, friend of Hamlet
Guildenstern, friend of Hamlet
Ghost of Hamlet Senior
Claudius, King of Denmark, uncle of Hamlet
Gertrude, Queen of Denmark, mother of Hamlet
Ophelia
Polonius, father of Ophelia
Laertes, brother of Ophelia
Hamletta, stepsister of Hamlet
Therapina, friend of Hamletta
Feminista, friend of Hamletta
Graveyard ghosts 1, 2, 3, 4 and 5

The action takes place in the state of Denmark, at the court and in a graveyard.

Hamletta, Therapina and Feminista act the dumbshow.

Children can take part as heralds and entertainers of the court. The audience are the graveyard and make graveyard noises.

Enter Prologue.

Prologue   This is the story of family secrets and lies
Causing madness and bloodshed, it's no surprise.
When Daddy dies and Mummy beds a new man
It's hard for the children who carry the can.
But our play's different with Hamlet's stepsister,
Hamletta – though the Bard missed her.
Now enter Hamlet from his summer vac:
See how his life will take a different tack.

Exit Prologue. Enter Hamlet and Horatio.

Hamlet   Sweet Horatio, my trusted friend
I know you'll stick with me to the end.

Horatio	How stands Denmark and its handsome prince? You look as if something's made you wince.
Hamlet	How should I feel? A father's sudden end – Then my mum with a new boyfriend. These adults and their so-called morals Only end up in family quarrels. Now Rosencrantz and Guildenstern Come right in and take a turn.

Enter Rosencrantz and Guildenstern.

Rosencrantz	We're on your side against Step-Dad But don't provoke him or he'll get mad.
Guildenstern	Avoid family strife – friendship's your beacon No-one can speak the truth like we can.
Hamlet	There's nothing like the support of my peers We can meet later and have a few beers.

Exeunt Rosencrantz and Guildenstern.

Hamlet	Although I've my share of trouble I'll find a way through – at the double.
Horatio	What's this I've heard about Laertes' sister – Is it true you'd like to tryst her?
Hamlet	I love Ophelia with youthful passion It's a love that parents cannot ration. If they're opposed, I'll need all my resources If she and I are ever to join forces.
Horatio	Hamlet, I don't want to give you an awful fright But the guards saw your dead father here last night. They seem to think that he was looking for you So I'll come along to see if it's true.

Enter ghost of Hamlet Senior and beckons Hamlet aside.

Ghost (*to Horatio*)	Wait over there Horatio There's some thing only Hamlet must know.

Horatio moves upstage.

Ghost	Son, I hate to add to your cares and woe But there is something you have to know. I was killed by my cruel brother So he could be king and marry your mother.
Hamlet	Unnatural! My uncle's the killer What horror's next in this spine-chiller?

Ghost	As I lay in the orchard for a snooze, He put poison in my ear – a cunning ruse. I rely on you to revenge your father But preferably without harming your mother.

Exit Ghost.

Hamlet	How am I going to avenge this treason? If I keep it secret, I may lose my reason. It's bad enough that my father's dead And soon after that my mother wed. Now here's old Daddy demanding revenge It's enough to send me round the bend.

Horatio moves down stage.

Horatio	Now the Ghost has gone away Tell me all that he did say.
Hamlet	This terrible secret is mine alone Though all I can do is sigh and moan.
Horatio	You're in hot water – you look afraid. If you need me, I'll come to your aid.

Exeunt Hamlet and Horatio. Enter Claudius and Gertrude, accompanied by Laertes and Polonius.

Claudius	I'm rough, tough Claudius the King And I can do most anything. I've got sweet Gertrude to be my wife.
(mutters aside)	(Shame I had to take my brother's life.)
Gertrude	I'm Queen Gertrude, devoted to pleasure Fancy clothes and a life of leisure When my husband died, I wed his brother, Hamlet thinks I'm a lousy mother.
Polonius	I'm Polonius, master of court faction Listen to my boy – a real man of action.
Laertes	I'm Laertes, come to say goodbye Back to study in France, so I must fly. But I'm worried about my dopey sister She loves Hamlet – I bet he's kissed her. She won't admit he's out of her league So she moans over him to the point of fatigue. I've tried to tell her to play it cool But she says that's not what she hears at school.

Exit Laertes. Enter Hamlet.

Claudius	Here's Hamlet, my newly acquired son Don't return to college, stay here for some fun. Give me a hug and listen to my homily: You're now part of my 'blended family'.
Hamlet *(scowling)*	I'm loyal to my dear old Dad His death poisons my life and makes me sad.
Gertrude	Come on, live in the here and now Stop beating your breast and mopping your brow.
Hamlet	Oh mother, heavens above! Don't you know what it's like to love? I do love you, but you make me cross You don't seem to realise that I'm the boss.
Claudius	Even though he doesn't like me crowned I'm sure that in time, he'll come round.

Exit court except Hamlet. Enter Ophelia.

Hamlet	Oh sweet Ophelia, you fill me with lust So come and kiss me, I insist you must.
Ophelia	I am Ophelia, a woman chaste –
Hamlet	But Ophelia, I yearn for your warm embrace.
Ophelia	Hamlet, you're so impatient for my kisses But I'd rather wait till I'm your missus. Now exit and end your lather Here comes my most respected father.

Ophelia points offstage, indicating that Hamlet should leave. Exit Hamlet.
Enter Polonius.

Polonius	As her dad, when there is no mother I do my best for her and her brother. I want Ophelia to stay my little girl. But she loves Hamlet, her head's in a whirl.
(to Ophelia)	Now Ophelia, with Hamlet, you must try to be cool Or he'll love you and leave you, that's the rule.
Ophelia	Oh Dad, though he makes me weak at the knees. I don't know whether it's all a tease. Whether it's love or moods that cause his glowers I've had enough. I'm off to tend my flowers.

Exeunt Ophelia and Polonius.

Enter Hamletta with Therapina and Feminista.

Hamletta	I'm Hamlet's step-sister, Hamletta's the name
	The mother was different, the father's the same.
	Not many people know I was banished from birth
	That fool Shakespeare ignored my worth.
	I suspect the new King did our Dad in – dead
	So he could get that Queen Gertrude into bed.
	Now they are wed, there's still no place for me
	In the latest version of their blended family.
	With all that ill feeling, I should go to ground
	But to look after Hamlet, I'll stick around.
	These are my friends, we're an all-girl group
	Masquerading as a theatre troupe.
Therapina	The family dynamic is very disturbing.
	It's a system that needs perturbing.
Feminista	My name is Feminista
	And I can recognise one sick mister.
	So next time Hamlet is ill at ease
	Interrupt one of his soliloquies.

Enter Hamlet.

Hamlet *(wracked by doubt)*	
	Did Claudius do it? Or is my mind defective
	Or is what's needed a good detective?
	Oh, I'm really feeling suicidal –
	Should I choose action or just remain idle?
Hamletta	Hamlet, we three studied drama at the University
	What you need is a mime on family diversity.
	It can point to the secrets parents hide
	When they act nice but are mean inside.
Hamlet	That's a great idea. As I'm no gumshoe
(cheering up)	You strolling players can put on a dumb-show:
	Show it to the court, don't waste time
	Call Mum and the King to see the mime.
	Gather, court! Ophelia, sit by my side
	In the front row. We've nothing to hide.

Enter all players except Ghost. The court gather to watch the mime piece on the 'blended family' acted by Hamletta and friends.

Player King and Player Queen are lovey together. King lies down to rest. Queen leaves him. Poisoner creeps in, takes off the King's crown and kisses it, puts poison in the King's ear. King dies. Queen laments. Poisoner pretends to lament. He woos the Queen and puts on the crown.

Claudius	The plot thickens, it's getting scary
	Have the children guessed? This is hairy!
	Though I feel pangs of remorse
	I'm the king – let events take their course.

Exit Claudius.

Hamlet *(to Ophelia)* I'm upset and don't know what to do
All I can think of is to take it out on you.
So get thee to a nunnery or some retreat
I've too many troubles for us to meet.

Ophelia	Oh Hamlet, why are you so mean?
	Do you find fault because I am keen?
	I'm off to commune with my flowers
	That will take me many hours.

Exit Ophelia.

Polonius	I think Hamlet is set to embarrass…
(*hides*)	So I'll just listen from behind this arras.

Exeunt court and players except Hamlet and Gertrude and Polonius (hidden).

Hamlet *(to Gertrude)* Did you like the mime, mother dear?

Gertrude	You have upset your Dad, I fear.
Hamlet	How dare you sully my father's name,
	When you married his brother? Have you no shame?
Gertrude	Your father was kind but Claudius is exciting –
	Oh Hamlet, can't we stop fighting?

Curtain shakes.

Hamlet	Is it a burglar or is it a rat?
	I can't bear either…
(*thrusts sword*)	…so take that!
Polonius	Alas, alack, for I am slain!
Hamlet	If that's the King, I'll strike again.

Strikes again. Polonius staggers out and dies. Enter Claudius.

Claudius	What now! I see murder and affray
	Be sure that Hamlet will regret this day.

Gertrude *(to Hamlet)* Oh dear, you've killed Ophelia's Dad,
Now I think you're really mad!

Hamlet	The old man was a stubborn mule
	Now I'm off to act the fool.

Exit Hamlet.

Claudius	Let's send him to England, he's causing bother,
	You're just soft on him 'cos you're his mother.
Gertrude	Even though his behaviour's out of order
	Let him stay here – I'll act as warder.
Claudius	No. But since he thinks we're fuddy duddies,
	Let's ask some help from his buddies.

Enter Rosencrantz and Guildenstern.

Claudius	Now, my friends, Guildenstern and Rosencrantz
	I bet you find it hard now student grants
	Are replaced by loans – a new regime
	Which messes up our rhyming scheme.
Rosencrantz	What do you say, Guildenstern?
Guildenstern	I say we've not exactly got money to burn.
Claudius	There's cash if you do a job for me and the Queen:
	You see, our son Hamlet needs a change of scene.
	I know you'd want to see him better.
	Take him abroad – and don't forget this letter.

Claudius shows letter to audience – it has message 'kill the bearer' – the audience see it but the others don't. Rolls up letter and gives to Rosencrantz and Guildenstern. Exeunt Claudius and Gertrude.

Enter Hamlet.

Hamlet	What's this – a holiday? That sounds like fun
	Rosencrantz and Guildenstern, let's head for the sun.

Exit Hamlet with Rosencrantz and Guildenstern. Enter Ophelia.

Ophelia	Now my garden's turned to weeds
	I'm overwhelmed by all my needs.
	My brother's gone, my father's dead
	Perhaps it was something that I said.
	One day these men will be death of me
	Oh well, I'll just go and sit by a willow tree.

Exit Ophelia. Enter Hamletta with Therapina and Feminista.

Hamletta	The situation's looking grim
	Ophelia's fit to do herself in.

She's living in such a dream
I wouldn't trust her near a stream.
The King ignored Gertrude's pleas
So Hamlet's been banished overseas.
Is this family under a curse?
How can I stop it going from bad to worse?

Feminista   It's no good standing frowning
Let's go and save Ophelia from drowning.

Therapina   Then she can come back in disguise –
That'll give Hamlet a nice surprise.

Exeunt Hamletta with Therapina and Feminista.

The audience are the graveyard. Enter Hamlet with skull.

Hamlet   I'm alive. I switched the scroll
And foiled my uncle's evil goal.
Now I find this skull – alas, poor Yorick!
This graveyard must be symbolic:
It stands for sadness and our buried hopes
It's not just me, the whole country's on the ropes.
While I bemoan the human condition
We must all endure the Con-Dem coalition.
That's what's rotten in the state of our nation
And now's the time for audience participation.

(to audience)   Let me hear your sobs and wails.

Audience participation: sobs and moans.

Hamlet   Now let's listen to some ghostly tales.

Enter from audience Ghosts 1, 2, 3, 4 and 5.

Ghost 1   I am the ghost of the NHS
They turned it into big business.

Ghost 2   And I'm the ghost of the welfare state
Greed and meanness sealed my fate.

Ghost 3   I'm the ghost of special needs
'Cos I no longer fit educational creeds.

Ghost 4   I'm the ghost of political burn-out
Democracy's busted, look at the turn out.

Ghost 5   I'm the Ghost of political coalition
Stitched together without your permission.

Enter Ghost of Hamlet's father.

Ghost   Yes I agree there's something rotten
But Hamlet have you forgotten?
You should do what your old dad says
And put an end to Claudius's ways.

Exeunt Hamlet and Ghost. Five ghosts return to audience and sit down. Enter Hamletta.

Hamletta   Just in case the message isn't getting through
Let me spell it out for you.
Parents could've come clean with kids
Instead they kept some things hid.
The children made what sense they could:
They did wrong, though motivated by good.
In the book, there's a fight and they die
And you and me are left to cry.

But today our version will end better
Thanks to me, Hamletta.
But first Laertes will take the stage
He enters upset and full of rage.

Exit Hamletta. Enter Laertes.

Laertes   I'm home from France at greatest speed
Driven by grief and emotional need
My Dad is dead, my sister's mental
I can't believe it was accidental.
I must challenge Hamlet to a duel
Or else I'll look a cowardly fool.

Enter Claudius.

Claudius   My condolences for your bereavement
You got here fast – that's quite an achievement.
You've come from Paris, which is quite far
Especially in the days before Eurostar.

Laertes   I'm after Hamlet, so out of my way
I intend to kill him without delay.
Thanks to him, my family's no more.
His death will even up the score.

Claudius   I've a plan. In the duel, fight fast and furious
Make him sweat, then he won't be curious
About the refreshing drink I'll slip him –
He won't notice as his eyes grow dim
That the drink is poison and his end is nigh.
He won't have time to say goodbye.

Claudius puts poison in cup.

Claudius *(aside)*   And to make doubly sure Hamlet gets his reward
                    I've poisoned the tip of Laertes's sword.

Enter Hamlet and Horatio.

Hamlet   After all my ups and downs
                    I'm ready to fight for Denmark's crown.

Horatio   Hamlet, I'm with you through thin and thick –
                    But watch out audience, I fear a trick.

Hamlet and Laertes fight.

Claudius *(aside)* Go on, Laertes – let rip!
                    I didn't tell him about the poisoned tip.

Gertrude   Go on son, beat him to pulp!
                    Pass me the drink – I'll take a gulp.

Claudius   Darling, stop – don't have a drink!
                    It's not as nice as you might think.

Gertrude   Sweetheart, you're doing what I can't abide.
                    Don't you tell me – *I'll* decide.

Enter Hamletta with Therapina and Feminista and Ophelia in disguise.

Hamletta   I don't like the carnage that I am seein'
                    It's all just way too Jacobean,
                    Where self-important men act tragic.
                    I'll stop the rot, as if by magic.
                    Instead of faction killing courtly faction.
                    We need time to think – so freeze the action.

Performers freeze. Therapina stops Gertrude drinking poisoned cup.

Therapina   Gertrude, there's been a mix-up
                    I recommend you give me that cup.

Feminista takes the swords from Hamlet and Laertes.

Feminista   Boys, I'm afraid you've been tricked:
                    One of you could die, by poison pricked.

Hamletta   I'm Hamletta, old Hamlet's first born, long exiled
                    Now I'm back – your step-sister and step child.
                    Sure, I know what it's like to suffer
                    Wisdom, not revenge, has made me tougher.
                    Instead of everyone getting so fraught
                    There's lessons for all the court.

> Instead of settling everything by the sword
> They can go to classes at the Mary Ward,
> Or their local education centre
> To find re-education and a mentor.
> If even Rosencrantz and Guildenstern try hard
> They may end up in a play by Tom Stoppard.

Enter Rosencrantz and Guildenstern.

Rosencrantz   After Hamlet switched the scrolls
                 We had to reappraise our goals.

Guildenstern   Yes, we went from student malefactors
                 To post-modern bit-part actors.

Rosencrantz and Guildenstern link arms.

Hamletta *(to Laertes)* Laertes, you should work on that anger of yours
                 I'm sure you could find a suitable course.

Laertes   It's true that I have become a bit wild
                 I must commune with my inner child.

Hamletta *(to Hamlet)* Hamlet, there's no need to become deranged
                 There's quite a lot that can be changed.
                 If you learn to accept your lot
                 You wouldn't be stuck in such a terrible plot.

Hamlet   My passion made me rant and rave
                 I'm sorry I sent Ophelia's dad to his grave.
                 I'll be a better man tomorrow.
                 I've only one last little sorrow –
                 Remember 'to be or not to be'?
                 I missed out on my famous soliloquy.

Feminista   Ophelia didn't drown, she went for a swim
                 And for some reason she's still keen on him.
                 Instead of suiciding, she's here in disguise
                 Let's hope that Hamlet turns out as wise.

Ophelia   *(dropping disguise)*
                 Hamlet, I know you think my love's too syrupy
                 But we can work it out in therapy.

Hamlet and Ophelia link arms.

Therapina   Now we need something to put right
                 Those erring parents who are none too bright.

Claudius   Although I may be addicted to force
                 I love Gertrude – don't make us divorce.

Gertrude	Hamlet, I chose him and I can make it work Even if he is a bit of a jerk.

Gertrude and Claudius link arms.

Hamletta	They did wrong and must live with their regret But they never set out to make Hamlet fret. Gertrude and Claudius can go on a cruise Out of harm's way, with time to muse.
Horatio	I said I'd stick around till the final curtain. I expect the players will all go on hurtin'. But at least the action has reached a plateau So now's the time for strawberry gateau.

THE END

IT'S PICASSO!

Picasso and the spirit of the 20th century

CAST

Setting the scene
Inventor, an eccentric genius
Familiar, the inventor's pet
Queen
Spirit of the 20th century

Late Picasso
Picasso
Jacqueline, a wife of Picasso
Paloma, daughter of Picasso
Francoise, girlfriend of Picasso

Mid-life Picasso
Olga, Russian ballerina, another wife of Picasso
Woman with two faces
Marie Therese, girlfriend of Picasso
Dora Maar, girlfriend of Picasso
Spirit of Fascism

Picasso, youth on the edge
Gertrude Stein, literary figure
Alice B. Toklas, cookbook author and Stein's partner
Harlequin
Sabartes, friend of Picasso's youth
Casamegas, friend of Picasso's youth
Germaine, loved by Casamegas

Child Picasso
Spirit of 19th century
Don José, father of Picasso
Conchita, sister of Picasso

Audience participation: the audience can recreate Guernica (the picture) and release doves of peace (made in paper beforehand).

SCENE 1
Setting the scene

The eccentric Inventor is sitting reading the paper. His Familiar is reading an animal paper.

Inventor	Hmm – 'Inventors get CBE'... Hang on, Familiar, that's you and me! We've made things the world has never seen, Like our zeitgeist scanner and time machine. Since we're to be honoured with a gong Say some words in your animal tongue.
Familiar	I'm your friend in animal skin We'll stick together through thick and thin. Magicians and inventors need an assistant. Though I'm not human, I'm very persistent.
Inventor	Now a special time has come The start of a new millennium. Usually we solve dangerous crimes Today we'll search for the spirit of our times. Whenever I say 'time machine' It means we shift historical scene.

Enter the Spirit of the 20th century.

Spirit of the 20th century	As Spirit of the 20th century I think you'll need some help from me. Although my own time has just expired Understanding the recent past is what's required.
Inventor	Pet, there's no need to ask. The nature of our coming task Is to discover the spiritual mystery Buried in our recent history. On this zeitgeist dial, you'll see indicated Whether our findings have been vindicated.

(gives zeitgeist scanner to Familiar)

Now let's travel in my time machine.
Wait! Who is this? Enter the Queen.

Enter Queen.

Queen	I've ruled for nearly sixty years Through wars, conflicts and vales of tears. Out of strife and conflagration We must find some inspiration.

Familiar *(aside, looking at the zeitgeist scanner)*
> The reading goes right off the screen
> When it registers the Queen.

Inventor
> Thank you Ma'am for your blessing
> We must start now – time is pressing.
> I fear it will be far from rudimentary
> To find the embodiment of the past century.

Queen
> I'll sit down and watch this play
> Ruling can wait for another day.

Exit Queen to sit in audience.

Inventor
> I don't want to seem perverse
> But I've programmed history in reverse:
> Events from the recent past
> Arrive the first – the others last.
> The scanner detects a universal soul
> Someone in the epic mould
> Man of genius, universal brother
> Like me – creative and an animal lover.

Familiar *(polishes scanner)*
> I'll polish our machine with Brasso
> My goodness, here comes Picasso.

Inventor
> The mystery starts at his peak of fame
> When he had become a household name.
> Then we check out the mid-life crisis
> (Though his work still fetched good prices).
> And if we need to test again,
> We can visit his early years in Spain.

SCENE 2
The late Picasso

Inventor, Familiar and Spirit of the 20th century remain on stage. Enter Picasso.

Spirit of the 20th century *(aside)*
> As you can see from his elderly gait
> This isn't early Picasso – it's the late,
> A man who is a universal entrancer.
> Let's ask him – he'll know the answer.

Inventor
> What is the secret of your longevity?
> And such enormous creativity?

Picasso	I'm in my eighties, very old Everything I do turns to gold. My every scribble is fêted Wherever I go, I'm celebrated. Yet a true artist must always dream on: Time runs out but I paint like a demon.
Inventor	Your talent may be heaven sent But I find your room a bit unkempt.
Picasso	All my art of myth and fable I keep right here on my kitchen table. The hallmark of genius is constant chaos It *looks* a mess – but what a pay-off.
Spirit of the 20th century	Picasso, about your genius, what part Stems directly from your lover's art?
Picasso	People think I'm a sexy old goat But I need a woman on whom to dote.

Enter Jacqueline.

Picasso	Meet my pretty wife, Jacqueline. What's more she's aged just nineteen.
Jacqueline	Picasso, genius of the day I'll keep you hidden right away I'll protect you from scandalous revelations Not to mention your friends and relations.
Picasso	I like an age differential It gives a relationship great potential. Say, half a century or more – That let's a woman know the score. Now my ego couldn't be any bigger I've become an international figure.
Inventor	Am I given to understand You're not much of a family man?
Picasso	Kids with their noise make me fume – Here comes Paloma with her perfume.

Enter Paloma.

Paloma	I'm Paloma. That means 'dove' But I never knew paternal love. My Daddy ignored me all life long – I just use his fame to sell my pong.

Exeunt Jacqueline and Paloma.

Picasso	Her mother was also very self-willed
	She fancied herself an artist, and was quite skilled.

Enter Francoise.

Francoise	We met at the end of the Second World War
	When Picasso was sixty-four.

Picasso	Together we championed liberty's cause
	Said 'Long live communism' and 'No more wars'
	She aspired to an artistic career –
	It just wasn't on, I fear.
	In everything, she wanted her own way.
	Well, I'm sorry, I just wasn't going to play.

Francoise	Listen Picasso, one thing's true:
	I'm a slave to love, but not to you.
	Your affairs all have one common format:
	First, the plinth – and then the doormat.

Enter Inventor and Familiar.

Inventor	Do you mean to say
	This family typifies the 20th century way?
	I have my professorial doubts
	Pet, get the scanner out.

Familiar scans Picasso with the zeitgeist detector.

Familiar	No, he's failed my zeitgeist test –
	This period's good, but not his best.
	Picasso, you've crested fame's highest arc
	But take us back to when you made your mark.

Exeunt Inventor, Familiar and Spirit of 20th century.

SCENE 3
The Mid-Life Picasso

Enter Olga. Picasso remains on stage.

Picasso	In the 1920s I gloried in success
	But couldn't hide my inner distress.
	I married Olga, a Russian dancer
	I thought her love would be the answer.

Olga	Before we met, he played fast and loose
	And I was in the Ballet Russe.

Picasso	Olga, you're delectable Let's marry and be respectable.
Olga	I decree an ordered life I want to be a society wife. Now we're rich, let's get a castle And leave behind all this hassle. Let's drive around in the latest cars Like 1920s movie stars.
Picasso	I'll do it, but all this stuff's boring I'd rather get on with painting and drawing.
Olga	If he's in a bad mood-io He just goes off down the studio.

Exit Olga.

Picasso	My wife has become estranged I'm so upset I feel deranged. At this stage I must remake myself in art So bring in a muse to play her part.

Enter woman with two faces.

Woman with two faces	I'm the woman with two faces I've got eyes and ears in odd places. First Picasso painted me as a nudist Now see my face – it's gone all cubist.

Picasso *(to Inventor)* Now you time-travel detective
I've messed up your sense of perspective.

Inventor *(from audience)* Take a look from the front, and from the side
See how genius takes imagination for a ride.
(Put differently, he's a troubled little squirt
Who chases anything in a skirt.)

Woman with two faces	Now I'll split into two parts And send two women to contest his heart.

Exit Woman with two faces. Enter Marie Therese.

Marie Therese	He took my arm outside the shops: Now he paints me and never stops.
Picasso	Marie Therese, our seamless love has no creases I'll paint you in my masterpieces.

They embrace.

Picasso	But wait! Who is that I hear knocking? I think it might be a young blue-stocking.

Dora Maar knocks and enters.

Dora   I'm a surrealist photographer
        Your most talented lover by far.
        I'll stay creative in my own right.
        I won't give in without a fight.

Picasso   Marie-Therese, I love you the most by far
        But you must take turns with Dora Maar.
(to Dora)   Dora, I'd like to break you in
        Hire a studio and live in sin.

Marie Therese Alas the day I was beguiled
        Picasso has left me with child.

Enter Olga.

Olga   I'm fed up with Picasso on parade
        Our marriage is over I'm afraid.

Dora *(to Picasso)* As equals we agreed an artistic affair
        But I'm the one who had the wear and tear.
        Life with you is a losing battle
        First, a model – then a chattel.

Exeunt Marie Therese, Olga and Dora Maar.

Picasso   Alas my marriage is collapsing
        As my mistress is expecting
        And soon I'll have the penalty of fame –
        A book of memoirs by my old flame.
        It's all too much. My inner pain
        Threatens to burst out again.

Enter Spirit of Fascism, Inventor and Familiar.

Spirit of Fascism In comes I, the evil fascisti
        Representing all that's bad and shifty.
        Picasso's spirit knows the score
        Soon Europe will be engulfed by war.
        I am the epitome of evil and sham
        Come to test the spirit of modern man.

Picasso   The spirit of fascism's abroad
        But I say art is mightier than the sword.

Inventor   Pet, raise your hackles and bare your teeth
        Save the continent from liberty's thief.

Familiar   I am the Inventor's familiar
        Get out of here or I will kill ya.

Familiar mauls the Spirit of Fascism.

Spirit of Fascism One day I'll be Europe's gaffer
       Meanwhile, feel the taste of my Luftwaffe.

Exit Spirit of Fascism.

Picasso   Then planes bombed a small Basque town
       They bombed and bombed and bombed it down
       So audience, as the world gets sicker
       I'll create my masterpiece: 'Guernica'.

Audience recreate 'Guernica' (e.g. waving cut-out shapes or sticking them on a large sheet of paper).

Inventor   Does this picture of despair and desolation
       Encapsulate a century's inspiration?
       Is our century's meaning really so bleak
       Or is your genius still playing hide and seek?
       Pet, the zeitgeist measuring tool!

Familiar points scanner at Picasso.

Inventor   Picasso, I think you're playing the fool
       If we examine this read-out
       We'll track our genius without a doubt.

Familiar reads scanner.

Familiar   The reading shown by my paw
       Proves we've yet to learn something more.
       I guess the meaning buried here
       Was found much earlier in your career.

Picasso   Yes, my personal vale of tears
       Began in the pre-war years.
       Some people say my genius did begin
       With my character Harlequin.

Inventor   Let's enter the period of blues and rose
       Where anything comes and anything goes.

Exeunt Picasso, Inventor and Familiar.

SCENE 4
Picasso on the edge.

Enter Gertrude Stein and Alice B. Toklas.

Gertrude Stein Hello audience, Stein's the name,
       Literary genius is my game.

	Paris is my stomping ground I rope in talent and invite them round.
Alice B. Toklas	I'm Alice B., my cooking is the best Gertrude's conversation does the rest.
Gertrude Stein	Now there's one young man I'd like to lassoo A Spanish painter called Picasso.

Enter Picasso with rolled up paintings.

Picasso	Gertrude, our shared mission is the avant-garde To make sure understanding art is very hard.
Gertrude	I'm creating a new fictional form To take the world by storm.
Alice B. Toklas	She's got an ego bigger than the state of Texas I believe shrinks call it 'narcissistic cathexis'.
Picasso	My paintings are filled with sadness It comes of living on the edge of madness. Sometimes my images are too much to handle When I show them, it creates a scandal.
Gertrude Stein	But there's no-one you can shock less Than me and my friend Alice B. Toklas.

Picasso *(unrolling paintings)*

> These are the rose period with a clown
> They're very expensive ones to own.

Gertrude Stein	All right Pablo, I'll try them – My rich brother will be round to buy them The only thing he's having none Of is your *Demoiselles d'Avignon*.

Exit Picasso. Enter Harlequin.

Harlequin	When you see me sad and moody It means Picasso's gone all broody. Having kids is a spiritual joy (Well, slightly less if it's a boy). His art shows the feeling of paternity Is our main link to eternity.

Exit Harlequin.

Gertrude Stein	Huh! You men are all of a piece I'm off round to see Matisse.

Alice B. Toklas	Even though Picasso's a sexist pig Something tells me he'll make it big.

Exeunt Gertrude and Alice B Toklas. Enter Inventor and Familiar.

Inventor	Pet, in the time machine – quick! We're getting nearer to what makes him tick. We may discover some revealing truth, If we see Picasso in his Catalonian youth.

Enter Picasso, Sabartes and Casagemas, arm in arm.

Picasso	I'm young and on the make Painting is a piece of cake.
Sabartes	I'm Picasso's friend Sabartes I like art and I like parties.
Casamegas	I'm Carlos Casamegas. We three will be big, we'll all be famous. Picasso is heaven-sent For a drug-addicted Catalan decadent.
Sabartes	We set out as arty draft dodgers And stuck together till we were codgers. Picasso's genius overshadows all others – But it's thanks to us, his Spanish brothers.

Exit Sabartes.

Casamegas	I fell in love with one of the Bohemian set Germaine – the nicest girl I ever met. She thinks I'm a right berk Because the physical side doesn't work. When I was back in Spain I told Picasso of my pain.
Picasso	Can't you see my spirit is sinking? Why don't you give up love and drinking? The reason for our bond of loyalty Is so you can all pay attention to me. I'm a teenage genius in turmoil. When my temper's on the boil, I want someone to vent my anger on: Casamegas, you're just a hanger-on! I'm fed up with your morbid refrain, Your hopeless love for Germaine. You love her but you don't own her – Now push off to Barcelona.

Casamegas   Alas while I sit and ponder
Absinthe makes the heart grow fonder.
I know, I'll throw a party for my friends:
If Germaine won't have me, then that's the end.

Enter Germaine, Sabartes, Inventor and Familiar.

Germaine   Carlos, I'm fed up with all your antics
I don't care if I drive you frantic.

Casamegas   I've an announcement to make:
Friends, my whole life is at stake.
Following my lover's last rejection
I'm the picture of dejection.
And so, Germaine, *voila pour toi!*

Casamegas shoots her and thinks he hits her but in fact he misses.

Dead! and so *voila pour moi!*

Casamegas shoots himself.

Germaine   He shot at me but I didn't die:
Now it's my turn to exit for a cry.

Exeunt Germaine and Sabartes.

Picasso   Carlos and I were bound by a code of honour
But I turned my back and now he's a goner.
Alas I ignored the misery he confided
So he went and suicided.
From now on, my life's racked by remorse.
Surely these events are the very source.

Familiar points scanner at Picasso.

Familiar   Not quite at 'max'...

Inventor   Perhaps the centuries' debate
Will yield the origins of his fate.

All remain on stage.

SCENE 5

The child Picasso

Enter the Spirit of 20th century.

Spirit of the   Now we're well time-travelled
20th century   Our mystery's quite unravelled.
This makes a potent 20th century mix
Of art, romance and politics.

Enter Spirit of 19th century.

Spirit of the 19th century	These hallmarks of future fame I claim in the 19th century's name. All the innovations you see Picasso bring Were driven from an earlier spring. His outlook isn't modern – it's antediluvian His origins are macho and Andalucian.
Spirit of the 20th century	On the contrary! His was a modern mind He left all that Spanish stuff behind.
Spirit of the 19th century	He wasn't a prodigy from nothing. Lots of times, he was only bluffing. His genius was formed by the Spanish middle-class-o That's the key to Pablo Picasso. The failings of his lacklustre Dad Were quite enough to send anyone mad.
Inventor	Let's see the psychological drivers for young Pablo Shown in this moving family tableau, Where his father and his sister Conchita speak Lines to make his heartstrings tweak.

Enter Don José with Conchita.

Don José	Honour your family and religion Be like me and paint a pigeon.
Picasso	To say so may cause a family rift, But dad, I've long surpassed your tiny gift.
Don José	Pablo, I see I'm just a failed dauber You're an artist of a different order.

Exit Don José.

Conchita	As well as your fight to be the family boss You must bear the hurt of sibling loss. After a long and painful illness I passed into eternal stillness.
Spirit of the 20th century	I fear the cause of all this hysteria Is Conchita's sad case of diphtheria.
Picasso	I was first touched by divine grace When I looked death starkly in the face. Conchita was my darling sister Since her death I've always missed her.
Conchita	However talented, death will cheat ya – That's the message from poor Conchita.

Exit Conchita.

Picasso	Through my life long creative panic I've been driven by this family dynamic Each female image I create Bears witness to Conchita's fate.

Familiar scans Picasso. Scanner registers 'MAX'.

Inventor	Yes, his rating is high enough for me: Art, politics and personal tragedy, A talent to shock and a mastery of form – He took the 20th century by storm. Picasso's a kind of super-male A monstrous hero of this tale. Our quest has been one long riot So let's go home for some peace and quiet.

Enter Queen.

Queen	The last century was one of the worst Let's hope for better in the twenty-first.

Spirit of the 19th century *(to Spirit of 20th century)*	We're both from the past, let's not quarrel The audience can decide the moral. What matters is what we co-create: That shapes the spirit of a future date.

Spirit of the 20th century	Now audience, each release a dove Speeding towards the skies above. Let an optimistic spirit dawn Let's celebrate our times, not mourn.

Audience release doves.

Inventor	Now we've seen the life of Picasso Let's enjoy our tea and gateaux.

THE END

JACK O'LANTERN AND THE WILD HORSE

Adapted from Comberbach Soul-Cakers Play, Cheshire,
with added graveyard epitaphs

CAST

Jack O'Lantern
Wild Horse, named Dick
Old Lass
Corpse 1, Anonymous
Corpse 2, Martha Snell
Corpse 3, Jane Kitchen

Hussar
Woman Potter
Joseph Glendowing
Radnor Ghost
Essex Ghost
Maiden Lilliard

Audience join in singing.

Jack O'Lantern enters leading the Wild Horse.

Jack O'Lantern   In comes I, the driver, Jack O'Lantern
With old Dick who's come to see you again.
He once was alive but now he's dead
He's nothing but a poor old horse's head
Stand up lad!

Horse prances and dances.

Jack O'Lantern   We've come to celebrate Old Halloween
And show strange sights you've never seen.
For this is the Festival of Death
So you might get scared or hold your breath!
But first some business – who wants to buy a horse?

Horse begs not to be sold.

Jack O'Lantern   Now ladies and gentlemen, just view around
Has there been a better horse on England's ground?
He's sound-footed and a splendid horse in any gears
And ride him as you can, he'll throw you over his ears.
This horse has an eye like a hawk, a neck like a swan
Every tooth in his mouth stinks like pickled onion.
Tongue like a lady's pocket book, fancy that!
And his ears are made out of an old box hat.

Horse prances.

Jack O'Lantern   Whoa boy!
Now Dick show you obey your best friends.

Horse bows.

Jack O'Lantern   And now do your worst.

Horse tries to bite him.

Jack O'Lantern   No-one will want to buy you now
So come on, let's get on with the show:
We're going to frighten you out of your skin –
The Horse can be in on this.

Horse shows he (or she) is pleased.

Jack O'Lantern   So let's begin
Now, where's the Old Lass?

Jack O'Lantern pulls Old Lass out of the audience.

Jack O'Lantern   Come on, let's look at the old gravestones
And shake some stories out of dusty bones.

At graveyard, Old Lass reads from a gravestone.

Old Lass   Here lies my good and gracious aunty
Whom Death has packed in his portmanty.

Jack O 'Lantern   Isn't that touching! Who else is buried here?

Corpses 1, 2 and 3 enter.

Jack O'Lantern   These three corpses look pretty queer.
Come on Dick, let's go and hide
I can see a good place over that side.

Jack O'Lantern and Horse rejoin audience.

Old Lass
and audience
(sing)   In a churchyard in a wood
OO OO OO OO AH AH AH AH
There a pale old woman stood
OO OO OO OO AH AH AH AH.

Saw three Corpses walking in
OO OO OO OO AH AH AH AH
They were tall and they were thin
OO OO OO OO AH AH AH AH.

Woman to the Corpses said:
OO OO OO OO AH AH AH AH
Will I look like that when I'm dead?'
OO OO OO OO AH AH AH AH.

Corpses to the woman said:

Corpses 1, 2 and 3 (scream)
AARGH!!

Jack O'Lantern (*from audience*) Please Corpses tell us all your story
    And I hope your death wasn't too gory!

Corpse 1 To all my friends I bid adieu
    A more sudden death you never knew.
    As I was leading the old mare to drink
    She kicked and killed me quicker'n a wink.

Horse cheers from audience.

Corpse 2 Poor Martha Snell, her's gone away,
    Her would if her could but her couldn't stay.
    Her had two bad legs, and a baddish cough
    But her legs it was that carried her off.

Corpse 3 Here lies Jane Kitchen
    Who when her glass was spent
    She kicked up her heels
    And away she went.

Jack O'Lantern Let's meet more ghosts as this is fun.
    Now tell your story one by one.

Enter Hussar, with sword.

Hussar I went and listed in the Tenth Hussars
    And galloped with them to the bloody wars.
    'Die for your sovereign – for your country die':
    To earn such glory, feeling rather shy,
    Soon I slipped home, but death then sent me off
    After a struggle with the whooping cough.

Enter Woman Potter, with jug.

Woman Potter Under this stone lies old Katherine Gray
    Changed from a busy life to lifeless clay.
    By earth and clay she got her pelf,
    Yet now she's turned to earth herself.
    Ye weeping friends let me advise,
    Abate your grief and dry your eyes,
    For what avails a flood of tears?
    Who knows, but in the run of years,
    In some tall pitcher, or broad pan,
    She in her shop may be again.

Enter Joseph Glendowing, wounded.

Joseph Here lies Joseph Glendowing
Glendowing Murdered near this town June 15, 1808.
    His murderers were never discovered!
    You villains! If you murdered me –

You bruised my head and pierced my heart
Also my bowels did suffer part.

Enter Radnor Ghost with a plant.

Radnor Ghost   I plant this shrub upon your grave, dear wife,
That something on this spot may boast of life.
Shrubs may wither and all earth must rot
Shrubs may revive: but you, I'm glad, will not.

Enter Essex Ghost with melon.

Essex Ghost   This disease you never heard tell on
I died of eating too much melon.
Be careful, then all you that feed – I
Suffered because I was too greedy.

Enter Maiden Lilliard with sword.

Maiden Lilliard *(with Scottish accent)*
Fair Maiden Lilliard lies under this stone
Little was her stature but great was her fame.
Upon the English lions she laid many thumps,
And when her legs were cutted off...

(kneels)   ...She fought upon her stumps.

Jack O'Lantern   She fought the Battle of Ancrum Moor
Way back in 1544.
When King Henry fought the Scots
But won only 800 graveyard plots.

(to audience)   Now our play has nearly run its course
That's almost all from me and the horse,
Except for a final homily
Before you get cakes and tea.
Remember our life is like unto a winter's day:
Some break their fast, and so depart away.
Others stay dinner – then depart full fed.
The longest age but sups and goes to bed.

Dear folks, then behold and see
As we are now, you'll one day be.
So use your talents, be kind to friends,
And if you quarrel, make amends.
We have to go, just time to say
Thank you all for being in our play.

THE END

Note

Devised from the Antrobus Souling Play (from Cheshire) performed around the Feast of All Souls on 2 November (i.e. the day after All Saints Day), and from humorous graveyard epitaphs dating from the 16th to 18th century (from *Graveyard Laughter* by Samuel Klinger). 'Souling' refers to a call for money to pay for masses for the souls of the dead.

KAPITAL MARX:
KARL MARX IN MAITLAND PARK

CAST

Prologue
Class Struggle
Proletariat
Global Capitalism
Builder 1
Builder 2
Karl Marx, known as 'Moor'
Fred Engels, known as Fred
Marx's mother
Mrs Marx, Marx's wife
Prussian police spy, Wilhelm Stieber
Wilhelm Liebknecht, 'Library'
Edgar Bauer, German refugee
Drunkard 1
Drunkard 2
Policeman 1
Policeman 2
Ferdinand, Prussian Minister of Interior
George Grey, British Home Secretary
Lenchen, housekeeper
Jenny, Marx's eldest daughter
Laura, Marx's second daughter
Tussy (Eleanor), Marx's youngest daughter

Audience participates by booing Global Capitalism.

They also make the sound effects for the builders' noise by chanting:

> Bang, bang, hammer, hammer,
> Hear the noise of builders' clamour

and join in the singing of 'The Internationale' at the end.

SCENE 1
Introduction

Enter Prologue.

Prologue   Karl Marx used to have a fearsome reputation
                 But lately he's undergone rehabilitation.

He used to be blamed for Mao and Stalin
But now he's become the media's darling.
In 2005 listeners of BBC Radio Four
Voted Marx the philosopher with the highest score.
He was born in 1818 and died in 1883
In London, although born in Germany.

He's come a long way from being a German refugee
Who wrote *Das Kapital* on political economy.
Marx put Class Struggle and Proletariat on the map.
So let's invite them now to take the rap.

Enter Class Struggle and Proletariat.

Class Struggle   I'm Class Struggle, the hidden spring of History
Of which Karl Marx dispelled the mystery.
He thought the revolution was imminent
But alas capitalism is still pre-eminent.

Global Capitalism (*interrupts from audience*)
I'm Global Capitalism, still the biggest and best
Of course Class Struggle should be repressed.

Proletariat   I'm Proletariat, still enchained
Since Marx's time what have we gained?
We've ipods and tellies but we work long hours
Because of Capitalism's far-reaching powers.

Global Capitalism Hoorah! Hoorah!

Prologue   Let's go back to Marx's arrival
When he came to London for his survival.
He was banned from Germany and from France,
Even Belgium wouldn't give him a chance.

Proletariat   That was due to the upheavals of 1848
(They were like the protests of May 1968)
When revolution seemed on the cards
And Marx and Engels were its foremost bards...

Enter Global Capitalism.

Global Capitalism   ...As they'd written the *Communist Manifesto*
Promoting communism with gusto.
But the 1848 risings were defeated
For I, Global Capitalism, won't be unseated.

Class Struggle: When we see Capitalism, we boo
Come on audience, join in too.

Audience	Boo! Boo!

Global Capitalism We caused the housing market to be overheated
That means we get rich and you get cheated.
So we'll bring on the construction crew.
Come on lads, it's your cue..
Builders play a part in Karl Marx's life
And that of Jenny, his long-suffering wife.

Enter Builders 1 and 2 (as Builders' Chorus).

Builder 1	We're the happy builders' chorus
House-building makes a profit for us.
Builder 2	We're building up and down the street
In winter rains and summer heat.

Builders1 and 2 *(together)* We make clouds of dust and heaps of noise
We're the industrious builder boys.

Audience	Bang, bang, hammer, hammer,
Hear the noise of builders' clamour.

Exeunt Builders' Chorus, Global Capitalism, Class Struggle and Proletariat.

SCENE 2
Soho, 1850

Enter Karl Marx and Fred Engels.

Karl Marx	I'm the prolific writer, Dr Karl Marx
With advanced ideas, I'm full of sparks.
I'm hopeless with money, I just spend it –
It's irresponsible, I can't defend it.
Marx's mother *(from audience)*	My son, I beg you to make capital rather
Than write about it…
Karl Marx	…That's enough, Mother.
Why don't you relieve my indigence
And give me an advance on my inheritance?
Marx's mother *(from audience)*	I don't want to encourage your idleness
Get a proper job or go into business.
Fred Engels	Allow me, Fred Engels to provide the lolly
Then you can relax and study and be jolly.
I'm happy to finance the fruits of your genius
Even if I have to be abstemious.

I'll even work for my father's firm
In Manchester, it's Engels and Ermen.
There I'll see Mary and Lizzie Burns
With whom I'll fall in love by turns.

I'll send you fivers in the post,
Cut in half so they won't get lost.

Karl Marx   The postman calls three times a day
So send me funds without delay.
I'll miss you Fred, my dearest friend
But the means will justify the end.

Fred Engels   Dear Moor, we'll write lots of letters.

Karl Marx   Farewell, we'll always be your debtors.

They hug. Exit Fred Engels to Manchester. Enter Mrs Marx.

Karl Marx   My dearest wife, now Fred's departed
Our many woes make me downhearted.

Mrs Marx *(weeping)* I was not brought up to scrimp and save
Misery will drive me to the grave.

Karl Marx   When I see tears rain down upon your bosom
I go off to read in the British Museum.

Exeunt Karl Marx and Mrs Marx.

SCENE 3
Soho, 1851

Enter Prussian police spy.

Prussian   I'm a Prussian police spy, Wilhelm Stieber
police spy   I think that this revolutionary's getting feebler.
He lives in Soho in poverty and squalor
While studying child employment horror.
I've followed Marx to a foreign land
In the pay of his wife's brother Ferdinand
Who wants from me a daily report
So I spy on Marx and mustn't get caught.

Prussian police spy moves to side of stage. Enter Karl Marx.

Karl Marx   I'm studying the misery of child employment
Detailed in the Blue Books of the government.
I'm amazed the British officials don't recoil
From such heart-rending accounts of children's toil.

> And Fred reports from the factories near him
> Of ragged children on a pittance – it's pretty grim.
> I use these harsh facts in substantiation
> Of my theory of capitalism's exploitation.

Enter German refugees, Wilhelm Liebknecht and Edgar Bauer.

Wilhelm Liebknecht	We're German refugees, we're Marx's mates We like drinking and political debates. I'm Wilhelm Liebknecht, 'Library' is my nickname I play chess with Marx, a noble game.
Edgar Bauer	They play at chess for many an hour Oh, by the way, I'm Edgar Bauer.
Karl Marx	I appreciate your genial bonhommie Distracting me from political economy.
Edgar Bauer	Come out for a drink in our usual mode At all eighteen pubs up the Hampstead Road.
Karl Marx	Fred's sent me a five pound note So I won't have to pawn my winter coat.
Prussian police spy *(to audience in stage whisper)*	They'll get drunk and talk loud I can eavesdrop from the crowd.

DUMBSHOW   *Marx, Liebknecht and Bauer drinking.*

Enter Drunkards.

Drunkard 1	Bloody foreigners in our bars!
Drunkard 2	We'll biff you and you'll bear the scars.

Exeunt Drunkards. Edgar Bauer trips over pile of paving stones.

Edgar Bauer	I can use this stone to break a gaslight.
Karl Marx	No one will see us – it's darkest night.

DUMBSHOW: *Marx, Liebknecht and Bauer break gaslights.*

Sound of police whistle. Enter Policemen 1 and 2.

Policeman 1	What have we here – some lager louts?
Policeman 2	Foreigners – they're not from hereabouts!
Wilhelm Liebknecht	Dear Moor, it's the police, we'd better flee!
Karl Marx	I know the way, down this alley.

DUMBSHOW	*Policemen chase Marx, Liebknecht and Bauer through audience and lose them, and exeunt.*

Prussian police spy	In modern times, as we all know Marx and his friends would get an ASBO. I'm off to report to Ferdinand That Marx is getting out of hand.

Exit Prussian police spy. Enter Ferdinand.

Ferdinand	I'm Ferdinand, Prussian Minister of Interior Annoyed my sister married an inferior. I'll ask the Prussian ambassador to write To the British Home Secretary to put this right And get Marx and his cronies deported On the basis of what my spy's reported.

George Grey, Home Secretary *(from audience)*

I'm the British Home Secretary, George Grey.
I'm informing the Prussian ambassador today
That mere discussion of regicide is permitted
So long as our Queen is not specifically targetted.
And so long as there's no definite plan,
I'm sorry we can't deport this man.

Ferdinand	His reply puts me in a rage Why won't he lock Marx in a cage? Now Marx and Engels are free to write Subversive articles by day and night.

Exit Ferdinand.

SCENE 4
Move to Grafton Terrace, 1856

Enter Prussian police spy at side of stage.

Prussian police spy	The Marx family fortunes have improved. To Kentish Town they've now removed. It's harder to keep up my spying. I'll lurk by the pub – it's worth trying.

Exit Prussian police spy to audience.

Enter Karl Marx, Mrs Marx and Lenchen carrying bags and bundles.

Karl Marx	Today's a very special day We've moved to Grafton Terrace – hooray!
Mrs Marx	Green fields surround us with horses and sheep This will be a peaceful place to sleep.

Karl Marx	Dear wife, thanks to your inheritance
	We've left behind Soho decadence.
	No more of that pestilential slum
	So why, dear wife, do you look glum?

Mrs Marx   What is this life but full of care?
            Without dear Lenchen, I'd go spare.
            In Soho three of my babies died,
            Buckets of tears for them I cried.

Karl Marx   More tears – I can't take another deluge!
            I'm off to the British Museum for refuge.

Exit Karl Marx.

Mrs Marx   Why is it every time I blub
            My husband's off to museum or pub?

Lenchen   He's not unfeeling, he shares your grief
            He writes and drinks to get relief.
(to audience)   I'm the housekeeper, faithful Lenchen
            Whose duties are too many to mention.
            I do the best I can in a foreign country
            When there's no food in the pantry.
(whispers)   And I too have a secret grief:
            My illegitimate son, in brief.

Mrs Marx   Yes, who was the father? You never said,
            Is it significant that his name's Fred?

Lenchen   On this matter, my lips are sealed.
            His Dad's name won't be revealed.
            Forget him, you've still got three daughters.
            Let's cherish them as the Good Lord taught us.

Enter Jenny and Laura and baby Tussy.

Jenny   I'm Jenny…

Laura   I'm Laura…

Jenny   …and this is Tussy.

Laura   That's her nickname, it rhymes with 'pussy'.

Jenny   Mama will you tell us a fairy tale?

Mrs Marx   How about *The Tempest?* It's about a gale.

Laura   Good, it's Shakespeare…

Jenny   …that's our great delight.

Mrs Marx Lenchen, go to the pawnshop as money's tight.
  Take this necklace and get what you're able.

Lenchen *(grimly)* It's the only way to put food on the table.

Exeunt Mrs Marx, Lenchen, Jenny, Laura and Tussy.

SCENE 5
Grafton Terrace 1861

Enter Builders 1 and 2.

Builders 1 and 2 *(together)* We're the happy builders' chorus
  House-building makes a profit for us.

Global Capitalism (cheers, from audience)
  Hoorah!

Builders 1 and 2 *(together)* We make clouds of dust and heaps of noise
  We're the industrious builder boys.

Audience Bang, bang, hammer, hammer,
  Hear the noise of builders' clamour.

Exeunt Builders 1 and 2. Enter Mrs Marx and Lenchen.

Mrs Marx Such noise and dust makes me demented
  Now the building boom has been invented.

Lenchen The urge for shelter is primordial
  So I'll fix you a refreshing lemon cordial.
  You lie down now and I'll brush your hair
  You're just recovering from that smallpox scare.

Mrs Marx That smallpox made me lose my looks
  No wonder Karl's buried in his books.
  I sent the girls to stay with Liebknecht
  But I miss their laughter in this empty nest.

Lenchen Dr Allen says they can return today.

Enter William Liebknecht and Jenny, Laura and Tussy.

Jenny We enjoyed our stay with Library
  But it wasn't the same because we missed you.

Laura And now we're back, we can hug and kiss you.

Children hug Mrs Marx.

Tussy Library's home is like a palace
  And I loved playing with little Alice.

Wilhelm Liebknecht	Where's the Moor? I fancy a pub crawl.
Mrs Marx	He's out, we'll tell him of your call. He's started *Das Kapital*, Volume One. He's so hard at work, a lot's been done. He's also suffering from huge carbuncles, His liver complaint and big furuncles.
Lenchen	Dr Allen prescribed him stout Which does no good, so I have my doubts.
Mrs Marx	Between his swellings and my mental torment Our household's in emotional ferment.

Enter Karl Marx.

Karl Marx	My dearest daughters, come to my arms!

Daughters run to hug him.

Karl Marx	Welcome home to this maison de larmes!
Jenny	That's 'house of tears' in translation You're still the best Papa in any nation.
Laura	When Mama was ill, we refused boarding school Because religious lessons were the rule.
Wilhelm Liebknecht	What lovely daughters you have sired But dear Moor, you look so haggard and tired.
Karl Marx	Library, I'm trying to explain surplus value It's a dreadful struggle, I can tell you. I'm a perfectionist so I keep re-formulating, As economic language can be intimidating.
Wilhelm Liebknecht	What about a chess game to clear your brain?
Mrs Marx	Oh, no! He'll get furious if you win again! When he loses he's foul to me all night I beg you consider my sorry plight.
Wilhelm Liebknecht	Instead we'll retire to the Lord Southampton pub While faithful Lenchen prepares some grub.

Exeunt Karl Marx and Wilhelm Liebknecht. Enter Prussian police spy at side of stage.

Prussian police spy	I'll follow to eavesdrop what I can After Marx and Engels, Liebknecht is the third man.

Exit Prussian police spy.

Lenchen	Yes, I brew the beer and bake the bread
	Patch the clothes and keep them fed.
	Feeding them is the hardest of all
	Especially when unexpected visitors call.
Tussy	And you're the best Lenchen in the universe
	You never complain when things get worse.
Lenchen	If only that were really true.
	Away with you all, I've work to do.
Jenny *(to Laura)*	Laura, come play the piano now we're home
	We could sing or perhaps recite a poem.

Exeunt Jenny and Laura.

Mrs Marx	I thought this move would answer my prayers
	But it's only added to our cares
	In Maitland Park we must keep up with the Joneses
	Even when we eat only turnips and bones-es.
	Now Karl is out on drunken capers
	I'll lie down with the vapors.

Exit Mrs Marx.

Lenchen	The girls learn piano like their betters
	While their parents write begging letters.
	Thank God for Engels, our loyal friend
	Without him we'd come to a sticky end.
Tussy	But I like it here, it's such a treat
	To know fifty children in the street.
	I ride Papa as my 'horsey' round the garden.
Lenchen	Your Papa doesn't mind the burden.
Tussy	I'm a tomboy running wild
	Because I'm Papa's communist child.
Lenchen	You're my sweetest, dearest tomboy
	Filling the house with smiles and joy.
	Make the most of your innocent youth
	Before life gets hard, that's the stark truth.
Tussy	I'm off out to play...
Lenchen	It's late, Tussy...
Tussy	...I must
Lenchen	So take some bread, here is the crust.

Exit Tussy. Enter Builders 1 and 2.

Builders 1 and 2 *(together)*	We're still the industrious builder boys
Builder 1	Still house-building with dust and noise.
Audience	Bang, bang, hammer, hammer, Hear the noise of builders' clamour.
Global Capitalism	They're forerunners, not an oddity New homes are a profitable commodity.
Audience	Boo! Boo!
Builder 2	We're still making lots of profit.
Lenchen	Yes, but the dust makes us cough, it Makes us splutter and wheeze. You'll bring this family to its knees.

Exeunt Builders 1 and 2.

Lenchen	I wonder what I can pawn today To keep the creditors at bay.

SCENE 6

1867 Marx's study, Modena Villas, Maitland Park

Enter Prussian police spy at side of the stage.

Prussian police spy	Now Karl Marx has moved up the road He's out of my league, he's à la mode. So this is where I take my leave I'm sure no-one is going to grieve.

Exit Police Spy. Enter Karl Marx, Mrs Marx, Lenchen and Tussy.

Karl Marx	People may think I'm a fuddy-duddy To be so happy in my new study. My books are my slaves, they await my orders As my mind roams free across the borders. My friend Library's returned to our homeland So when I need someone to lend a hand I send Jenny and Laura to take notes for me-um From the Blue Books in the British Museum.
Mrs Marx	Thanks to Wilhelm Wolff and your inheritance We've got a new house with a grand entrance. At Modena Villas, none of us frets As we've been rescued from our debts.

	I was so glad to escape from the builders' noise And now we've room for pets and Tussy's toys.
Tussy	Yes, our dogs, cats and a bird called Dickie.
Lenchen	If a cat gets the bird, that could be tricky!
Tussy	I'd better go and check on the poor bird I couldn't bear him to be murdered.

Exit Tussy.

Mrs Marx	Now *Das Kapital* is published – Volume One – The nightmare's been lifted, we can have some fun.
Lenchen	It's taken him years and years to write He'd sleep in the day and work all night.
Karl Marx	Next there'll be Volumes Two, Three and Four.
Lenchen	Oh dear, I didn't realise there was more!
Karl Marx	I owe it all to Fred's devotion I couldn't support myself…
Mrs Marx	…What a notion!
Karl Marx	Let's fast forward a couple of years I'm still writing, my wife's still in tears. If I had my life over again, I'd never marry, that's too much pain. And I still endure those huge carbuncles My liver complaint and blasted furuncles. We're at 1870, an important date When the Paris Commune challenged the state. The Commune's demise was a bitter pill But my dear Fred moved down to Primrose Hill.

Enter Fred Engels.

Fred Engels	At last I've retired from Engels and Ermen I'm relieved to be shot of the family firm. When Mary Burns died suddenly, I was sad Now I'm with her sister Lizzie, that's not so bad.
Karl Marx	We can meet together every day As daily discussions are the only way To develop a radical ideology Of politico-economic sociology.
Fred Engels	You'll have an annual allowance from me. Will that be sufficient? We'll have to see.

Karl Marx	At last you're back, my life's complete.
Fred Engels	I'll come every afternoon, what a treat!
Karl Marx	And you can join our Sunday jaunt Up to Hampstead Heath as is our wont.
Fred Engels	I know Lenchen prepares a delicious spread.
Karl Marx	It'll be like old times, dearest Fred. We can get away from my troubles and cares Like my daughters' choice of love affairs. Lafargue, Longuet and (in the future) Lissagary What attracts my daughters to a revolutionary? And if these rascals weren't bad enough – They're French! That puts me in a huff!

Enter Lenchen with picnic basket.

Lenchen	Mr Engels, you can help to carry the basket You're a family friend, so I dare to ask it.
Fred Engels	Of course, I'll help willingly, give it to me Let's be off when you've gathered the family.

Enter Mrs Marx, Jenny, Laura and Tussy.

Karl Marx	Lead on my dear ones, the Heath beckons We've got plenty of food, enough for seconds. Audience, I invite you all to come along To join in our walk, our talk, our song: Food is the music of love, I say So let's make the most of this sunny day.

Exeunt all to Hampstead Heath for a picnic singing 'The Internationale'.

> So comrades come rally
> And the last fight we must face
> The Internationale
> Unites the human race.

SCENE 7
Epilogue

Enter Class Struggle, Proletariat and Global Capitalism.

Class Struggle	We leave Marx and Engels to their brief respite And thank them that they helped workers to unite. Their theories inspired trade union movements The 40-hour week and such improvements.

Proletariat	We forget that working conditions we enjoy today
	Were won by workers who went without their pay.
	From Marx and Engels they drew inspiration
	For their struggle against gross exploitation.
Global Capitalism	Marx was correct about the arms trade
	War won't stop while profits are made.
	Governments will never make obstruction
	To the growth of weapons of mass destruction.
Proletariat	He was right on some things and wrong on others
	So read *Das Kapital* yourself, sisters and brothers.
	Then decide for yourself about Karl Marx
	Who spent his last years in Maitland Park.

THE END

LITTLE GIRL WITH THE KIND HEART

Or, Getting Rid of Daddy's Girlfriend

CAST

Narrator	Maid
Old Man	Dog
Little Girl	Baba Yaga
Stepmother	Thin Black Cat
Mouse	Cows
Gates *(played by two people)*	

The audience is the wood, and five audience members are given handkerchief, can of WD40, comb, meat and loaf for the Little Girl to find. The audience makes the sound of the loom:

> Clickety clack, clickety clack
> Come on shuttle, forward and back.

The audience put their hands in the air to become a forest when the magic comb is thrown down.

Children in the audience are invited to become cows and drink the imaginary river.

SCENE 1

At a hut in the forest

There is a table in front with bread and jam. A shed to one side.

Enter Narrator with cast (except for Stepmother).

Narrator
Come on audience, assemble cast
Here's a tale from times gone past.
So please let your minds run free
And imagine things you'll never see:

The Narrator indicates cast members one by one, who then leave the stage as directed.

Narrator
A cat that weaves, a mouse that talks...

Exeunt Thin Black Cat and Mouse.

Narrator
A witch who through the forest stalks,
A maid, a dog and gates who play their part...

Exeunt Baba Yaga, Maid, Gates and Dog.

Narrator
To help a little girl with a kind heart.
Now here's an old man who lives alone

                    In the forest – a happy home,
                    And in the years since his wife died
                    His little daughter is his only pride.

Exit Narrator.

Old Man   Here we are in our little hut
                    The table's set, the loaf is cut.
                    Let's have a lovely slice of bread.
                    On top there's some jam to spread.

Little Girl   Here we are, safe in our little wood.
                    After tea, I'm allowed to play if I'm good.
                    We're happy together, just we two.
                    But first I've got some chores to do.

The Little Girl does chores.

Old Man *(to audience)* Life is hard as a single dad
                    So I'll get the girlfriend to share my pad.
                    I'll put an end to my lonely sorrow,
                    And ask her to move in – right now.

Enter Stepmother.

Old Man   Darling, let me introduce your stepmother
                    She's come to share our life together,
                    To join our household and have jam for tea.
                    It'll be so much nicer now we're three.

Old Man   Now I'll just have a little rest
(to Stepmother)   While you run the house as you know best.

Old Man sits down.

Stepmother   You're the prettiest girl I've ever seen
                    But now we start a new routine.
                    Clean the table, scrub the floor,
                    Wash the dishes, then come back for more.
                    Now husband, I'm doing her a favour.
                    She must do her share of household labour.
                    Hurry girl, you idle shirker –
                    You'll never grow to be a worker.

                    This place is thick with dust.
                    There's no jam for tea – just this crust.

Stepmother gives crust to Little Girl, who accepts in bewildered silence.

Stepmother   What! No 'thank you' for your bread?
                    Go and eat it in the shed!

Exeunt Old Man and Stepmother. Little Girl goes to shed.

Little Girl	Oh dear, I'm so unhappy. I much preferred it with my pappy. And now I've upset step-mummy There's just this crust for my tummy.

Enter Mouse.

Mouse	Hello, I'm Mouse, whenever I appear 'Scratch, scratch' is what you'll hear.

Little Girl	Hello Mouse, you look famished. With this crust I've been banished. You've not eaten for a long, long time – Would you like a bit of mine?

Little Girl gives crust to Mouse who nibbles.

Little Girl	Have some more. What still hungry? Eat up – I won't be angry.

Mouse eats up crust.

Mouse	Little girl, since you've been so nice Let me give you some advice. Your stepmother's sister to Baba Yaga, The wicked witch of this saga. So if you are asked to go and see her, Look for me – I'll be near.

Exit Mouse. Little Girl returns to table. Enter Old Man and Stepmother.

Old Man	I'll go and pay my friend a visit. I like a pint. I wouldn't miss it. Besides, I'll skip the fuss and bother, While these two get to know each other.

Exit Old Man.

Stepmother	You lazy girl! I'll keep you in your place And take that smile right off your face. You've had things too much your own way. You must realise that I'm here to stay. But you've one way out of your disgrace: Go over to my sister's place, And ask to borrow a needle and thread. Then I'll read you a story before you go to bed.

Little Girl *(aside)*	Oh no – remember the mouse's warning! I may never see another day dawning.

(to stepmother)   Mother, I'll do anything you say –
                      Only please think, I don't know the way.

Stepmother *(pinching Little Girl's nose)*
                      Feel this? It's your nose.
                      Just follow that! Now off you goes.
                      And since you like something to munch,
                      Take this package for your lunch.

She puts stones wrapped in a towel into Little Girl's basket.

Little Girl *(aside)* First my step-mum raves and rants.
                      Then she sends me to my aunt's
                      Oh! I'm frightened out of my skin.
                      I wish I could see that mousey-kin.

Stepmother   Fetch me back that needle!
                      Now off you go! Skedaddle!

Exit Stepmother. Little Girl moves towards woods. Enter Mouse.

Mouse   Scratch, scratch. It's me. Guess who!
                      Little girl, I'll tell you what to do.

Little Girl   Thank you. My errand fills me with dread,
                      But first let's have some jam and bread.

Mouse   Yes, I will join you in a nibble.

Little Girl takes out lunch and unwraps it.

Mouse   Oh no! Your lunch is full of pebbles.
                      Now that deed is really foul.
                      But you may as well keep the towel.
                      And let me give you one more tip:
                      If you see anything useful, pick it up.

Girl leaves stones and puts towel in basket. Exit Mouse.

SCENE 2

In the woods

Girl remains on stage. Enter Narrator.

Narrator   Let's recap. The mouse is always nibbling.
                      Her step-mum's sent her to her sibling.
                      I wonder what fate awaits her
                      As she approaches Baba Yaga's lair.
                      So watch the little girl as she travels
                      And see how our tale unravels.

Little Girl	Now what were little mousey's words?
	The best advice I ever heard:
	Just pick up anything you find,
	And remember, carry on being kind.

She walks through audience.

Little Girl	Oh I think I'll come to grief.
	But what's that? – a handkerchief.

She picks up handkerchief, puts it in basket, and walks on.

> What's next in my woodland sortie?
> Here's a can of WD40.

She picks up WD40, puts it in basket, and walks on.

> Now that I am far from home
> Here on the ground I see a comb.

She picks up comb, puts it in basket, and walks on.

> I'm afraid of Baba Yaga's traps.
> Oh, here's meat. I'll take some scraps.

She picks up meat, puts it in basket and walks on.

> As I approach my aunt's with dread,
> I'll just pick up this loaf of bread.

She picks up loaf, puts it in basket and exits.

SCENE 3

Deeper in the woods

At the front of the stage. Enter Narrator and Little Girl.

Narrator	Soon we'll meet the devil of our saga.
	Please imagine the home of Baba Yaga,
	The bony-legged, the witch
	Who has the things with which to stitch.
	Tall gates bar the way to a dirty yard.
	Inside a fierce dog stands guard.
	And Baba Yaga's hut walks around,
	On hen's legs, instead of on the ground.
	(That's according to the folklorists:
	It's a good job we're not purists.)
	Now see the little girl approach the gates
	On her errand to test her fates.

Exit Narrator. Enter Gates, and (behind) Dog and Maid.

Gates   Oh no, we're really old and dusty
And our hinges are very rusty.

Little Girl   How lucky that I found some oil.
Have some, Gates, to ease your toil.

She oils the gates with her WD40 and goes through.

Maid   Boo hoo! My mistress works me all day long.
Then I feel the edge of her sharp tongue.
No matter how I go on trying,
She's so cruel I can't stop crying.

Little Girl   How lucky that I thought of keeping
This hanky to stop you weeping.

She gives handkerchief to Maid.

Dog   Woof, woof! I'm underfed and a danger.
I'll attack you, little stranger.

Little Girl   Now then, here's a loaf to guzzle.
What a pity I didn't find a muzzle.

She gives loaf to Dog. Enter Baba Yaga. Baba Yaga sits and weaves. Enter Narrator.

Narrator   Inside the hut we see the witch of doom
Busy working at her loom.
The little girl will surely come to grief
When she meets Baba Yaga's iron teeth.
As the shuttle flies forward and back
We hear the sound go 'clickety clack'.
Now audience, it's vital for our plot
That you make the sound. Give it all you've got.

Again: clickety clack, clickety clack
Come on shuttle, forward and back.

Audience   Clickety clack, clickety clack
Come on shuttle, forward and back.

Narrator   Alright, that's enough, stop that.
Don't forget, in the corner, there's a cat.

Enter Thin Black Cat.

Little Girl   Good day aunt, to you, my best,
My mummy's sent me with a small request
For a needle to mend a stocking.
(to audience)   Oh dear, my knees are knocking.

Baba Yaga *(aside)* Good day, pleased to meet you
      Especially as I'm going to eat you.
      Sit here, take my place at the loom.
      I'll fetch the needle from the other room.

Little Girl sits and weaves.

Audience   Clickety clack, clickety clack
      Come on shuttle, forward and back.

Baba Yaga goes to edge of stage.

Baba Yaga *(to Maid)* Maid, light a fire, heat scalding water
      So I can boil my sister's step-daughter.
      She'll be a nice little feast
(to Little Girl) Now keep weaving little niece.

Narrator prompts audience.

Audience   Clickety clack, clickety clack
      Come on shuttle, forward and back.

Little Girl *(to cat)* Catkin, have you had nothing to eat?
      It's lucky I have some scraps of meat.

She gives meat to cat who eats it.

Thin Black Cat That snack had a welcome taste
      Now I've a plan if you'll make haste.

Baba Yaga *(from edge of stage)*
      Now then my little beauty
      Are you weaving and doing your duty?

Narrator prompts audience.

Audience   Clickety clack, clickety clack
      Come on shuttle, forward and back.

Little Girl   Yes, please do tell me catkin
      How I can escape and save my skin.

Thin Black Cat What you must do, little girl with kind heart,
      Is tiptoe out and get a head start.
      Baba Yaga will follow with a terrible growl
      When she's near, throw down your towel.
      It will turn into a great river,
      Which will put her in a dither.
      She will try and chase you home.
      That's when you throw down your magic comb.

	The audience will become a great big thicket. That should be just the ticket.
Little Girl	But if she hears the loom stop the clickety clack Baba Yaga will come running back.
Thin Black Cat	Don't worry, I'll sit and do the weaving, So she won't hear when you're leaving.

Narrator prompts audience.

Audience	Clickety clack, clickety clack Come on shuttle, forward and back.

Little Girl leaves, Cat takes over the loom. Enter Dog.

Dog (*sees Little Girl*)	Whoever it is, I'll kill you dead. Oh, it's the little girl who gave me bread.

Dog sits down and lets her pass. Enter Gates in closed position.

Gates	Because our hinges have been oiled Baba Yaga will be foiled.

Gates open and Little Girl passes through and runs downstage.

Baba Yaga (*from edge of stage*)	
	Are you weaving my little sweet Before you have your bath-time treat?

Narrator prompts audience.

Audience	Clickety clack, clickety clack Come on shuttle, forward and back.
Thin Black Cat	Yes, auntie, the loom's still going And the shuttle is to-ing and fro-ing

Baba Yaga (*shouts from edge of stage*)	
	That's not the voice of my little niece She can't have escaped in one piece!

Baba Yaga enters in a rage.

Baba Yaga	Cat, why didn't you tear her eyes out?
Thin Black Cat	You always made me go without. I never had anything to eat But the little girl gave me scraps of meat.
Baba Yaga	Gates, why didn't you squeak out When the little girl tried to sneak out? Maid, why did the bath take such a time? On my word, you'll pay for your crime.

	And you, pathetic hound, Why didn't you pull her to the ground?
Gates	All those years you never eased us. That little girl with oil pleased us.
Dog	All those years I ate only crusts of bread. The good little girl gave me a loaf instead.
Maid	All those years I served you without a prize! Then she gave me a hanky to dry my eyes.
Baba Yaga	Even though she's had a head start I can catch her in my witch's cart And beat the ground with my broomstick, So I'll catch her up pretty quick.

She runs after Little Girl, chasing her into audience.

Little Girl	I'm running fast and my lungs are straining But the wicked witch is quickly gaining. I can hear her dreadful howl What shall I do? – throw down the towel.

She throws towel between her and Baba Yaga.

Baba Yaga	Oh no! My way is barred by a magic river. I'll summon my magic cows come hither. Cows, please drink this imaginary water Then I'm quickly off to slaughter.

Children mime drinking river. Baba Yaga continues pursuit.

Little Girl	No matter how fast I run Baba Yaga quickly comes. Oh no, I must get home! My last try is this comb.

She throws down comb. Audience put up hands. Little Girl exits safely through audience.

Baba Yaga	Oh, no, it's turned into a magic thicket. It's not fair, it's just not cricket. The going's just too tough, I'm going home, I've had enough.

Exit Baba Yaga.

SCENE 4
In front of Old Man's hut

Enter Little Girl. The Mouse is in the hut.

Little Girl — Even though Baba Yaga's been outdone
I've still got to face my step-mum.
Where's the shed? I think I'll hide
Till I meet someone who's on my side.

She looks in shed and meets the Mouse.

Mouse — Scratch, scratch. Now go and tell your father
About your trip to Baba Yaga.

Little Girl leaves shed and goes to table where Old Man and Stepmother are sitting. Exit Mouse.

Stepmother — Oh no, how an earth did you survive?
No-one's ever come back alive.

Little Girl — Dad, oh daddy, step-mum sent me to a witch.
Luckily I got back without a hitch.
Mousey-kin helped a lot,
Or I'd have ended in the cooking pot.

Stepmother — Don't believe her girlish fancy.
I'm innocent of necromancy.

Old Man *(to Stepmother)* When I slipped away to town
You tricked me and let me down.
I should have seen through you before.
Leave! Never again darken my door.

Exit Stepmother.

Old Man — Now we're rid of that belledame
Let's sit and have some bread and jam.

Little Girl — Yes, it will be just like our former life
Before you got yourself a wife.
We were such a happy house,
But daddy, please can we ask mouse
To join us for our tea?

Enter Mouse, who sits at the table with them.

Little Girl — It's how I like it – just us three.

THE END

MUMMERS PLAY FOR LAMMAS:
DEATH OF THE SUMMER LORD

written with Martin Jakes and Paul Dalton

CAST

Ceres, Goddess of the Corn	Doctor Slack
Turkish Knight	Friar Tuck
George a Greene	Puck
Eezum Squeezum	Dragon
Sabra, King of Egypt's daughter	Ophelia

Play can be preceded by an optional song for players and audience to the tune of 'Turali, Turali':

SONG

Tonight we've a play for harvest time
As Ceres will tell in appalling rhyme
The Summer Lord will die so he'd better watch out
For the Turkish Knight will give him fair clout.

Chorus
Turali, Turali, Turali-o
Turali, Turali, Turali-o
Our play is a circle like those in the corn
About death and renewal and being reborn

For now it is Lammas and the evenings draw in
And the day loses power and the darkness will win
So tonight for your pleasure the tale is retold
Sit back and relax and let the story unfold.

(Repeat chorus)

Enter Ceres.

Ceres   Here comes I, Ceres, Goddess of the Corn
Bringing harvest plenty as the year draws on
For the summer now is past its height
So George must be killed by the Turkish Knight.
Look, here comes the Turkish Knight
So fierce with sword a-shining bright.

Enter Turkish Knight.

Turkish Knight   Before with George a Greene I spar
Let me recount the story so far.

> Full seven months I've lain in the forest dark
> Waiting for Lammas, and to make my mark.
> Now that night is winning over day
> The time is here to have my way.
> George a Greene is my age old foe
> Now it's his turn to die, I'll have you know.

Enter George a Greene.

George a Greene	In steps I, George a Greene, a champion bold With my sword, I won three crowns of gold. Did I hear you mention my name? The Turkish Knight – not you again!
Turkish Knight	The moment's come, so draw your sword For now I'll be your master and lord.

Skirmish between George and Turkish Knight.

Enter Eezum Squeezum and Fair Sabra, interrupting the fight.

Eezum Squeezum	In comes I, old Eezum Squeezum On my back I carry my beezum And here's the King of Egypt's daughter Come to see the Summer Lord's slaughter.
Sabra	For the Turkish Knight must have his Queen Once he's killed George a Greene.

Eezum Squeezum grabs Fair Sabra's hand.

Eezum Squeezum	I've got Fair Sabra in my hand I'll grab her money and her father's land.
Sabra	Let go you evil piece of dirt And get your hands from under my skirt. I've come here for a rendez-vous With the Turkish Knight, and not with you.
Turkish Knight	I forgot I arranged to meet you Sabra.
Sabra	Typical!
Eezum Squeezum	Come over here and let me grab 'ya.

Sabra escapes Eezum Squeezum's grasp.

Eezum Squeezum	I think I'll go and find a woman After all I'm only human.

Exit Eezum Squeezum.

Ceres	Oh George, oh George, your time is nigh.
George a Greene	So cleave to me before I die.
Ceres	Oh George are you getting Cere-is (serious)?
George a Greene	Lust is sending me delirious.
Ceres	Look behind and take your guard The Turkish Knight's approaching hard.

Fight resumes between George and the Turkish Knight.

George a Greene	Oh pardon me, oh Turkish Knight May I not live just one more night: Sensual pleasures are to me mysterious At least give me one more night with Ceres.
Turkish Knight	Your hour is up and your reign is over You have no time to take a lover. When Yuletide comes with wind and rain The crown of power will be yours again.

They fight, George is killed.

Ceres	So George is dead, no chance to yield Is there a doctor in this field?

Enter Doctor Slack.

Doctor Slack	Did I hear someone calling me? As a matter of fact, I'm an M.D. Some people think I'm a bit of a quack But call on me, I'm Doctor Slack.
Ceres	The King is dead and must be reborn To ensure the success of next year's corn.
Doctor Slack	This young man looks woebegone What he needs is some mogadon.
Sabra	That sort of prescription is pretty pathetic Please give me something homeopathic.
Doctor Slack	Enough of your alternative notion I'll fix you with Slack's Own Potion.

Doctor revives George a Greene.
Sabra dances towards the Turkish Knight to become his wife.

Turkish Knight	Now that I am King again Let the marriage feast begin.
Sabra	Yes, I'll agree to be your bride.
Turkish Knight	Then I can face anything by your side.

Turkish Knight and Sabra embrace.

Sabra	Here comes Earth, Air, Fire and Water To wish us joy from every quarter.

Enter Friar Tuck, Puck, Ophelia and Dragon.

Friar Tuck *(hiccups)*	Here comes I, earthy old Friar Tuck – hic To join in the party and wish you good …luck.
Puck	I'm Puck of the Air, the playful sprite I'll play some tricks on you tonight.
Dragon	You think that we exist no more, But where there's fire, there are dragons galore.
Ophelia	I'm watery Ophelia, of love I'm dead So don't fall in the river, fall into bed.
Friar Tuck	I've waited years for the lovely Ophelia Come over here and let me feel 'ya.
Ceres	Now you've heard from each element, We'll continue with our merriment. Thank you friends for listening to our story We hope you didn't find it too gory. For as surely as night must follow day The son must end his father's sway And find his own authority To set his self-expression free.

Cast and audience sing chorus:

> Turali, Turali, Turali-o
> Turali, Turali, Turali-o
> Our play is a circle like those in the corn
> About death and renewal and being reborn.

THE END

Note

Inspired by a brief mention of a play called *Death of the Summer Lord* reported in a libel case brought by the Earl of Lincoln to the Star Chamber in 1601. In the villages neighbouring South Kyme in Lincolnshire, revellers continued their May festivities into August, and went too far in allowing their summer 'Lord of Misrule' to provoke their real Lord, who took offence.

NICOLETTE AND AUCASSIN

CAST

Narrator
Garin, Count of Beaucaire
Aucassin, his son
Bolgar of Valence, enemy of Garin
Soldier, a follower of Bolgar
Nicolette

Timothy, a shepherd
Andrew, a shepherd
King of Topsy Turvy
Queen of Topsy Turvy
Topsy Turvy Handmaid
The Topsy Turvy army
(played by children)

The audience take part by throwing missiles in the Topsy Turvy battle.

SCENE 1

In the county of Beaucaire in medieval France

Enter Garin and Aucassin.

Garin   No, Aucassin, I will not hear of it!
It's stuff and nonsense every bit.
Your duty, son, is to fight and win
Your reputation in the battle's din,
Not to mope and get upset
Over an upstart beauty like Nicolette.

Aucassin *(ignoring his father)* How futile, how tiresome is this argument
When my soul rages in eternal torment.
Wreathed in beauty like the misty morn
Is the fairest woman ever born,
Golden like an evening sunset –
My heart, my hope, my Nicolette.

Garin   Oddsblood! You foolish youth!
Listen while I tell the truth.
You must defend our ancient town –
That's the way to win renown.
You can't wed someone of lowly birth.
Find a lover to match your social worth.
And if you simply will not listen –
I'll clap your girl in my highest prison.

Exit Garin.

Aucassin   Nicolette, you are my morning, night and noon:
Our wedding day can't come too soon.

My father will shut you up in jail,
Leaving me to weep and wail.
But even though you are behind bars,
My love will stay constant as the distant stars.
I'll suffer to think how sad you'll be –
But you won't be half as sad as me.

Enter Garin.

Garin   Aucassin, come quick, we're under attack!
I beg you show the punch you pack.
Act like you've got some common sense:
Our enemy's here, Count Bolgar of Valence.
So act like a future ruler of Beaucaire,
And fight like a lion in his lair.

Aucassin (*still ignoring his father*)
Oh Nicolette, when I think of your lovely face
It makes my pulse stir and my heartbeat race.
(*to Garin*) Father, if you think I'll fight in your army
I'm sure you're absolutely barmy.
All my energy is fixed on one celestial vision.
I couldn't fight – except on one condition.
Promise to let me and her get wed
Then I'll go out and kill 'em dead.

Enter Bolgar and soldier upstage; Garin draws sword.

Garin   Dolt! Dunce! Idle day-dreamer!
It's foolish to persist in this amour.
For what count affairs of the heart
When fights and blood and warfare start?

Bolgar and soldier advance.

Bolgar   I am Count Bolgar, heir to our ancient feud.
Warriors of Beaucaire, I hope you're in the mood.

Bolgar and Garin fight.

Aucassin (*to Garin*) Then let my last word be this:
I'll fight if I can have a single kiss.

Garin (*over shoulder to Aucassin while fighting Bolgar*)
All right, I agree. You and I can't quarrel more.
Now take your sword and fight this war.

Aucassin fights Bolgar and soldier. Garin withdraws upstage.

Aucassin Here I come – Aucassin the warrior!
My love will overcome any barrier.

> Take that you rascals and rogues –
> I'll fight you off in droves.

Bolgar and soldier overpower Aucassin.

Aucassin	I say! Unhand me sirs! Desist. Lay off!
Soldier	This is a pretty one – a real toff.
Bolgar	We'll carve him up and ruin his love life Before he ever gets himself a wife.
Soldier	Let's truss him up and skewer him whole Before we hear more about his immortal soul.
Aucassin	But if I'm dead, and not around any more, How can I be Nicolette's paramour? Once I'm tortured and, well, dead I'll never more compose verses in my head. In fact this treatment makes me mad So I'll catch Count Bolgar and take him to Dad.

Aucassin breaks free, kills soldier, captures Bolgar and takes him to Garin.

Aucassin	This is a real mind-bender I beg you to accept the enemy's surrender And sort out some diplomatic compromise. Now hurry and let me claim my prize. That single, fleeting moment's bliss When I can give my Nicolette a kiss.
Garin	Son, you've demonstrated your ability And surprised me by your virility But first a kiss, then you'll ask for her hand – No, son, you're living in cloud-cuckoo land. Whatever you say, I know better. She's locked up. Now just forget her.
Aucassin	I can't believe it. I've been taken for a dupe. Well, Dad, I'm going to land you in the soup. I'm going to set Count Bolgar free So he'll live to be your enemy And fight and make life tough.

Aucassin releases Bolgar.

Aucassin	Off you go. That's it. I've had enough.
Bolgar	Thanks very much, you love-lorn loon. I'll be back fighting – very soon.

Exit Bolgar.

Garin   Fool! Monkey! Oh feckless son,
        Look what you've gone and done.
        Well, that's it – you're off to prison.

Exeunt Garin and Aucassin.

SCENE 2.
Imprisonment

Aucassin is in prison upstage. Nicolette is to the side in a tower.
Enter Narrator.

Narrator   Well, that almighty cock-up
        Saw Aucassin consigned to the lock-up.
        For a prize courtly lover
        He seems to get in a lot of bovver.
        His father now departs this tale
        Having done service as the alpha male.
        To show that true love has its pains
        Both hero and heroine are left in chains.

        But now it's time to catch a glimpse
        Of the beauty that's bewitched our prince.

Exit Narrator. Enter Nicolette.

Nicolette   Here I am, Nicolette, locked up in this tower.
        Count Garin has me in his power.
        He won't accept me as his daughter-in-law
        Because my parents were lowly and poor.
        Although in point of fact I'm orphaned
        And brought up here in this strange land.
        But Aucassin loves me for myself
        And I love him too for love, not wealth.

        But while I'm locked up, love lies idle
        And restraint makes my spirits bridle.
        I may not have much high technology
        But I can still do some escapology.

Nicolette escapes.

Aucassin   Here I am, in prison I languish –
        For love I suffer such pain and anguish.
        Only the thought of her fair face
        Will help me survive this disgrace.

Nicolette approaches.

Nicolette	Psst! Aucassin, listen, it's me.
	I was in prison, but now I'm free.
	Your dad tried to keep me out of the way
	But I shinned down the drainpipe and got away.
	Buck up, they're going to hunt me down
	Until I give you up and leave this town.
	But if our hearts must be broken

(passing ring through prison bars)

	Then take this ring as my love token.
Aucassin	Oh this will always be my treasure
	To remind me of love's boundless pleasure.
	Your leaving sends me round the bend.
	I'll kill myself. It would be the end.
Nicolette	Men! You just sit around moping
	Leaving us women to do the coping.
	While you ramble on at length
	It's women's love that has the strength.
Aucassin	My darling, I acknowledge your sincere intent
	But I just can't accept your argument.
	Women love with their eyes and noses
	All the way to the tips of their toes-es.
	But by a strong heart men's love is exalted.
	It's inescapable and can't be faulted.
Nicolette	Aucassin, my dearest, be that as it may
	If I hang around, there'll be hell to pay.
	Your father's men are in hot pursuit
	So I must flee your love – however cute.

Exeunt Nicolette and Aucassin.

SCENE 3
In the forest

Enter Narrator.

Narrator	This is a tale of a funny sort
	Aucassin's love has come to nought.
	He hasn't managed yet
	To get anywhere with Nicolette.
	First he was free and she was jailed;
	Then she escaped and he was nailed.
	Now Garin releases Aucassin from prison torment
	Though his soul is in a lover's ferment.

Fair Nicolette to the forest has fled,
Knowing that Garin wants her dead.
Let's see now how she fares
In among animals and their lairs.

Exit Narrator. Enter Nicolette.

Nicolette   Here I am in this fearsome forest
                   On the run – I feel quite harassed.
                   I'm getting desperate, I don't mind confessing.
                   In these dark woods, it's quite depressing.

Enter shepherds Timothy and Andrew carrying their lunch.

Timothy   I'm Timothy. Of shepherds I'm the best

Andrew   And I'm Andrew. I'm tired, I'd like a rest.

They sit down and eat their lunch.

Nicolette *(aside)* Wait a moment, here are some yokels.
                   That's it – when lost, ask the locals.
(to shepherds)   Hallo,
(aside)   …they may be able to do me a favour.

Timothy *(to Nicolette)* Hallo,
(to Andrew)   …who's here – a right little raver.

Andrew   What do we want with a fragrant beauty?
(to Timothy)   We're minding our flocks and doing our duty.
                   We're just shepherds. Let's not get involved.

Timothy *(to Andrew)* You're right. Let's be resolved.

Nicolette   Hey, you guys, you know Lord Aucassin –
                   Give him a message if you see him passing.

Andrew   I knew it. That type always use you.
(to Timothy)   Then they turn round and accuse you.

Timothy
(to Andrew)   No, play our cards right and we're on a winner
(to Nicolette)   Hallo there love, we're having our dinner.

Nicolette   Tell him, if you see him, mates
                   That a precious jewel awaits
                   Him – a jewel and treasure beyond compare
                   Something wonderful and very rare.

Andrew   No we couldn't possibly comply
                   Why it would be a downright lie.

Jewels and prizes don't make sense.
Nothing round here is worth two pence.

Nicolette *(holds out a five pound note)*
Oh please do what I've proposed.
Will a fiver make you more disposed?

Timothy *(takes money)* Now what you've said is really funny
But we've no objection to your money.
We don't mind repeating that load of tosh
While we're sitting here having our nosh.

Nicolette   Great. Now I'm off to rest in that bower
And get my head down for half an hour.

Nicolette retires to bower and lies down. Enter Aucassin.

Aucassin   How I hate this deep dark wood
I only came because they said I should.
But I'm beginning to have my doubts.
I'm lost as to my whereabouts.

(to Timothy and Andrew)
Hallo, good day. I say you chaps
I hope I'm not disturbing your midday nap.
But you don't happen to have seen
Passing this way a beauty queen?

Timothy   What us? Now, have we? A pretty bird?

Andrew   There's none round here, or we'd have heard.

Aucassin   Perhaps this ten pound note
Will give your memory a jolt?

Aucassin proffers ten pound note.

Timothy   No, no – but if it were, say, twenty
Then we might remember plenty.

Andrew   Well, someone did pass this way,
A pretty woman, would you say?

Timothy   She had some far-fetched idea
That priceless treasure was hidden near.

Aucassin *(giving twenty pound note)*
This is good news – here take this cash.
Find her? I'm going to have a bash.

Andrew   Let's exit and go and celebrate
And leave this fool to meet his fate.

Exeunt Andrew and Timothy.

Aucassin *(looking around)* Hallo, a bower, I'll look round here.
     I can't wait for Nicolette to appear.
     With this excitement I can hardly stand,
     When I think about our love's that's banned.

Aucassin falls over.

Aucassin   Oh no, my shoulder's dislocated
     What pain! I'll have to be sedated.
     Oh, I'm really cross, I'm so upset
     Just when I was looking for Nicolette.

Nicolette *(sitting up)* I recognise that manly sound.
(emerges from bower) Dear Aucassin, it's me! Darling, well found!

Aucassin   Oh Nicolette, my heart feels new
     From the moment I set eyes on you.
     But before I tell you more,
     I must confess, my shoulder's sore.

Nicolette   Oh, Aucassin, lover of great renown
     Don't say you've gone and fallen down.
     Now I'm not much of a physician,
     But I'll soon have that shoulder back in position.

Nicolette manipulates Aucassin's shoulder.

Nicolette   Darling, although we're back together
     I forsee some stormy weather.
     Don't forget your father's made us outlaws.
     He'll find us and kill us without good cause.

Aucassin   Well, I don't want that. Perish the notion.
     We'll away to sea and sail the ocean.
     Hand in hand, we'll stride toward the sunset.
     Two constant lovers, Aucassin and Nicolette.

SCENE 4
In Topsy Turvy land

Enter Narrator.

Narrator   They go to sea but don't get excited
     To see our lovers temporarily united.
     They get ship-wrecked on a foreign shore
     Washed up in a place never seen before.

In Topsy Turvy, all is upside down –
Judge for yourself if their ideas are sound.
And in addition to the role reversal,
There's a battle scene with no rehearsal.

Exit Narrator. Enter Aucassin and Nicolette.

Aucassin   Those storms have made me feel quite queasy
                  But in this land my duty is clear and easy:
                  I'll make my name with noble deeds
                  And crush opponents like broken reeds.

Nicolette   Hang on, you never know with foreign tribes
                  First of all, we should check out the vibes.

Aucassin   All right, let's go and see the king.
                  He's in charge, he'll pull some strings.
                  But which way? Shall we follow the Pole Star?

Enter King of Topsy Turvy at other side of stage.

Nicolette   No, over there…
(indicating King of Topsy Turvy across stage, next to bed)
                            …look, the royal four poster!

King *(in labour)* This is too much for a king to endure
                  First it hurts then it hurts some more.
                  I've carried this babe for months, hung up my sabre
                  Now birth pangs too, that's a poor division of labour.
                  And all that mess when my waters broke
                  Now I'm fully dilated and it's no joke.
                  I feel sick, and fear that I'm going to vomit or
                  Faint, and need the foetal heart monitor.

                  Oh here it comes! My kingdom for a massage
                  To ease the baby from its passage!
(gives birth)   I've never been so tired in all my life.
                  But what I want to know is – where was my wife?

Nicolette   Come on stop that self-pity and groaning!
                  A bit of hard labour and you don't stop moaning.
                  You men, you make such a fuss,
                  Take my advice and leave child-bearing to us.

Aucassin   You're a king, this isn't proper behaviour.
                  You should be a hero and a national saviour.
                  It just isn't fine and logical
                  For a man to be so gynaecological.

So come on you knock-kneed monarch,
Put an end to this childbed lark!
From now on you must do your duty –
Or you'll get more than a baby's bootee!

Aucassin kicks King out of bed.

King
Hey man, don't get so uptight!
I know those old values are hard to fight.
But you should hang loose, relax, just be –
Instead of coming on like Mad Max III.

Aucassin
Let's get this straight: I'm a knight
So show me where to go and fight.

Nicolette
I hope this won't turn into a squabble.
The men in this play have caused enough trouble.

King
Well, if you insist, I'll give you a guided tour.
And first, we'll see the Topsy Turvy war.
Come over here for a sight you've never seen:
The one in charge is the Topsy Turvy queen.

Enter Topsy Turvy Queen and Handmaid, with Topsy Turvy army.

Queen
Yes, I'm the Topsy Turvy regina.
I like a scrap, there's nothing finer.
Here is my strange assorted army –
Only four foot tall and their weapons are barmy.

Handmaid
I'm the second in command
I take charge of this fighting band.
Instead of missiles, tanks and scuds,
We've sponges, socks and other duds.
So kids take up the things you've brought to throw.
Wave them, show them, let them know.

Queen
Right troops, form up in battle ranks
And let's begin our foolish pranks.

Handmaid
First rank, advance and throw!
That's it, over there! Now back you go.

Topsy Turvy army throw soft missiles.

Queen
Come on and take the plunge,
Throw those objects, hurl that sponge.

Topsy Turvy army throw again.

Handmaid	Now everybody else, give hard knocks! Hit 'em with your weightless socks.

Topsy Turvy army throw again.

Queen	Cease fire! I think we've got them beat! Let's watch our noble heroes now retreat.
Aucassin	No it isn't proper knightly combat To be assailed by a furry wombat. I'll show you how, Cowabunga! With my sword I'll come among ya. (That's a slogan from a TV craze That once was big in bygone days).

Aucassin rushes forward and disperses children.

King *(restraining Aucassin)*	Aucassin, stop this, hold on, chill out. This is a friendly battle, not a rout. In Topsy Turvy we always fight our friends. It's just our way of passing the weekends.
Queen	I agree. Aucassin is just too warlike If it was up to me he'd be on his bike. How about Nicolette as PM – no one will match her Certainly not that Margaret Thatcher.
Nicolette	I know you think I must be soppy To fall in love with someone stroppy, But I must stick with Aucassin I love him and he's my man.
King	Fall in love? Pah – that's as maybe! I'm off home to feed the baby.

Exeunt all.

SCENE 5
Homeward bound

Enter Narrator.

Narrator	So Topsy Turvy land, so upside down Didn't suit our knight of great reknown. With Nicolette he stayed awhile Until Dame Fortune sent another trial. When a pirate band descended Their short-lived happiness was ended.

They were kidnapped and taken separate ways
And our heroes were lost in a lover's maze.

For many months they live apart,
Though each has a place in the other's heart.
So, what's in store? A tragic end or a get-together?
First hear from one and then the other.

Exit Narrator. Enter Aucassin.

Aucassin   After many adventures and hard knocks
My ship was cast upon the rocks.
And by chance it was the very coast
Of Beaucaire, the land I love the most.
Mum and Dad have died. I'm head of state
But still my heart is like a heavy weight.
It's a pity therapy's not invented yet
As I'm all cut up over Nicolette.

Withdraws upstage. Enter Nicolette in disguise as minstrel.

Nicolette   First of all I was snatched by buccaneers
And taken in pirate ships far and near.
I almost went to an early grave,
Then I was sold to be a slave.
I was sent to work without a wage
In the royal city of Carthage
Until the discovery of my nativity
Put an end to my captivity.

I found I was born the daughter of the king
But stolen at birth and never knew a thing.
Then they began to treat me well
And dressed me like a courtly belle.
They intended me for the marriage mart
But Aucassin still ruled my heart.
So I disguised myself as a troubadour
And from court to court began to tour.

I sing of love and how hard it is to bear.
Now I've arrived at the court of Beaucaire.

(sings)   Ladies and gentlemen, hear my song
Of broken hearts and love gone wrong
How Aucassin and Nicolette loved each other
And then lost track of one another

But Nicolette keeps him in her heart
And longs for him though they're far apart
She's in Carthage where she's part of the royalty
But still Aucassin commands her loyalty.

Aucassin *(moving to Nicolette)*
At last I hear the answer to all my prayers
In this minstrel's songs and airs.
Nicolette alive – can this be true?
Minstrel, is this woman known to you?

Nicolette
Yes, I think she could be traced
I daresay she's longing to be embraced.

Aucassin
Tell her my feelings are unchanged.
Tell her with love I am deranged.
After months and months of separation
I invite her to help me rule our nation.

Nicolette
All right, but don't forget
It may take months to find Nicolette
And though it may seem to you that ages pass
When she comes, it'll seem just like a flash.

(to audience)
The poor man lives in a fantasy world.
He can't see I'm not a boy, but his own girl.
I can't bear to shatter his illusion.
It would cause too much confusion.

I'll just nip round the back and see you later
After a few words from our narrator.

Exit Nicolette to change out of her disguise.

Aucassin
Now I must endure this uncertain wait
Before I can be reunited with my mate.
It makes me miserable and sad
Any more delay will drive me mad.

Enter Narrator. Aucassin and Nicolette can enact the narrative in a dumbshow.

Narrator
Nicolette sheds her disguise
While Aucassin just cries and cries.
But her absence is very short
And in her true self returns to court.
When Aucassin sees his Nicolette
We see him at his happiest yet.
They fall into each other's arms
And gaze upon each other's charms.

And after one night chastely separate
At last Aucassin weds his Nicolette.
They are the lord and lady of Beaucaire
And finally all pleasures share.

This is the end of our tortured tale
Of how love kept true and did not fail.
And so we bid you all adieu
And wish good fortune to all of you.

THE END

ODYSSEUS IN TRANSIT

With additional lines for Hermes by Penny Cloutte

CAST

Poseidon, the sea god
Athene, daughter of Zeus
Cabin Boy
Boatholder *(who holds model boat)*
Odysseus, King of Ithaca and hero of Trojan War
Penelope, wife of Odysseus, at home during Trojan War
Eurylochus, a sailor
Polites, a sailor
Perimedes, a sailor
Sailor 1
Sailor 2
Sailor 3
Lotus Eater 1
Lotus Eater 2
Circe, a goddess
Handmaids to Circe
Hermes, the messenger god
Siren 1
Siren 2
Scylla, a six headed monster *(played by one to six people)*
Charybdis, a whirlpool *(played by at least two people)*
Calypso, a demi-goddess

Roles for children:

Fishes with Poseidon (red snappers, octopuses and squids)
Handmaids for Circe
Lions and wolves for Circe

The audience plays the winds, the ocean, and sings a dirge of lamentation, to the tune of 'Ten Green Bottles'. They help rescue sailors from the Lotus Eaters.

The action takes place on the wine-dark sea and various islands.

Audience (sings to tune of '10 Green Bottles')
>   We're 20 Greek sailors sailing on the sea
>   20 Greek sailors sailing on the sea
>   5 washed overboard, oh dearie dearie me
>   15 Greek sailors sailing on the sea.

Enter Poseidon and Athene.

Poseidon   I am Poseidon who makes Odysseus his sport:
>   My winds blow him from port to port.
>   The reason he made me mad
>   Is that I was the Cyclops' Dad.
>   My one-eyed innocent son
>   Was blinded in front of everyone.
>   Now Odysseus suffers in the wine-dark sea –
>   That'll teach him to anger me.

Athene   I'm the goddess Athene, proud and goddess-y
>   The true heroine of 'The Odyssey'.
>   Mortal Odysseus will need me at his side
>   When Poseidon blows him far and wide.

Poseidon   Audience, help us play the storms
>   Way beyond shipping forecast norms.
(leads audience in imitating winds)
>   Blow from the East, blow from the West
>   And put these sailors to the test.
>   Blow from the North, blow from the South
>   Puff out your cheeks, and bulge your mouth.

Children enter as fishes around boatholder who plunges the boat up and down.

Poseidon   You children as fishes swirl around
>   The boat which plunges up and down.
>   You sailors lean into the icy blasts
>   While sails are battered against the masts.
>   At last we'll let the winds abate
>   Leaving the crew in a sorry state.

Exeunt Poseidon and fishes and boatholder. Enter Odysseus with Cabin Boy. Enter Penelope at opposite side of the stage area.

Cabin Boy   I'm this good ship's cabin boy
>   I'm on lookout and shout 'land ahoy!'
>   Here's our captain Odysseus, famed for guile.
>   He's from Ithaka, that rugged isle.

Odysseus   In comes I, the renowned Odysseus
On my way home to see my missius.
We've left behind the Trojan Wars
But keep landing on unknown shores,
While my queen Penelope waits at her loom
Watching for my sail from a turret room.

Penelope *(at a distance)* I weep and wail and shed my tears –
My husband's not back after ten long years.
I fear a man's heart can be defective
Especially if there's no working time directive.
And Odysseus is so late home
I sometimes wonder if he prefers to roam.

Athene   What a patient woman she's been
Let's return her husband to this faithful Queen.
However, that happens in next year's play.
Bring on what's left of the sailors, to start today.

Exit Athene and Penelope.

Enter Eurylochus, Polites, Perimedes, and three sailors.

Odysseus   Admire my man-management skills
As our story unfolds its thrills.
Come on you trusty sailors
My brilliant leadership will never fail us.

Eurylochus   I'm Eurylochus, one of this heroic band
I hope we'll return safely to our native land.

Polites   I'm Polites. We'll never let you down
Until you return home to claim your crown.

Odysseus   Now before adventures grab your attention
I must confess to some apprehension.
I left Troy with my brave crew
But on the way, I lost a few.
Cyclops and Lystragonians tested our bravery
But next we're up against women's knavery.
So let's sing a little song
Lamenting how things went wrong.

Audience *(sing)* We're 15 Greek sailors sailing on the sea
15 Greek sailors sailing on the sea
5 died in battle oh dearie dearie me
10 Greek sailors sailing on the sea.

We're 10 Greek sailors sailing on the sea
10 Greek sailors sailing on the sea

> Cyclops ate 4, oh dearie dearie me
> 6 Greek sailors sailing on the sea.

Enter Cabin Boy.

Cabin Boy I come in again, the cabin boy
To tell you I see land ahoy

Exit Cabin Boy.

Perimedes I'm Perimedes of this gallant crew.
It's been tough, but we've come through.
After being tossed by storms for many a day,
We'll cast anchor here in this tranquil bay.
We'll take on water, have a hearty meal
Then look around and get the feel...

Enter Lotus-Eaters 1 and 2 in a trance.

Polites They're vegetarians – I can tell at a glance
Though they seem to be in something of a trance.

Lotus Eater 1 We're lotus eaters on our desert isle
Take lotus and stay with us a while.

Odysseus I'm sure these harmless meat abstainers
Cannot do anything to detain us.

Lotus Eater 2 Men, forget heroics with this easeful drug
Embrace our languor in a sensual fug.

Polites The winds have blown and blown
I'm overdue the chill-out zone.
I'm sick of hard work and desolation
I'll take some lotus for consolation.

Perimedes Me too, I'm ready for the easy life
Better than going home to duty and the wife.
Veggies, you have us in your power –
We just crave the lotus flower.

Odysseus It makes me quite neurotic
To see good men wasted by a narcotic.
Come audience seize the rope and help me tug
To rescue my men from the lotus drug.

Rope wrapped around Eurylochus, Perimedes and Polites. Odysseus with audience hold both end of ropes and pulls them away from Lotus Eaters.

Athene cheers audience on.

Athene *(from audience)* Lotus makes them weak and dopey
So audience, pull hard on the rope-y!

Eurylochus and Odysseus cry out.

Eurylochus	Odysseus you can rave and rant We want to nibble on the lotus plant.
Odysseus	You can't become devotees of the weed And leave your mates in their hour of need.

Sailors rescued.

Lotus Eater 1	Wow, have it your way, dudes.
Lotus Eater 2	Leave us to our hippy foods.

Exeunt Lotus Eaters.

Odysseus	By acting like the boss I can dull my sense of loss. Let us now flee from this cursed shore And learn what fate next has in store.

Enter Poseidon with children (fishes), boatholder.

Poseidon	Blow from the East, blow from the West And put these sailors to the test. Blow from the North, blow from the South Puff out your cheeks, and bulge your mouth.

Audience blow.

Exit Poseidon. Enter Cabin Boy.

Cabin Boy	Land ahoy!

Exit Cabin Boy. Enter Athene.

Athene	Another windswept isle: now meet the owner – The sexiest lady in all of Homer.

Exit Athene. Enter Circe (humming).

Circe	I'm the beautiful enchantress named Circe To wandering sailors I show no mercy. I lure them with sensual guile to my door So they'll stay with me for evermore.

Exit Circe.

Odysseus	Are these beautiful sounds a warning, Or is a new adventure dawning. My curiosity is insatiable Though sometimes danger is non-negotiable.
Eurylochus	We should leave quickly before we come to harm.

Odysseus   Not so fast, this place has a certain charm.
                  Eurylochus, we'll draw lots to explore this isle
                  You toss a coin, do it with style.

Eurylochus *(tosses the coin)* Tails!

Odysseus   Tails it is, take half the men and go forth
                  We'll stay here – you set off North.

Exeunt Odysseus, Perimedes and Polites.

Sailor 1   After weeks battling on stormy high seas
                  This looks like the place to take our ease.

Sailor 2   I see servants to meet our every need
                  And, wow, fine food to satisfy our greed.

Enter children as lions and wolves, roaring and howling.

Eurylochus   I fear the lions and wolves around the grounds
                  Fawning on us and making dreadful sounds.

Enter Circe and Handmaids with bottle of oil.

Circe   Come in fine fellows, make yourselves at home
                  Wallow in luxury – no more need to roam.
                  You look worn out with all your toil
                  Girls, bathe them, anoint them with oil.

Sailor 3   This looks to me like paradise on earth

Eurylochus   I'm suspicious, I'll give her a wide berth
                  Something about her makes my flesh creep.
                  My motto is: 'Look before you leap'.

Eurylochus retreats to the edge of the stage.

Circe   Now you're all relaxed and off your guard
                  I'll take my wand and strike you hard.
(hits sailors) Behold, you're now all bristled swine.
                  Come to your sties – so get in line!

Circe herds sailors as pigs.

Sailors   Oink, oink!

Exeunt Circe, Handmaids and sailors as pigs in procession. Eurylochus remains.

Eurylochus   Oh no, I can't think of any fate nastier
                  I must run tell Odysseus of this disaster.

Enter Odysseus.

Odysseus	Eurylochus, why have you returned all alone?
Eurylochus	Alas, Odysseus, our friends are lost and gone Circe's turned them into stupid pigs They're snuffling acorns among the twigs. How can we make amends, Now we have lost our dearest friends?
Odysseus	This is my fault, don't be furious It happened because I'm always curious. I'll set off now to win them back You stay here, just point me out the track.

Exit Eurylochus. Odysseus sets off to Circe's palace.

Enter Hermes.

Hermes	I'm Hermes the messenger. My feet have wings – Athene sent me to help with things. Your crew have gone to the House of Circe An enticing place, when a sailor's thirsty! Beware her girls and their loving cup – If you take even so much as a sup Of her wonderful food or delicious wine, In the blink of an eye you'll become a swine!
Odysseus	I need your advice on what to do So I can rescue my errant crew.
Hermes	Round at the back of the Pig and Whistle You'll find your men all covered in bristle. Spellbound by Circe – she's sexy, not holy. To help you, eat this herb called moly.

Exit Hermes. Enter Circe and Handmaidens.

Circe *(making to woo Odysseus)*
                    Welcome to my home, you handsome stranger.

Odysseus *(aside)* She's lovely but I smell danger.

Circe   I'll entertain you like royalty.

Odysseus *(aside)* But I must remember my men's loyalty.

Circe   Come taste my exquisite potion
                  My girls will rub you with scented lotion.

Odysseus   You're a beautiful lady of great charm
(aside)   I must remember she intends me harm.

Circe *(raises wand)* Now I'll strike you with my wand.

Odysseus *(raises sword)* Stand back: my sword is in my hand.

Circe
Who are you that can resist my wile
You must be Odysseus, renowned for guile –
I was going to enchant you but instead
I think I'll invite you to my bed.

Odysseus
Since you're a goddess, I've no choice but to obey
But promise no mischief from this day.

Circe
Promise! If you're going to be my lover
We must learn to trust each other.
I'll give your men their human form
If you keep my body warm.

Enter all sailors (including Eurylochus), no longer pigs.

Sailors
We appreciate the sacrifice you've made for us
But now we'd like to go home, Odysseus.

Odysseus
Sleeping with Circe the enchantress
Caused me very great distress.
I only did it to save my crew
Oh, Penelope, I'd rather be with you.

Circe
Odysseus, go, if that's how you feel –
My heart is hard, but not made of steel.
First, let me warn you of the strife
You must pass through to see your wife.
Siren songs will stop you in your tracks
Unless you plug your ears with wax.
Then monster Scylla will play her tricks,
Snatch your men and eat all six.

Or choose Charybdis, but take your Gortex
If you go near that whirling vortex.

Exit Circe.

Odysseus
I'll be a leader like Tony Blair
And tell them the truth, or it wouldn't be fair.

(to crew)
Now chaps, our plans have hit a minor glitch
We'll meet some maidens whose songs bewitch.

(gives wax)
Take this wax and plug your ears
That'll be an end to your fears.
Then do as I say, and tie me to the mast
I guarantee that'll get us safely past.

(aside)
Mentioning the monster and the whirlpool
Would only scare them – I'm no fool.

Polites   These plugs will be a boon
To shut out any sexy tune.

Perimedes   Strong binding is a must
To restrain our leader's lust.

Sailors tie Odysseus and plug their ears. Enter Sirens singing in French.

Sirens   Viens chéri, viens mon coeur,
Viens dedans mes bras sensuels
Viens chéri, viens mon cœur
Ne résiste plus nos charmes cruels.

Sweetheart come, sweetheart come
Come within my sensuous arms
Sweetheart come, sweetheart come
Resist no more our cruel charms.

Siren 1   We're Sirens, half clad females with a fishy tail
We lie in wait on rocks to trap the silly male.

Siren 2   If you want a woman who is kinky
My body's unusually slippery and slinky.

Odysseus   Men – forget my instruction!
Untie me: I choose seduction.

Eurylochus   Perimedes, I can't hear a sound
But Odysseus must be more tightly bound.

Sailors tie Odysseus more. Exeunt Sirens.

Odysseus   Untie me, unplug your ears
Now we'll face our greatest fears.
Here come Scylla and Charybdis –
I don't know how we'll outlive this.

Sailors untie Odysseus. Enter Charybdis, whirling and Scylla at opposite sides.

Charybdis   Up and down we vomit spume
Come, Odysseus, meet your doom.

Scylla   Lose six men in our monstrous jaws
Odysseus – the choice is yours.

Charybdis   Up and down we vomit spume
Come, Odysseus, meet your doom.

Scylla   Lose six men in our monstrous jaws
Odysseus – the choice is yours.

Odysseus	Oh no, I've lost my sense of direction –
	It's worse than in the general election.
	OK sailors, I say rush past Scylla
	The other way is sure to be a killer.
Scylla	I've six heads and can't be beaten
	Your boat won't pass until we've eaten.
	Come on, heads, one to six,
	Grab a sailor, take your picks!

Scylla grabs sailors. Exeunt Scylla, Charybdis and sailors.

Odysseus	Following Scylla's monstrous purge
	Audience, let's complete our soulful dirge.
Audience	We're 6 Greek sailors sailing on the sea
	6 Greek sailors sailing on the sea
	Scylla seized 6, oh dearie dearie me
	No Greek sailors sailing on the sea.
	We're no Greek sailors sailing on the sea
	No Greek sailors sailing on the sea
	6 lost at sea, oh dearie dearie me
	Odysseus all alone a-drifting on the sea.
Odysseus	Oh no – now I've lost all my men
	I don't know if I'll ever get home again.
	But look, I see Calypso's isle
	And here's the demi-goddess with her smile.

Enter Calypso.

Calypso	Odysseus stop drowning or waving
	Stay here and be my plaything.
	My island will become your home
	So what, if it's rather monochrome.
	I'll give you food and clothes in the latest fashion
	And make you the object of my passion.
Odysseus	I won my fame for being wily
	I'll stay awhile and live the life of Riley.

Exeunt Calypso and Odysseus. Enter Athene.

Athene	Odysseus thought all would be fine:
	Bed, board and concubine.
	But seven years makes casual love pall –
	Now he wants his wife back after all.

Enter Odysseus weeping. He sits off to one side.

Odysseus   I lived the life of an adventurous guy
                        Now I'm stuck here and don't know why.

Enter Calypso.

Calypso   Seven long years we've been going steady
                        I won't lose you – I'm still not ready.

Odysseus   O how I miss Penelope
                        I wish her arms would envelope me.

Calypso   Live-in lover, you'll get an earful –
                        I just don't see why you're so tearful.

Athene   We can't leave him in Calypso's arms
                        Zeus will send Hermes to break the charm.

Enter Hermes

Hermes   Time's up Calypso, I've cooked your goose:
                        These events are decreed by Zeus.
                        Odysseus doesn't want to shack up
                        And now he's got immortal back-up.

Calypso   I'm the daughter of a god, half-divine
                        I don't have to toe the party line!

Hermes   Your demi-god charms don't hold a candle
                        Against the power of my flying sandal.

Calypso   You're right: my plans are on the rocks
                        Thanks to your golden Birkenstocks.
                        He'll no more be my domestic slave
                        I'll set him free on the ocean wave.

Exit Hermes.

Calypso *(to Odysseus)* Odysseus, the end of your voyage is near
                        I'm chucking you out on your ear.

Exit Calypso.

Odysseus   It's nineteen years since I saw my wife –
                        Could I adapt to the quiet life?
                        After my exploits and wild adventures
                        Will I be just an old man with dentures?
                        Audience, you'll leave me on the brink
                        But first, let's hear what our goddesses think.

Enter Lotus Eaters 1 and 2.

Lotus Eaters 1   We offered forgetfulness for your trouble
and 2 *(together)*   But you would go and burst our bubble.

Enter Circe.

| Circe | I offered lust and sexual stews
When it came to loyalty, you chose your crew's. |

Enter Sirens.

| Sirens | You ignored seduction's chorus
And put big adventures before us. |

Enter Scylla and Charybdis.

| Scylla
and Charybdis | Wayward man, admit your error:
We showed how women inspire terror. |

Enter Calypso.

| Calypso | OK, you're married – we can live over the brush
That's my idea – what's the rush?
But then you spurned my loving kisses
In favour of returning to your missis. |

| Athene | In this play I'm a bit part narrator
But in Part Two I'm the Gladiator.
So, you writers, it will be my goal
That in Part Two I have a bigger role.
And Odysseus, you'll only cease to roam
With the promise of excitement at home. |

| Odysseus | See how I've had to confront my feminine side?
Alas, it's left me nowhere to hide.
I set my course from one bed to another
And put off returning to a wife and mother.
I dithered about and blamed my crew
When the truth was: I didn't know what to do.
Audience, in Part Two, I'll do what I oughta
But now it's time for puddings and torte. |

THE END

SONG SHEET FOR ODYSSEUS IN TRANSIT

Audience (sings to tune of 10 Green Bottles)

Practice before the start – Poseidon prompts.

> We're 20 Greek sailors sailing on the sea
> 20 Greek sailors sailing on the sea
> 5 washed overboard, oh dearie dearie me
> 15 Greek sailors sailing on the sea.

After scene setting, before the adventures – Odysseus prompts.

> We're 15 Greek sailors sailing on the sea
> 15 Greek sailors sailing on the sea
> 5 killed in battle, oh dearie, dearie me
> 10 Greek sailors sailing on the sea.

> We're 10 Greek sailors sailing on the sea
> 10 Greek sailors sailing on the sea
> Cyclops ate 4, oh dearie dearie me
> 6 Greek sailors sailing on the sea.

After Scylla and Charybdis – Odysseus prompts.

> We're 6 Greek sailors sailing on the sea
> 6 Greek sailors sailing on the sea
> Scylla seized 6, oh dearie dearie me
> No Greek sailors sailing on the sea.

> We're no Greek sailors sailing on the sea
> No Greek sailors sailing on the sea
> 6 lost at sea, oh dearie dearie me
> Odysseus all alone a-drifting on the sea.

PENELOPE ON ITHAKA

Loosely adapted from Homer with reference to
'The Penelopiad' by Margaret Atwood

CAST

Athene, goddess
Helper *(to Athene)*
Odysseus
Penelope
Margaret Atwood
Maid 1, Candy
Maid 2, Mandy
Maid 3, Sandy

Suitors 1, 2 and 3
Eurecleia, old nurse
Telemachus
Eumenius, a shepherd,
Argos, Odysseus'dog

Audience join in songs.

Enter Athene and Helper.

| Athene | I'm doing the Prologue, I'm the Goddess Athene.
I'm a fan of Odysseus, because I'm keener
On Ancient Greek heroes than their boring wives.
I helped Odysseus, and gave him nine lives. |

Helper   I'm the helper. Last time, we heard from Odysseus
So in this play the star is his missius.

Enter Odysseus (in distance).

Odysseus   Help me Athene, I'm in a shipwreck
I'm sinking in seawater up to my neck.

Athene   For someone supposed to be the master
Odysseus has known rather a lot of disaster.
Still, I don't want him to lose heart –
I'll fly to his side and play my part.

Odysseus   Please someone give me a helping hand
So I can make it safely onto land.
Help me I don't want to end by drowning
When I was going home to my crowning.

Exit Odysseus.

Athene   He'll soon meet up with pubescent Nausicaa
She'll take him home to her ma and pa

| | Then he'll be on his way home at last |
| | He's been away 19 years, so he's not fast. |

Helper | Let's leave him to it and meet his wife
| To learn the story of her life.

Exeunt Athene and Helper. Enter Penelope.

Penelope | I am Penelope, Odysseus' faithful wife
| Left on Ithaka to my widow's life.
| Grief would drive me stark staring crackers
| If it wasn't for my son, Telemachus.
| My husband's become famous in history
| But what I thought remained a mystery.

Enter Margaret Attwood.

Margaret | Until, I, Margaret Atwood, wrote 'The Penelopiad'
| That's a made-up word to rhyme with 'Aeniad'
| Otherwise it could have been 'The Penelopussy'
| A made-up word to rhyme with 'Odyssey'.

Penelope | Thank you, Margaret.
(to audience) | Homer said that for 19 years
| I twiddled my thumbs and shed my tears
| But when a husband goes off with his troop
| A wife gets busy with her women's group.

Margaret | Think of her as a lunar high priest virgin
| With the maids who do her urging.
| There's twelve maids and her – let's be clear
| It adds up to the months in the lunar year.

Exit Margaret. Enter Maids.

Maid 1 | I'm Candy, the first of Penelope's twelve maids,
| We're young and fresh with beautiful braids.
| We've come to prepare the next moon ritual,
| We know what to do, it's quite habitual.

Maid 2 | I'm Mandy, second Maid, loyal to Penelope.
| We try to stop her getting mopey.
| She's our priestess and we're her acolytes.
| We prepare offerings and other treats.

Maid 3 | I'm Sandy, third Maid with a strong pair of hands,
| I've an eye for men from many lands.
| When I want a man, I go with a suitor,
| One of the young blades as we're not neuter.

Exeunt Maids. Enter Suitors: they pass by in a line, carousing.

Suitors *(Singing to tune of '10 Green Bottles')*
>20 bad suitors carousing in the Hall
>20 bad suitors carousing in the Hall
>When Odysseus returns, we're in for a fall
>There'll be no bad suitors carousing in the Hall.

Suitor 1
>We're the greedy suitors, behaving badly
>Hoping that Penelope will love one of us madly.
>This is before the days of I-pods and computers
>So we're just hard-drinking, loutish suitors.

Suitor 2
>Husband gone, wife boo-hooing
>It's open season for our wooing.

Suitor 3
>She has to give us bed and board.
>The one she chooses wins her treasure hoard.

Exeunt Suitors. Enter Nurse.

Nurse
>I'm the old nurse, Eurecleia, I speak my mind,
>I'm quite crotchety and quite unkind.
>Now Telemachus is no longer a young lad,
>He needs some contact from his roving dad.
>And I don't like the suitors running riot,
>It's getting out of hand – I can't keep quiet.

Penelope
>I lead the life of a single mum
>I can tell you it isn't all fun.
>If I choose a suitor, Tele gets a step-dad
>It's all enough to make me sad!
>I'm overwhelmed by indecision
>And quite worn down with this attrition.
>I know! I'll make a virtue of stalling –
>Even if they say it's a woman's calling.

Nurse
>But my Queen, you can prevaricate no more
>You must move on from the Trojan War.
>The suitors are ruining your son's inheritance
>While you lead them all a merry dance.

Penelope
>I'll say I'll wed when I finish Laertes' shroud
>It's a clever plan of which I'm proud.
>By day I sit weaving at my loom
>By night I unpick it in the gloom.

(to audience)
>Audience, imagine that my tricks and sobbings
>Has bought a few years from those suitor bobbins.

Nurse

While you weep and wail
Their behaviour's beyond the pale.
Why not let slip how you weave and unweave
So they'll get furious, fed up and leave.

Enter Maids.

Penelope

My maids, go forth to spread the rumour
You can do it with a sense of humour.
Let your suitor lovers know that the shroud
Will never be finished, that I'll never be wooed.

Sandy

I've got a hot date with one tonight
I'll spill the beans if you're sure it's right.

Candy

And I've got an admirer I could tell,
Then we'll summon back Odysseus with a spell.

Mandy

People don't appreciate the power of prayer
Yes, we'll bring him back from God knows where.

Exeunt Penelope, Nurse and Maids. Enter Telemachus.

Telemachus

I'm Telemachus, prince of Ithaka
It's hard having a dad who's so mythical.
He left me with no male on whom to model
Which meant my adolescence was no doddle.
How I hate those suitors, but I feel powerless –
They laugh and accuse me of cowardice.
But since my dad took the army off to Troy
What can I do, left alone and just a boy?

Enter Athene (in disguise).

Athene

Telemachus, I'm a friend of your father
If I were you, I think I'd rather
Take a boat and seek for news
It's better than staying here with the blues.

Telemachus

You're right I'm ready to spread my wings
But how do I arrange these things?
This is before the days of the gap year,
I need captain, crew and a boat to steer.

Athene

I'm off to the harbour to gather a crew,
A trusty captain and a boat for you.
So meet me at dawn at the end of the pier
I'll get you safely out of here.

Exit Athene.

Telemachus	At last an adventure's come *my* way
	I feel this is my lucky day.
	I'll take the chance to leave this isle
	And go off to Sparta for a while.

Telemachus is about to rush off. Enter Nurse.

| Nurse | Telemachus, why are you in such a hurry? |
| | You look excited, that makes me worry. |

Telemachus	I'm going abroad now to seek some news
	Of dad. I feel, I've nothing to lose.
	If the Gods are with me, I'll bring back father.
	Till I've gone, keep it secret from my mother.

| Nurse | May the Goddess speed your most noble quest |
| | I'll keep your secret, it's for the best. |

| Telemachus | I'll never forget your devotion |
| | When I return, you'll get promotion. |

Nurse	Away with you, from this bag of bones
	Leave me to deal with your mother's moans.
	May the Goddess bless your mission
	And save your youth from perdition.

Exeunt Nurse and Telemachus. Enter Maids and Suitors in two lines.

| Suitor 1 | We're happy boozers and best buddies |
| | You can't say we're fuddy-duddies! |

| Suitor 2 | We're fine and dandy, yanky doodling |
| | You all look hot for some canoodling. |

| Sandy | We're not expected back till daybreak |
| | We want some fun, we're on the make. |

| Suitor 3 | Well come on lads, look smart and hearty |
| | Let's take these maids off for a party. |

| Suitor 1 | We'll take a break from the ice-cold Queen |
| | As these good-looking maids look pretty keen. |

| Candy (*whispers*) | You're wasting time with Queen Penelope |
| | You'll never make her your royal trophy. |

| Mandy | By day she works away at her loom |
| | By night she unravels it to spell your doom. |

| Suitor 2 | In that case we'll each woo a merry maid |
| | Before your youth and beauty fade. |

Suitor 3	As for the Queen – her behaviour's sinister She prevaricates more than our own prime minister.

Suitors and Maids go off giggling. Enter Penelope and Nurse.

Penelope	I've been looking for my son and heir I can't seem to find him anywhere.
Nurse	You know, he's become a headstrong youth So I dread to tell you the very truth About your son (on whom you dote) – He left at sunrise on a speeding boat!
Penelope	I guess he's gone after our wandering king Now I despair of everything!
Nurse	My Queen, you must pull yourself together He left with a fair wind and fine weather. You must let him loose from his mother's skirts You can't protect him from life's hurts.

Enter Suitors.

Suitor 1	We finally rumbled your wicked plot. You unravel your weaving and pretend you've not.
Suitor 2	Queen Penelope, thanks to your schemings You've turned us mortal men into demons.
Penelope	How dare you impudently blame A beleaguered Queen, and besmirch my name!
Suitor 3	We're sick of your double-crossing plan You've got three days to choose a man.
Penelope	I will not curse you, I'll restrain my ire Because you will drown in muck and mire!

Exeunt Suitors.

Nurse	We must gather the maids for a temple ceremony They must learn new chants to do from memory.
Penelope	Yes, we'll cast a powerful protective charm To keep my darling son from harm And we'll use magic so Odysseus hears verbatim About the wicked suitors' ultimatum.
Nurse	If Odysseus gets wind of a possible battle He might hurry back –

Penelope (*interrupts*)　　　　　Stop your prattle!
　　　　　　　　Now I know you're talking nonsense:
　　　　　　　　Get busy with the candles and incense.

Exeunt Penelope and Nurse.

RITUAL

Enter Penelope with ceremonial feather leading Maids holding candles or branches of rosemary aloft.

Penelope　　　　　To the Wind and Stars, let us pray together
　　　　　　　　Protect Telemachus with this feather.

Maids　　　　　As he sails the ocean's brim
　　　　　　　　We offer the Goddesses our hymn.

Penelope (*leads audience participation, to tune of 'My Bonny'*)
　　　　　　　　Odysseus lies over the ocean
　　　　　　　　Telemachus lies over the sea
　　　　　　　　My dear ones are over the ocean
　　　　　　　　Oh bring back my dear ones to me.

Enter Nurse.

Nurse (*aside*)　　　　There'll be one hell of a battle –
　　　　　　　　The suitors will fall like slaughtered cattle.

Exit Nurse.

Maids (*with audience to tune of 'My Bonny'*)
　　　　　　　　Bring back, oh bring back
　　　　　　　　Oh bring back my dear ones to me, to me
　　　　　　　　Bring back, oh bring back
　　　　　　　　Oh bring back my dear ones to me.
(*offering food*)　　　　Athene, we ask you, take this offering
　　　　　　　　To save our loved ones from their suffering.

Exeunt Maids and Penelope. Enter Athene and Helper in disguise.

Athene (*from afar*) I accept your offerings. I'm on your side
　　　　　　　　I'm sending both home with the morning tide.

Helper　　　　　I hope you're keeping up with our narration
　　　　　　　　Now we'll fill you in with some information.

Athene　　　　　We told of Odysseus at the start
　　　　　　　　Meeting young Nausicaa with her innocent heart.

Helper　　　　　After he told her folks his story
　　　　　　　　They lent him a ship to come home in glory.

Athene	But the sailors didn't want to risk their own neck For if Poseidon saw them, he'd cause a shipwreck.
Helper	So while Odysseus deeply slept They dumped him ashore and away they crept.

Enter Odysseus.

Odysseus	I feel refreshed by that healing sleep I'd better climb the cliffs, though they look steep.
Athene	Welcome stranger, are you stranded?
Odysseus	I am, can you please tell me where I've landed?
Athene	This isle is famous far and wide Look around, smell the air, let that be your guide.
Odysseus	I smell the herbs of home, is this my sacred ground?
Athene	Yes, it's Ithaka!
Odysseus	Finally, I'm homeward bound!
Athene	You're near but you've got a battle to face Wicked suitors have overrun your place. You need an old beggar man's disguise To shield you from your enemies' eyes.
Helper	Here, wear this poor man's jerkin So they don't suspect you, when you're lurking.

Athene touches Odysseus and he becomes an old man (i.e. she gives him a shepherd's coat).

Athene	The only way to win Ithaka back Is to make your way to your shepherd's shack.

Exeunt Athene and helper. Enter Shepherd.

Shepherd	I'm Eumenius, the shepherd. I see a stranger But funny, my dogs did not scent danger.
Odysseus	I'm a shipwrecked man but I have good will I'm just an old man with a belly to fill.
Shepherd	I see that like me you're of working stock Come in stranger, drink soup from the pot.

Knock at the door. Enter Telemachus.

Shepherd	Telemachus! You're back from the ocean wave.
Telemachus	Yes, the gods protected me from a watery grave.

Shepherd   This calls for a feast and celebration
I'll kill a fat pig and offer his blood in libation
Or if meat fills you with scorn
I'll see if I can find a bit of Quorn.

Exit Shepherd.

Odysseus   The shepherd is happy, you made his day
Tell me, have you been long away?

Telemachus   I went to Sparta for news of my dad
But rumours and stories – that's all they had.

Odysseus   Look no farther, just look into my face
You've found your dad in this humble place.

Telemachus   I fear a trick, I've so longed to meet you
Now I'm stunned – I can hardly greet you.

Odysseus   It's no magic, I have no charms
I am your father, come into my arms.

Odysseus and Telemachus hug.

Odysseus   Now I need you to swear an oath
That this will be secret to protect us both
And don't breathe a word to your mother –
I don't want any fuss and bother.
The suitors are going to meet their doom
Within a few days they'll share a tomb.

Enter Shepherd with sausages.

Telemachus   Eumenius, I treasure your hospitality
So different from the suitors' animosity.
Tomorrow, bring this stranger to dine
At the palace on our own fatted kine.

Shepherd   Audience, just to soften up the mood
Here's a sentimental interlude
Before the killing. Yes, it's 'man meets dog'
Except that this one's sleeping like a log.

Enter old dog Argos who lies on cushions, asleep.

Audience *sing*   King Odysseus had a farm
E-I-E-I-O
And on this farm he had a dog
E-I-E-I-O
With a woof woof here and a woof woof there

Here a woof, there a woof
Everywhere a woof, woof
King Odysseus had a farm
E-I-E-I-O.

Odysseus	What's that old dog lying on the dung heap?
Shepherd	It's Argos, the pup Odysseus trained to leap Over the meadows after rabbits and deer.
Odysseus	Is it really you, old Argos, lying here?
Argos	Yes it's me your faithful hound Don't worry I won't make a sound. My master, I've stayed alive for this day Now I can die happy, thank the Gods, I pray.
Odysseus	Your loyalty, Argos, has stood the test.
Argos	I'm going now to my doggy rest.

Argos dies. Exeunt Argos and Shepherd. Enter Penelope.

Penelope	I'm glad you're back but I'm angry and hurt I'm your mother but you treat me like dirt.
Telemachus	Save your protest mother, and all the rest Welcome this stranger – I brought him as a guest.

Enter Suitors carousing.

Suitors (*sing*)	20 bad suitors carousing in the Hall 20 bad suitors carousing in the Hall When Odysseus returns, we're in for a fall There'll be no bad suitors carousing in the Hall.
Telemachus	I've just got home from my trip abroad And I see you're still here for your bed and board *(indicates Odysseus)* Give this beggar some morsels from your plate Respect his human though decrepit state.
Suitor 1	Give him a push and make him stumble He's far too proud, we'll make him humble.
Suitor 2	He needs our help, he wants our crumbs So jab him with your fingers and thumbs!
Suitor 3	Yes, give him a good hammering We're not soft like David Cameron.
Suitor 1	He needs taking down a peg Like that jumped-up Nick Clegg.

Penelope	Your ill-breeding drives me to despair!
	You're so arrogant – why don't you care?
	He may have news of my husband's fate
	I'll give him protection from your hate.
(to Odysseus)	I apologise for the suitors' bad behaviour
	I long for my husband to be my saviour.
Odysseus	I met him once in a foreign port.
Penelope	Well, then you are most welcome in our court.
(to Suitors)	You asked me to choose one of you
	So this is what I'm going to do:
	We're going to have an archery contest
	The winner will wed me and I won't protest
	You'll use Odysseus' giant bow
	And string it in front of us from top to toe.

Suitors take turns attempting and failing to string bow.

Suitor 1 *(tries bow)*	That can't be hard, we bet it's easy
	Gosh – it's quite a challenge. I'm feeling queasy.
Suitor 2 *(tries bow)*	Let me try my hand.
	No, I'm afraid it must be jammed.
Suitor 3 *(tries bow)*	My one at home is really tough –
	No, I just can't work this old fashioned stuff.
Telemachus	For marks out of ten, you all get zero.
	This bow only responds to a real hero.
Odysseus	If no-one can do it, let me have a go.

Enter Athene and Helper.

Athene	Cor, I've arrived just in time to join the show.
	With my sidekick I'll go to any length
	To help Odysseus in a test of strength.

Odysseus strings the bow.

Suitors	We are amazed, we gasp with horror.
Odysseus	Now let's clean up this Sodom and Gomorrah.
Telemachus	My Queen, I want you out of harm's way
	The suitors are going to rue this day.
Penelope	Hang on! Why are the men centre stage
	Just because they're on the rampage?
	Does the audience have to follow the boys
	For the killing with their murderous toys?

I'm the Queen, so audience stay with me
The maids will let us know what we don't see.

Exeunt suitors being chased by Odysseus.

Athene   Good, we like to be the only females around
Especially here on the battleground!
Now the suitors will get their come-uppance.

Helper   I never liked them, I don't care tuppence.

Exeunt Athene and Helper. Distant sound of battle and screams.

Penelope *(awaiting reports from the Maids)*
What's going on – I can't help fretting!
Sounds like some terrible blood-letting.

Enter Candy.

Candy   The suitors are all falling like flies
Every time I look, another one dies.

Enter Mandy.

Mandy   There's blood from the ceiling to the floor
Everywhere I look is covered with gore.

Enter Sandy.

Sandy   The maids are summoned to clean up the mess
We do the dirty work, just as you'd guess.

Candy   It's a horrible task, nasty and distressing
At least we can give our lovers a final blessing.

Exeunt Maids leaving Penelope alone with Nurse.

Penelope   I'm worried for the maids, I fear for their fate.

Nurse   You can't intervene, you'll be too late.

Exit Nurse. Enter Odysseus.

Penelope   Audience, I'll ask for one more proof of identity
Odysseus made our marriage bed from a living tree.
(to Odysseus) You are the victor, you may have my husband's bed
But you must drag it next door until we're wed.

Odysseus   That bed has roots deep in the earth
I can't move the bed, for all I'm worth.

Penelope   Then you must be Odysseus returned from the dead
Only you and I know the secret of our marital bed.

Odysseus   Will you accept me back, my patient wife
To be your partner and share your life?

Penelope | I must call my maids to plan celebrations
| Offerings to the Goddess and special libations.

Odysseus | No, I've hung them all from the palace tower,
| As they were all in the suitors' power.
| Every maid had a suitor lover
| I couldn't risk any of them becoming a mother.

Penelope | You killed my maids? What every one?
| I can't believe what you've just done!
| I'm dizzy with grief, you have no notion
| How I loved them all with deep devotion.

Odysseus | In our custom, bastard sons of dead suitors
| Would be honour-bound to kill and loot us.
| Yes, I understand temptation, I'm no prude
| But it wasn't worth the risk of a blood feud.

Penelope | They were my companions for 20 years
| Now they're gone, I've nothing left but my tears.

Odysseus | They were killed for reasons of state
| I see you're upset but it's just too late.

Penelope | My joy at our reunion is mixed with sorrow
| I'll plan a ritual for the maids tomorrow.

Enter Telemachus.

Odysseus *(to Telemachus)* You've proved your manhood in a fight
| The slaughter was a patriarchal rite.
| Now you've won renown
| I can hand over my royal crown.
| You will be King of Ithaka as your reward –
| I won't stick around: I'd just get bored.

Penelope | But Odysseus, you've only just got home.
| Do you really have such an urge to roam?

Odysseus | Yes, but I'll stick to a radius of fifty miles
| And return often to your womanly wiles.

Telemachus | Yes, father, but now we've finally met
| I hope you'll drop in, please don't forget.

Enter Athene and Helper.

Athene | I've flown in to tell the moral of this tale
| That marriage without compromise is bound to fail.
| Penelope's adapting to her husband's return
| While Odysseus has something to learn:

He spent nineteen years talking about going home
When really he prefers to roam.

Helper   But now he's old and feels antique
He finds the spirit is willing but the flesh is weak.
So when rain pours down, he doesn't seek
To be anything other than a stay-at-home Greek.

Enter Nurse.

Nurse   You might think I'm old and sour
But I've sucked up to those in power
And seen the back of those immoral ladies
Who now have been sent to live in Hades.

Telemachus   My mother's a woman of great capacity,
Infinite resource and perspicacity.
Remember how she lived and fought
Without a penny in child support?
Well, now her life is going through upheaval
But she won't despair or whine or snivel.

Enter Margaret.

Margaret   Was she a faithful wife or a hopeless dummy
A moon goddess or a loving mummy?
I say Odysseus' slaughter was an insult
To our Great Minoan Mother cult.
The old reward for his success
Was a single year with the Moon Goddess.
Then *he* gets slaughtered – that's the rules
Instead he shed the blood of maids and fools.

What you saw was our earthy women's larks
Traduced by barbarous patriarchs.

Penelope   Thank you all. But be that as it may
I am the heroine of this play
I thank you all for coming along
Now please join in our final song.

Penelope (*sings to tune of 'My Bonny'*)
Odysseus came home from the ocean
And brought catastrophe
He hung all my maids without warning
And this is a sorrow to me.

Sorrow, a sorrow
And this is a sorrow to me, to me.

233

Sorrow, a sorrow
And this is a sorrow to me.

The loss of my maids it was tragic
They were too young and too lovely to die.
So women hold on to your magic
It's something no money can buy.

Magic, your magic
It's something no money can buy, can buy.
Magic, your magic
Is something no money can buy.

THE END

QUEEN'S CHAMPION

A play in seven adventures,
based on the novel and TV drama by Shaun Sutton

CAST

Trumpeter
Queen Elizabeth
Lord Burghley, her minister
Fidian, steward of Penlynden Hall
Servant 1
Servant 2
Sir Henry Penlynden
Don José, nephew of Sir Henry
Hal, friend of Don José
Servant 3
Roger, son of Sir Henry
Toby, kitchen boy
Sir Thomas Wycherley, villain
Master Allan, villain
Ralph, groom at Penlynden Hall
Rumbell, cook at Penlynden Hall
Old Bart, shepherd

Cook Hannock
Ayrton Castle servants
(non-speaking)
Guard 1
Guard 2
Guard 3
Additional guards
(non-speaking)
Beaconess 1
Beaconess 2
Mary Brandon
Don Alonso
Servant at Wycherley Manor
(non-speaking)
Courtier to Queen Elizabeth I
Lady Allingham, lady-in-waiting

Audience cheer, take sides in the fight in Penlynden Hall, make a human wall
of rocks in the cave and join in the toast to the Queen at the end.

PROLOGUE

Trumpeter plays 'Greensleeves'. Enter Queen Elizabeth.

Queen Elizabeth   I'm Queen Elizabeth, her Royal Highness
Whom history knows as Good Queen Bess.
I'm at the height of my successful reign
But Popish plots are still my bane.
We suspect the Spanish Armada's on the way –
This will have a bearing on our play.
Catholic Spain wants to invade our land:
To remove Protestantism is their plan.

Here comes Lord Burghley my trusted minister
Who deals with treason and anything sinister.

PRELUDE 1
The Court

Enter Lord Burghley.

Lord Burghley   My lady, traitors infest this land
                    Both far away and near at hand.

Queen Elizabeth But on the Queen's Champion I can depend:
                    That's Sir Henry Penlynden, my trusted friend,
                    Who at a ceremony in his Hall tonight
                    Will pass to his son Roger the statuette bright
                    And so make young Roger my champion bold
                    Though he's only fourteen years old.

Lord Burghley   I'll scour the land for traitors
                    All those Spaniards really hate us.

Exeunt Lord Burghley and Queen Elizabeth.

PRELUDE 2
Penlynden Hall

Enter Fidian and servants. Servants scurry about getting ready for Sir Henry Penlynden's banquet.

Fidian   I'm Fidian, steward of Penlynden Hall
                    With servants at my beck and call.

Servant 1   Master Fidian, where should go the stools?

Fidian   Round the tables, are you all fools?

Servant 2   Master Fidian, the musicians don't know what to do.

Exeunt servants, running.

Fidian   Practice their tunes, haven't they a clue?

Don José enters fighting with swords with Hal. Don José wins.

Don José   So Hal do you admire my Spanish style?

Hal   Let's just practice all the while.

Fidian   Don José, as Sir Henry's nephew, stop this fight.

Don José   Hal and I are practising for the contest tonight.

Fidian   Don José, then I beg you to practise elsewhere.

Don José (*to Hal*) Later, Hal, in the courtyard I'll fight you there.

Exit Hal. Enter Servant 3.

Servant 3 (*nervously*)   Master Fidian…. Sir Henry…
Sends for his only son…

Fidian   You must call him Master Roger:
I will see it is done.

Exit Servant 3.

Don José   If you seek Roger, he's is on the roof on high.

Fidian   Up on the roof! Is he trying to fly?
Though my aged bones protest
I'm driven to do whatever's best.

Enter Roger and Toby sliding down roofs. Fidian climbs to rooftop.

Fidian   Toby!

Roger   It was my fault, I brought Toby up here.

Fidian   Your pardon, Master Roger, Toby's at fault I fear
He knows for a kitchen boy this is out of bounds
I can't have him wandering the grounds.

Toby slithers down roof.

Fidian   Keep still boy and listen to me.

Toby   I can't at all, sir, can't you see?

Roger laughs.

Fidian   There is nothing to laugh at young Master
These roofs are dangerous; it could be a disaster.
Your father wishes to speak to you
He has been waiting 15 minutes, that won't do.

Roger   Master Fidian, I regret you had to climb so high
I just love the roofs I don't know why.

Exit Roger.

Fidian   Toby, do you wish me to send you away?

Toby   Please don't, I'll do whatever you say.

Fidian   Return to the kitchen and ignore Roger's call
Remember you're paid to work at the Hall.

Exeunt Fidian and Toby.

PRELUDE 3
Sir Henry's Study

Enter Sir Henry and Roger.

Sir Henry   I'm Sir Henry Penlynden, devoted father and lord.
Since Master Allan left, my paperwork soared
But today is the day you must take on the role
Of Queen's Champion in heart and soul.

Sir Henry opens secret compartment, and Roger lifts out statuette of Queen's Champion.

Sir Henry   Guy Penlynden received this 200 years ago
When he saved Queen Isabella's life, as we know.
He was only 14 when he discovered a plot
His noble deed was never forgot:
As each Penlynden heir reaches the age of 14
He becomes the next Champion to the Queen.

Roger   Oh Father it shines, it looks like gold
I'm honoured that it will be mine to hold.

Sir Henry   Now the Spanish Armada has set sail
We must defend the Queen, without fail.

Roger   If the Spanish land on our Sussex coast
Brave Toby and I will fight the most.

Exeunt Sir Henry and Roger.

PRELUDE 4
Treason at Queen Elizabeth's Court

Enter Queen Elizabeth.

Queen Elizabeth Now happens a scene which gives me shame
When a villain blackens Sir Henry's name
Even though I hid behind the dais
I was taken in by Sir Thomas' bias.

Queen Elizabeth withdraws. Enter Lord Burghley, Sir Thomas Wycherley and Master Allan.

Sir Thomas
Wycherley   Lord Burghley, I bow beneath your fame
Sir Thomas Wycherley is my name.
With these Spanish letters I can accuse
Sir Henry Penlynden! It's shocking news
That he intends to betray our nation.

| Lord Burghley | This is a very serious accusation |
| | How came these letters into your keeping? |

Master Allan	I, Master Allan found them when peeping
	Into a secret compartment in Sir Henry's study
	It's a conspiracy dark and bloody.
	When I was Roger's tutor at Penlynden Hall
	He nearly caught me, it was a close call.

Lord Burghley withdraws to confer with Queen Elizabeth in secret.

| Queen Elizabeth | But I thought Penlynden was one I could trust. |

Lord Burghley *(to Wycherley)*	Even so, question him we must.
	Our Queen commands you, with a troop of horse,
	To bring her the Penlyndens as a matter of course.

Exeunt Lord Burghley and Queen Elizabeth.

Sir Thomas	He's been duped by my dastardly plan
Wycherley	Now I need your treachery, Master Allan:
	You must ride ahead to Penlynden Hall
	And make them resist me when I call.
	Tell them there's a rebellion in the West
	So they'll defend Penlynden Hall with the best.

| Master Allan | A little bending of earthly laws |
| | Can be forgiven – for a higher cause. |

| Sir Thomas | I'm also a secret Catholic plotter |
| | But my aim is to see Elizabeth totter! |

Exeunt Sir Thomas and Master Allan.

FIRST ADVENTURE
Banquet at Penlynden Hall

Banquet in progress. Fidian, Hal and Don José are on stage.
Enter Toby, Ralph, Rumbell and Old Bart.

| Toby | Back at Penlynden hall the party's started |
| | Meet the servants, brave and stout-hearted. |

| Ralph *(holding bar)* | I am Ralph the groom of massive stature |
| | I will bend this iron bar iron without fracture. |

Rumbell	I'm Rumbell the cook and I'm going to bet
	That this iron bar will defeat you yet.
	And if at this mighty feat you fail
	Then you must drink a yard of ale.

Ralph bends the iron into a circle. All cheer.

Toby   Here's Old Bart, who rescued me on the moor
                        And brought me to Sir Henry's door.

Old Bart   You'd found my ram in a thicket
                        And saved him when you could have nicked it.

Enter Sir Henry and Roger.

Sir Henry   Good servants gather round
                        Now let's hear the trumpet sound.

Trumpeter sounds fanfare.

Sir Henry   My son, though you are but 14 years of age
                        You have a good heart and manly courage.
                        This golden figure of chivalry is yours
                        As Queen's Champion, you defend our shores.

Big cheers from audience and all.

All   God save Penlynden! God save Master Roger!

Master Allan rushes in.

Master Allan   Old friends, I've come to sound the alarm
                        And warn you of forthcoming harm.
                        The Queens soldiers have joined a revolt
                        Of rebels in the West, it's the Catholics fault.
                        We must defend Penlynden: they're heading here
                        I've bolted the main door, so never fear.
(secretly laughs and explains to audience)
                        I'm plotting their downfall
                        Really, I didn't shut it all.

Sir Henry   Fidian, take Roger to the attic and hide.

Master Allan   Let me remain at young Roger's side.

Sir Henry: Oh, alright. You once were his teacher,
                        And your warning is a redeeming feature.

Exeunt Roger, Fidian and Master Allan.

Sir Henry *(to audience)* Now audience, interrupt your revels
                        Now take sides, for or against the rebels.

*Enter Sir Thomas, some of the audience side with him and there follows a
mock fight with shouting and cardboard swords.*

Toby   I will foil their evil plot
                        Watch me throw the apples I've got.

Toby throws apples at the assailants, i.e. Sir Thomas's followers. Next, Sir Henry is wounded.

Hal	We're determined not to be defeated But Sir Henry, let your wound be treated.
Sir Thomas *(shouts)*	Surrender now and stop your defiance!
Don José	No, we won't join your treacherous alliance.
Sir Thomas	Then we'll burn Penlynden to the ground.
Don José *(to Sir Henry)*	What about Roger? He mustn't be found My Spanish honour will make me fight – Giving in just wouldn't be right.
Toby	Roger could escape from the roof with my rope.
Sir Henry	Go too, Ralph, Rumbell, and Hal – it's our only hope.
Old Bart	I may be old but I'll come along I'm loyal and resourceful, though not so strong.

Ralph, Rumbell, Old Bart, Toby and Hal head for the attic to join Fidian, Master Allan and Roger. All escape via the rope and exeunt round the back.

Sir Thomas takes wounded Sir Henry and Don José prisoner. End of fight.

Sir Thomas	I will take these captives to London town.
Don José	It's you who are traitors to the crown.
Sir Thomas	Ayrton Castle will be our first lodging We'll hunt for Roger, wherever he's dodging.

Exeunt Sir Thomas, Sir Henry and Don José.

SECOND ADVENTURE
Escape through woods to Blake's Mill

Enter the fugitives Ralph, Rumbell, Fidian, Hal, Old Bart, Toby, Roger, Master Allan, all arm in arm – but Master Allan rather reluctantly.

Ralph	This is near Blake's Mill, as I'll be bound Though I long to lie upon the ground.
Roger	Let's take a rest among these trees We're tired and hungry, on our knees.
Rumbell	I'm as empty as a parson's purse I'll become a bag of bones if this gets worse.

Hal	We could sleep to get our strength again We'll be all right if it doesn't rain.
Old Bart	I learned the way by tracking sheep At Blake's Mill we can have a sleep.
Fidian	Rumbell, you take Toby to a local farm Where the farmer will keep him safe from harm Then hurry back with food and ale While we wait here down in this dale.
Toby	I'm nearly Master Roger's age, I don't want to leave If I miss the adventure, I'll surely grieve.
Fidian	Do what I say, or you'll move me to anger.
Toby	Master Roger, have my apple for your hunger.
Roger	Oh Toby, you're such a faithful friend I hope we meet up before the end.

Exeunt Rumbell and Toby.

| Master Allan | Fidian, let me have a part to play
In my humble, self-sacrificing way.
While you all go to Blake's Mill and rest
I'll wait and bring Rumbell, that'll be best. |
| Fidian
(to audience) | All right, let's see how your plan goes.
Something about him gets up my nose. |

Exeunt Ralph, Fidian, Old Bart, Roger.

| Master Allan | Now they've gone I have to rush
To get Sir Thomas to stage an ambush.
When he knows we'll turn out the winners
I expect he'll mock those protestant sinners. |

Exit Master Allan.

THIRD ADVENTURE
Ayrton Castle, rescue and death

Enter Rumbell and Toby.

| Rumbell | Here we are at Ayrton Castle
I hear Cook Hannock's quite a rascal.
Our plan is to rescue Roger's dad
I didn't tell the others – they'd think we're mad. |

| Toby | We'll mingle with servants in the melée |
| | No-one will notice we're tired and smelly. |

Enter Cook Hannock and servants.

| Cook Hannock | Who will take supper to the prisoners' hole? |

| Rumbell | What prisoners are they, upon my soul? |

| Cook Hannock | Two Penlyndens in disgrace. |

| Rumbell | We'll take the trays to that dark place. |

Rumbell and Toby pick up trays of food.
Exeunt Cook Hannock and servants.
Enter two guards with Don José as prisoner.

| Guard 1 | Put the prisoners' food upon this table. |

Rumbell *(in high whining voice)*
I so fear the Spaniard, I'm not able
If he looks at me, he'll strike me dead.

Guard 1 *(to Guard 2)* Let's fill this sorry fool with dread
We'll make him face the Spaniard's evil.

Guards drag Rumbell to Don José while Toby stealthily seizes the swords of the guards.

Guard 2 *(to Rumbell)* You tun of wind, look upon the devil!

Don José and Rumbell knock guards to the ground.

| Don José | We'll lock up these guards in Sir Henry's cell: |
| | Wait here on guard, please, Rumbell. |

Exeunt Don José and Toby with guards as prisoner. Enter Sir Thomas.

| Sir Thomas | I thought I'd come to gloat and sneer |
| | But look, the brave rescuer is here. |

Sir Thomas and Rumbell fight, Sir Thomas wins.

Re-enter Don José to fight Sir Thomas.

Don José	As a child I learnt my swordplay in Castille
	So Sir Thomas, feel the blows I deal.
	My mother was Sir Henry's sister
	But she and dad were killed by Spanish twisters.

Don José wins and holds Sir Thomas at sword point. Enter Toby doggedly supporting the wounded Sir Henry.

| Sir Henry | Do not kill Sir Thomas, it wouldn't be right. |

Sir Henry	Do not kill Sir Thomas, it wouldn't be right.
Don José	He showed no mercy to you last night.
Sir Henry	We're not murderers, we're men of honour.
Don José	But we can't leave till he's a 'goner'.
Sir Henry	If I come too, I'll cause delay So I'll guard him while you get away.
Sir Thomas	You're not out of the castle yet You'll get lost in the passages, I'll bet.
Toby	I'm little and quick, I'll find the way.

Exit Toby.

Rumbell *(angrily)* Come back boy! Come back I say!
(to Don José)   We'll go back through the kitchens the way we came.

| Sir Henry | When Toby returns, I'll tell him the same. |

Don José *(handing Sir Henry his sword to guard Sir Thomas)*
                May God protect you on this Earth
                Sir Henry you are a man of worth.

Exeunt Don José and Rumbell.

Sir Henry *(to Sir Thomas)* Tell Roger not to fear for me.
                He's the Queen's Champion to defend the free.

| Sir Thomas | Your son will soon be in my power
Thanks to Master Allan, warped and sour.
He sent your servants to Blake's Mill
Into my ambush. He wishes you ill. |

Enter Master Allan behind Sir Henry, with dagger secretly.

| Sir Henry | Oh, what a foul intrigue
You and Master Allan are in league. |

Sir Thomas *(to Sir Henry)* Come, kill me and go and warn the Don
                One thrust, and you could save your son.

Sir Henry hesitates.

Sir Thomas *(to Master Allan)*
                Strike man!

Master Allan stabs Sir Henry who slumps to the ground.

| Master Allan | He's dead. His body's limp
Once, he was strong. Now I'm a wimp
For this is a shameful deed I've done. |

Sir Thomas   Come, we ride to Blake's Mill to seize the son.
And take him to the Castle's keep.
Quick, let's surround them as they sleep.

Exeunt Sir Thomas and Master Allan. Enter Toby. Sir Henry stirs weakly.

Toby *(to Sir Henry)* It's me, sir, Toby, I'll bring you aid.

Sir Henry   Too late, my son has been betrayed
I am nearly dead and gone
Go to Blake's Mill, save the Queen's Champion.

Sir Henry dies.

Toby   Now Rumbell and the Don are freed
I must find them with the greatest speed,
Tell them, Sir Henry's dead, and the ambush,
And we're betrayed so we must rush.
I do hope Roger is not suffering
While events give him a buffeting.

Exit Toby.

FOURTH ADVENTURE
Escape from Blake's Mill

Ralph on watch. Fidian, Hal, Old Bart and Roger asleep. Sound of horses.

Ralph *(waking Fidian)* I hear horses, please wake, Master.

Fidian   If it's not Rumbell, it's a disaster.

Fidian, Hal, Old Bart and Roger get up.

Sir Thomas *(from outside)* You're surrounded so you better disarm
Surrender now or you'll come to harm.

Ralph *(pointing to 3 barrels)* Leave the soldiers to Hal and me.
There's hope yet
Roger and Fidian, in you get:
These barrels will save the lives of three.

Hal   When the soldiers see them coming
Out of the way they'll start running.

Ralph   You too, Old Bart, don't be grumpy
Some straw will make the ride less bumpy.

Old Bart   I'll go in the barrel if it will save my skin
We'll meet you later at Brandon's Inn.

Fidian, Roger and Old Bart roll away in the barrels and escape.

Ralph fights soldiers. Enter Sir Thomas who fights Hal.

Sir Thomas *(to Hal)* Where is Roger, tell me, sir,
(fights with Hal)   No? Then I'll kill you, cur!

He thrusts at Hal, who dies. Enter soldiers who capture Ralph.

Sir Thomas *(to Ralph)* The boy Penlynden where is he?

Ralph	Not here.
Sir Thomas	Don't hide the truth from me.
Soldier	Perhaps in the barrels they got away.
Sir Thomas	So find the barrels without delay.
	Leave the prisoner here so I can play with him
	Maybe I'll kill him on a whim.

Master Allan rushes in.

Master Allan	The beacons are lit, every one
	Which means the Armada has begun.

Enter Beaconesses with ribbon of beacons between them.

Beaconness 1	We're beaconnesses who make a fiery chain
	To say the Armada's come from Spain.
Beaconness 2	The flames leap from hill to hill
	The war's begun, for good or ill!

Exeunt Beaconnesses.

Ralph *(to Master Allan)* You betrayed young Roger, I'm in a fury
I'll see you hung by judge and jury.

Master Allan	Your rage puts me in a dreadful fright
	So I'll run off into the night.

Exit Master Allan.

Sir Thomas	Now that beacons light the sky
	I see I've got bigger fish to fry.
	I must ride home to Wycherley Manor
	To lead conspirators to the invaders' banner.

Exeunt Soldiers and Sir Thomas. Enter Rumbell, Don José and Toby.
They greet Ralph.

Rumbell *(to Ralph)* Old Mountain, you look the worse for wear.

Ralph	At least I'm alive, I'm touched you care.
Don José	But Hal lies dead, God grant him peace I mourn my friend's abrupt decease. We will return to make a proper burial I shall miss Hal, brave and mercurial.
Rumbell	The beacons are lit in our hour of danger As England rises to defeat the stranger We must get to Brandon's Inn, God willing.
Don José	I fear there will be further killing. If my family hadn't been killed by the Inquisition I'd be part of the Spaniards' expedition.

Exeunt towards Brandon's Inn, but not arriving till Master Allan and Roger have spoken and left.

INTERLUDE
At Brandon's Inn

Enter Roger creeping out of a window with statuette.

Roger	We reached Brandon's Inn and sheltered But alone with my guilt I sweltered. I've endangered Toby and so many friends I must surrender to make amends.

Enter Master Allan.

Roger	Master Allan, fancy seeing you – To tell the truth, I'm in a stew. But if I just tell the whole true story I'm sure it'll turn out hunky-dory.
Master Allan	To surrender to the rebels would be folly Let's go to Sir Thomas, yes, by golly.
Roger	Would he free my father? That's my concern.
Master Allan	Yes, I'm sure he will, as you will learn. As you know, I'm a very good planner So let's make our way to Wycherley Manor.

Exeunt Master Allan and Roger. Enter Mary Brandon, Ralph, Rumbell, Toby and Don José.

Mary Brandon	Who comes there out of the dark?

Rumbell	Penlyndens! hurry, this is no lark
Mary Brandon	You can stay till daylight then you must go 'Sir Henry's a traitor', is what I know
Don José *(to Mary Brandon)*	Thank you for your bravery: Be assured, we mean no knavery.

Enter Old Bart.

Toby	How was the barrel, how far did it go?
Old Bart	I'm covered in bruises I'll have you know Where's young Hal, didn't he come along?
Don José	He was killed by Sir Thomas, at Blake's Mill But there's news that if possible is worse still: Sir Henry Penlynden has drawn his last breath Sir Thomas also brought about his death.
Old Bart	That's very sad, these are bad times.
Don José	Sir Thomas will answer for his crimes.
Fidian	Sir Henry dead, I must tell his son and heir, He's Sir Roger now – to do and dare.
Toby	My dear friend will be tested by this news I do hope he can beat the blues.
Fidian	Oh now I'm really desolated Roger's gone, oh no, he should have waited.
Old Bart	Now I remember what Roger said That he wanted to prevent further bloodshed By going to the rebels, offering to surrender.
Fidian	Oh the innocent child, so young and tender!
Mary Brandon	Don't try to deceive me with your talk of 'rebels' You are the traitors, in terrible troubles The troopers came to arrest you with good reason Because the Penlyndens are charged with treason.
Don José	At last I make sense of my confusion Sir Thomas and Master Allan have been in collusion. In order to hide their Catholic plan They accused Sir Henry, an innocent man.
Fidian	We must denounce them without further ado.

Don José	Without proof, no-one will believe you We must follow Sir Thomas and make him confess To his dastardly deeds and his dirty business.
Ralph	I know Wycherley village, it's down by the sea.
Fidian	Then we need horses but they cost a fee.
Toby	I saw horses and a cart right here in the stable.
Old Bart	Well, Mary, I'm glad that to help you're able. Explain now why you've special cause – Tell the audience and get applause.
Mary Brandon	Yes, I wanted a little cameo role To show the goodness of my rustic soul. Bart saved me from drowning when I was a tot And near drowned himself, so now I've got An irredeemable debt to the kindly Old Bart. I'll get food for your journey with a grateful heart God speed your errand and watch over you God bless Penlyndens and guide what you do.

FIFTH ADVENTURE
Outside Wycherley Manor and cave

Enter Fidian, Ralph, Rumbell, Don José, Old Bart, Toby.

Ralph	Just imagine some time has passed And we've travelled very fast…
Rumbell	Here, to Wycherley Manor, the plotters' HQ. Now we'll rest, and work out what to do.
Fidian	I must rest my weary bones again I fear.

Fidian lies down.

Don José	Old Bart and Toby must stay with Fidian here. We need adults in their prime To revenge this awful crime. While we climb the cliffs down to the beach To see if from there the Manor we'll reach.
Rumbell	There may be a cave, dark and deep, Leading to a staircase steep.

Exeunt Don José, Ralph, Rumbell round the back.

Old Bart   They think you're young and I'm an old 'un
                      But you're quick and I'm cunning – both are golden.

Toby *(looking into the distance)*
                      They're looking for a path, why didn't they take me?
                      I'm used to cliff scrambling, how unfair life can be!

Fidian wakes.

Fidian   Toby, run after the others as fast as you can
                      Then report back to me so I know their plan.
                      Now let's fast-forward with narrative brio
                      To see what's happening to our trio.

Exeunt Toby and Fidian.

In Cave. Enter Guard 3 and Rumbell.

Rumbell *(from behind)* It's a good job we are brave
                      Now I've found Sir Thomas' cave.

Guard 3   Stop! Who goes there?

Rumbell fights with guard, is losing when Ralph enters and knocks the Guard to the ground, dead.

Rumbell   Good job you came – he gave me a scare.

Don José enters.

Don José *(to Ralph and Rumbell)* Give this body a watery grave
                      Meanwhile I'll look inside this cave.

Exeunt Ralph and Rumbell with body of guard to audience.

Don José *(withdraws towards back)*
                      Here's a door into Sir Thomas's den.

Toby runs forward and shouts.

Toby   There's a big boat coming with lots of men!

Re-enter Don José and Ralph and Rumbell.

Toby   Fidian sent me and on the way
                      I saw it. Please let me stay.

Don José   That'll be a Spanish envoy I expect
                      I'll meet him and show him due respect
                      You're Sir Thomas' servants, that's your disguise
                      While I take the Spaniard by surprise.
                      By the way, I've a suspicion
                      This cave is where they store their ammunition.

Enter Don Alonso.

Don Alonso	For Spain and the faith! Why Don José it's you! I'm Don Alonso, we once met at an embassy do! You are for Spain, sir, for the cause I have with me secret letters for Sir Thomas.
Don José	I remember you, you're from Granada How long since your boat left the Armada?
Don Alonso	Four days, but they're moving up the coast. I must see Sir Thomas – that matters most.
Don José	Sir Thomas left this morning to ride to Dover I'll guard the letters, just hand them over.
Don Alonso	Only to Sir Thomas himself – I'm no fool.
Don José	Then I'll have to challenge you to a duel. We'll fight according to the Spanish way Let the best Don win the day.

Toby, Rumbell and Ralph withdraw to watch. Don Alonso and Don José fight. Don Alonso loses and hands letters to Don José.

Don José	Toby guard Don Alonso, while I read these letters Bind his arms – what can we use for fetters?
Toby	There's no rope so I'll use my shirt I'll bind him tight but it won't hurt.
Don Alonso	I'll soon struggle free And light a candle so I can see.

Enter Queen Elizabeth (on high).

Queen Elizabeth	Wycherley's plotting, Sir Henry's dead England's future hangs by a thread. The Armada's sighted on the waves Whilst we watch adventures in the caves. The servants are all doing their bit And Toby is using his native wit, Leaving our Spaniard in the dark – Will it lead to a fateful spark? Fidian and Old Bart have tired of their wait And approached the manor to learn of Roger's fate. And what of that innocent young son? Let's take a look at what's going on.

Exeunt all.

SIXTH ADVENTURE
Wycherley Manor

Enter Sir Thomas, Master Allan and Roger and Servant.

Master Allan	Roger, this is Sir Thomas, a powerful man He's going to help you, he really can.

Roger   Sir Thomas, you are one who knows the best
Please listen to my most serious request.

Sir Thomas *(to Roger)* First you must sleep and take your ease.

Exit Roger with servant.

Sir Thomas   Tell me how you got him here, please.

Master Allan   I said you'd save Sir Henry from his doom.

Sir Thomas   I'm bad, but you're the worst villain in this room!

Master Allan   I've committed murder, that's my shame.

Exit Master Allan.

Sir Thomas *(to himself, wickedly)*
           Soon, you'll add more killing to your name.
           Now where's my Spanish messenger? Why's he late?
           I've got a revolution to facilitate.

Shouting heard; it is Old Bart and Master Allan fighting offstage.

Sir Thomas   Sounds like a quarrel in the yard
                   It's time I acted and called the guard.

Enter Old Bart and Master Allan fighting. Old Bart knocks Master Allan down. Guards seize Old Bart. Master Allan gets up.

Sir Thomas *(to Master Allan)* Who is it that made you fall?

Master Allan *(whispers to Sir Thomas)*
           It's Old Bart, the shepherd from Penlynden Hall.
           How did he know that Roger's here?

Sir Thomas   Where are your friends? You've nothing to fear.

Old Bart   I shall not tell you...

Sir Thomas   ...Even if I offer you gold?

Sir Thomas proffers money to Old Bart, who snorts with contempt.

Sir Thomas   Then we'll fight a duel, come be bold!

Explosion: the audience makes a human wall to represent rocks across the cave entrance. Sir Thomas, Old Bart and guards scatter.

Enter Queen Elizabeth on high.

Queen Elizabeth The explosion in the cave
Sent Don Alonso to his grave.
His candle set gunpowder alight
And made that bang which gave us all a fright.
It made a prison of the cave's refuge
And trapped our heroes under a rocky deluge,
Which is acted by the audience arm in arm.
So will our heroes come to harm?
See: the mouth of the cave is firmly stopped.
The staircase to the manor? – it's firmly locked.

Enter Don José (holding letters), Ralph, Rumbell, Don José and Toby.

Toby I hear footsteps behind the locked door
Perhaps we won't be here for ever more.

Enter Sir Thomas.

Sir Thomas How came the powder to explode?
You're trapped with that rocky load.

Ralph We'll hold you prisoner here with us!

Ralph and Rumbell make to capture him.

Sir Thomas No Roger's upstairs, we've played you false.
Master Allan brought him, I'll have you know.
He'll be killed if you don't let me go.

All are amazed and desist.

Sir Thomas You're sentenced to an evil doom
Locked in darkness and in gloom.

Exit Sir Thomas round the back.

Toby They won't kill Master Roger, will they?

Rumbell Sir Thomas blusters, that's his way.

Ralph Learning Roger's here is a mighty shock
We'll clear a path through the rock.

Queen Elizabeth on high.

Queen Elizabeth As the Penlyndens dig there's a big rock fall:
Audience – make a crumbling wall
When a crack appears, Ralph holds up the boulder:
He has a giant's strength in his shoulder.

Toby *(snatching the letters from Don José)*
>   I'll take these to Fidian, I'll get through the crack.

Exit Toby through a crack between audience members.

Rumbell   It's too dangerous boy, you must come back!
>   That Toby he's a little felon
>   He won't do what his elders tell 'im.

Queen Elizabeth All right, end of audience participation –
>   Now back to the plot to end our nation.

Enter Toby with letters, and Fidian to front left hand of hall.

Fidian   I've been waiting here for Old Bart
>   But to tell the truth I've been losing heart.

Toby   I've found out Roger is in Sir Thomas' power.

Fidian   I must go and find him; no time to cower
>   If by dawn I've not returned,
>   Deliver the letters, the truth must be learned.

Exeunt Toby and Fidian. Enter Sir Thomas and Master Allan.

Sir Thomas   You ride with Roger to Elizabeth's court
>   Or all our plans will come to nought.
(hands him a stiletto dagger) Hide this stiletto in your clothes
>   Use it to kill the Queen we loathe
>   While she speaks to Roger, you'll strike
>   Her dead, that's what we'd like.

Master Allan   My sins have caused me so much grief
>   Perhaps this final act will bring relief.

Exit Master Allan.

Sir Thomas   I've not seen the old shepherd for a while
>   I can use him for my evil guile.

Enter Guards 1 and 2 with Old Bart.

Old Bart   I'm saying nothing so you can save your breath.

Sir Thomas   I trapped your friends below in the cave of death
>   I'll make you join them, that's what I'll do.

Old Bart   Rather that, than live with the likes of you.

Sir Thomas   You can deliver my message to the Don,
(waving letter) Ho ho, you'll soon all be dead and gone
>   To make you suffer while you rot
>   I'll vouchsafe the details of my plot.

Sir Thomas gives Old Bart a letter and exits. Exeunt Old Bart and Guards 1 and 2 to the cave. Enter Fidian

Fidian
I hope Sir Thomas' threats are hollow;
As they take Bart, I'll secretly follow.
If he's locked away, I'll steal a key.
I'll find Roger, if it's the death of me.

He secretly follows them to the cave. Don José, Rumbell and Ralph are digging in cave.

Enter Old Bart from back.

Old Bart
I have Sir Thomas' message for the Don.

Don José *(reading letter)* Oh no! Allan and Roger ride to London.
Roger will beg the Queen for his father's life
Which will lead to her death…

Rumbell
What dreadful strife!

Don José
If Allan succeeds it'll cause consternation
And implicate Roger in the assassination.

Enter Fidian from the back.

Fidian
Is young Master Roger here?

Rumbell
Oh joy, oh heaven you're our saviour.

All exeunt the cave.

Ralph
I'll take a fast horse from the stable
And ride to London as fast as I'm able.

Don José
I'll await Sir Thomas' return
To avenge Sir Henry, with anger I burn.

Fidian
Rumbell, you and me and Old Bart
Will join young Toby in the cart.

Enter Toby.

Toby
I was just off to deliver the letters
When I met you, freed of your fetters
We're united again, this is exciting
We're back on course for adventure and fighting!

Exeunt Fidian, Rumbell, Old Bart, Toby.

Don José
I wonder if I'll have hours to wait
Before Sir Thomas is back to meet his fate.

Sound of horse's hooves. Enter Sir Thomas.

Don José	Sir Thomas, now draw your sword
	I need to avenge the death of my Lord.

Sir Thomas and Don José fight duel. Don José wins.

Sir Thomas	I die, and all my scheming has come to naught
	Unless Allan succeeds at Elizabeth's Court.

Sir Thomas dies with evil cackle. Exit Don José.

SEVENTH ADVENTURE
Elizabeth's Court in London

Enter Master Allan, Roger and Courtier.

Master Allan	We need an urgent audience with the Queen.
Courtier	Only those with news of the Armada will be seen.
Roger	The Court is so busy, we're lost in the crowd
	But I must plead for my father as I've vowed.
Master Allan	Pipe down, while I look out for Lord Burghley
	He's our only hope, the courtiers are surly.
Courtier	Make way for Lord Burghley, at once, I say.

Enter Lord Burghley.

Master Allan	Sir Thomas Wycheley has sent us from far away,
	This is Roger Penlynden, of whom we discussed.
Lord Burghley	Where's Sir Thomas? He's the one I trust.
Master Allan	He's away with the troops, I'm here in his place.
Lord Burghley	I'll take the boy and check with Her Grace.
Master Allan	My duty's with Roger, let me stay by his side.
Lord Burghley	Stay in the ante-room, my patience you've tried!

Exit Master Allan. Enter Lady Allingham.

Lord Burghley	Gracious Lady Allingham, look after this lad
	He's so weary from the journey's he's had.
Lady Allingham	You look sorely in need of rest
	Sleep will restore your youthful zest.
(takes Roger's hand)	Your childish hands are freezing cold
	We must see the Queen, she must be told.

Exit Lord Burghley. Enter Queen Elizabeth.

Queen Elizabeth The Spanish Armada is it drawing near?

Lady Allingham No, madam, but young Roger Penlynden's here.

Queen I'll see him in memory of happier times.

Enter Roger who sinks on one knee.

Queen Rise boy and explain your father's crimes.

Roger Ma'am, my father's still loyal to the Crown.

Queen Didn't Master Allan tell you as you came down?

Roger What is it that he should have said?

Queen I'm sorry to say that your father is dead.

Roger faints.

Lady Allingham He's fainted but it's not his fault
He just needs some smelling salts.

She revives him with smelling salts.

Queen Find Master Allan, bring him straightaway.

Enter Master Allan.

Queen Master Allan, you have a debt to pay
Your villainy is awful, it takes away our breath
That you never told Roger of his father's death.
Now beg forgiveness, though it tear your heart.

Roger You knew of his death? What was your part?

Master Allan Ma'am, you're gullible, with innocent brow
I killed him, just like I'm doing now…

Master Allan screams and attacks Queen with stiletto dagger. Roger leaps to protect Queen and is stabbed. Lady Allingham struggles with Master Allan.

Lady Allingham Villain, you have something of the night
I'll defend the Queen with all my might.

Enter guards who jump on Master Allan and take him away.

Enter Lord Burghley.

Elizabeth My Champion has saved me from a knave
Even so it was too close a shave.

Lord Burghley We'll need a wall of silence, we must take care
We'll say a madman attacked the Penlynden heir.
No-one must know of the attack on the Queen

It must be hushed up, like it never has been.
We can't afford a Hutton Inquiry,
The impact would be politically fiery!

Ralph arrives on horseback.

Ralph   I arrive, late and saddle-sore
                     To pick young Roger off the floor.

Ralph picks up Roger.

Roger   Ralph, please take me back to Penlynden Hall
                     Where I can recover from it all.

EPILOGUE
Back at Penlynden Hall

All characters still alive are in the Hall.

Fidian   The weeks pass by in a flash
                     As we go back to the party bash.

Musicians play.

Toby   Sir Roger's wounds now are mended
                     And so our play is nearly ended.

Roger   Here at Penlynden Hall is the final scene
                     Where we welcome our good Queen.

Queen Elizabeth   History proved that I was harder
                     Than that horrible Spanish Armada.

Toby   Though Roger's lord and I'm a servant boy
                     Lasting friendship is our joy.
                     Now, as the youngest I propose a toast
                     To the Queen we love the most.
                     All drink a toast to the Queen.

Queen Elizabeth   Our adventures end in a happy mood
                     So let's tuck into party food.

THE END

Note

Based on the 1950s BBC TV drama for children and subsequent novel by Shaun Sutton. To make filming fun for the actors, including a young Jane Asher, Shaun Sutton organised lots of parties, with a cake featuring a Queen's Champion statuette on top. From 1969 to 1981 Shaun Sutton was Head of Drama at the BBC, and was made OBE in 1979. In retirement, shortly before his death in 2004, he gave us every encouragement to adapt this play for Beth's sister Kath's birthday.

RAVERS AND STUNNERS

The lives of the Pre-Raphaelite painters

CAST

Prologue
Sir Joshua Reynolds, (nicknamed 'Sir Sloshua')
John Ruskin, famous art critic
Effie Ruskin, his wife
(Dante) Gabriel Rossetti, artist, poet
Holman Hunt, famous artist
John Everett Millais, famous artist
Ned Burne-Jones, famous artist
Professor Gabriele Rossetti, father of Gabriel
Christina Rossetti, poet, sister to Gabriel
Maria Rossetti, sister to Gabriel
Lizzy Siddall, Gabriel's lover
William Morris, writer and designer
Janey Morris, neé Burden, wife of William Morris, lover of Gabriel
Fanny Cornforth, Gabriel's mistress in later life
The Pre-Raphaelite children (of Burne-Jones and Morrises)
William Rossetti, Gabriel's elder brother

The Pre-Raphaelite children join in skipping.

Audience jeer at Sir Sloshua, chant PRB (for Pre-Raphaelite Brotherhood), throw apples and skip.

The action starts in 1848 and lasts several decades.

Enter Prologue.

Prologue   This play is about poetry and art
                        Which are close to each and every heart.
                        You can watch our Pre-Raphaelite brothers
                        Parade their ideas and oppress their lovers.
                        Though their art is beautiful to behold
                        We can watch their relationships unfold.
                        See the men enjoy their vices –
                        While the women make sacrifices.

                        Watch them as they all get pally
                        Will they choose greatness or a blind ally?
                        First, enter the elders whose debate
                        Will set the context for their fate.

Exit Prologue. Enter Sir Sloshua, Ruskin and Effie.

Sir Sloshua	I, Joshua Reynolds, make my entry I paint portraits of the landed gentry.
Ruskin	Rubbish! I am the famous John Ruskin I'll put your portraits in the dustbin. Art must stand above society fashions: It's all about beauty and natural passions And strives to record nature's immensity. The best art evokes life's full intensity.
Effie (*aside*)	His words hide that our marriage is a sham. Without divorce I'm in a jam.
Sir Sloshua	Painting has made me a wealthy man. My art sells – let's see if yours can.
Ruskin	Bring on the talent that's up and coming We'll give Sloshua a good nose-thumbing.

Enter the members of the Pre-Raphaelite Brotherhood (Gabriel, Holman Hunt, Millais and Burne-Jones) who lead audience in thumbing noses at Sir Sloshua.

Gabriel	I'm Gabriel Rossetti I spread my talents like confetti. Here are the rest of my whole sick crew Gang members, say halloo.
Holman Hunt	I'm Holman Hunt, in love with the Middle East Painter of 'Scapegoat', poor benighted beast.
(*to Sir Sloshua*)	Compared to me, you're boring and trite Our work is heartfelt, so we must be right.
Sir Sloshua	Art is about tradition and loads of money I say your ideas sound a bit funny.
Millais (*taking Effie's arm*)	
	I'm the childhood genius, John Everett Millais, I'll be famous without delay And although my love is scarcely muttered Effie knows where her bread is buttered.
Burne-Jones	I'm Burne-Jones. Our art is vibrant We like life with a bit of excitement. We go to Hampstead, singing while walking And stay up till dawn, just talking and talking.
Sir Sloshua	I've nothing to say to you renegades, You've no future. You won't make the grade.

Exit Sir Sloshua.

Ruskin
: That's got rid of someone frightful
  Now I'll be master and you – disciples!

Effie
: Stop! I married you for your renown,
  Alas, in bed you let me down.

Millais
: Ruskin, *my* genius and love of life
  Has won the heart of your own dear wife.
  So now we're going to elope
  While I will advertise Pears Soap.

Effie
: I'm off with Millais leaving you in the lurch
  To spend your time looking at some old church.

Exeunt Effie and Millais.

Ruskin
: Betrayed, confounded, I'm mad with rage
  I'll retire to become a Lakeland sage.

Gabriel
: Ruskin, before you go, I'm a bit short today
  I need a fiver – could you see your way?

Ruskin tips Gabriel a fiver and exits.

Gabriel
: Our gang needs a name known wide and far
  So give us a P

Hunt, Burne-Jones and audience
: P

Gabriel
: And give us an R

Hunt, Burne-Jones and audience
: R

Gabriel
: Give us a B

Hunt, Burne-Jones and audience
: B

Gabriel
: What's it spell?

Hunt, Burne-Jones and audience
: PRB!

Gabriel
: Yes, it sounds good
  It's our Pre-Raphaelite Brotherhood.
  Let's put the initials in our pictures
  Then become art history fixtures.

Burne-Jones
: Come on Pre-Raphaelite boys
  Let's go drinking and make lots of noise.

Holman Hunt
: Here's where I leave this merry band
  And go off to the Holy Land.

Exeunt Holman Hunt and Burne-Jones.

Gabriel	To show my talent is no flash in the pan,
	I'll introduce the Rossetti clan.

Enter Gabriele senior, Christina and Maria.

Gabriele senior	I'm his dad, I used to write poems.
	Exiled from Italy, I sought asylum.
	Citizenship test? I'm afraid I'll flunk it
	And get a hard time from Mr Blunkett.
	Since my English is so scanty,
	I'll make my living translating Dante.

Christina	I'm Christina, I must care for our dad.
	In my teens it drove me mad.
	I'm oppressed by the social norm,
	I have no alternative but to conform.

Gabriel	My older brother earns the family bread
	So I can take up art instead.
	My other sister I won't mention
	Focus on me – that's my intention.

Exit Gabriele senior.

Christina	My other sister is called Maria.
	My love for her feels unclear.
	While my father goes off hobbling
	I'll write a poem about some goblins.

Gabriel	You've no future without a wedding –
	Left on the shelf is where you're heading.

Maria	It's true. My life's work ends in a nunnery
	While the men enjoy fun and flummery.

Exeunt Maria and Christina. Enter Burne-Jones.

Gabriel	Now we'll form a salon, write a magazine
	And be the best the world has ever seen.
	We live life to the full, with gusto
	So hear this, our manifesto.

Burne-Jones	Romance and passion we'll unleash
	And sell our paintings to the *nouveaux-riches*.
	We'll reject that Royal Academy twaddle
	And take real-life women for our model.

Gabriel	Long neck, full lips, luxuriant hair
	We'll paint beauty to make men stare.

Burne-Jones   Now here's the answer to love's riddle
Enter please Miss Lizzy Siddall.

Enter Lizzy.

Lizzy   Millais painted me as Ophelia in a stream
I epitomise the Pre-Raphaelite dream.
I started life as a shop-girl
Now Gabriel I'll become your top girl.

Gabriel   Miss Siddall, please don't think me rude-io
If I ask you to come to my studio.
We can live together, you're my muse
You can look after me if I get the blues.

Burne-Jones   Please don't think life is all serious and bland
With our idealistic Pre-Raphaelite band.
We're not just artistic cranks
We like fun and merry pranks.
So audience, before we get uptight
Please join in our apple fight.

Apple fight with Lizzy, Gabriel, Burne-Jones and audience.

Burne-Jones   Enough! life's not all an orange pippin!
On with our tale: it's very gripping.

Exeunt all except Gabriel and Lizzy.

Lizzy   I'm not just here for you to lech
Remember I can also draw and sketch.

Gabriel   Whilst I recognise your talent
On one point I won't relent;
You can't be introduced to polite society.
I love you but you must stay home quietly.
Forget thoughts of wedded communion.
I'm off to paint the Oxford Union.

Exit Lizzy. Enter William Morris.

Gabriel   Just when our finances are all to cock
Here's William Morris who's of wealthy stock.
I've heard he's very idealistic
As well as being a bit of a misfit.

Morris   I want to put an end to society's ills
It's a pity I've got no social skills.
And in addition to being rather gruff
I find this painting rather tough.

Exit Morris. Enter Burne-Jones.

Gabriel   Now let's go out and look for girls
Ask them to pose, and paint their curls.
We need a stunner for our Arthurian themes
To keep alive those Pre-Raphaelite dreams.

Burne-Jones   We idealise women in the medieval manner
But lust blinds us when we meet a stunner.

Enter Janey and Bess.

Janey   I'm Janey Burden, with my sister Bess
Eighteen and never known a man's caress.

Bess   See those two men – why are they staring?

Janey   I'd say they have aristocratic bearing.

Burne-Jones *(to Janey)* You're right. Though we're very respectable
We must paint you – your looks are delectable.
Bess, your looks aren't quite so enriching
Off you go and do the stitching.

Exeunt Bess and Burne-Jones.

Janey   Alright, I'll be an artist's model
Compared to the slums, it's a doddle.

Gabriel   Oh no, help! I'm smitten
By this Pre-Raphaelite sex-kitten.
But I'm living with Lizzy Siddall
My heart is split right down the middle.
Not one but two amazing stunners
I've won the double – just like the Gunners.

Exit Gabriel. Enter Morris with portrait.

Morris   Janey, please don't think I'm behaving rashly
But I'll paint you in clothes from Laura Ashley.
I may be inept but I'll work like a Trojan
I can't paint but please read my slogan.

Morris shows back of portrait to Janey. It reads 'I can't paint you but I love you'.

Janey   Obviously I prefer Gabriel Rossetti
But he's elsewhere – he might forget me.
A poor girl can't choose
I'll be Morris's wife and Gabriel's muse.

Exeunt Janey and Morris arm in arm. Enter Burne-Jones.

| Burne-Jones | He loves Janey with a deep devotion |
| | But she loves another – oh unhappy notion. |

Exit Burne-Jones. Enter Christina and Lizzy.

| Christina | Lizzy, I've noticed you're always mournful |
| | Is it because my brother's scornful? |

| Lizzy | He won't marry me, the thickhead. |
| | I have to take refuge in my sickbed. |

Christina	He goes round town like a dandy
	Treating women like eye-candy.
	We stay home and do the sewing
	Our talents repressed, our tears flowing.
	Still for me it could be worse
	At least I write a little verse.

Exit Christina.

| Lizzy | Men! They want you to applaud them. |
| | I'm going to end it all with laudanum. |

Takes poison and dies. Enter Gabriel.

Gabriel	Now Lizzy's dead and I was to blame:
	I neglected love in pursuit of fame.
	I'll bury my poems in her grave
	And go distraught and rant and rave.

Exit Gabriel. Enter Janey.

Janey	I'm the blessed damozel, the adored lady
	But my boring husband is driving me crazy.
	He knows everyone and he's so busy
	Dashing here and there makes me dizzy.

Exit Janey. Enter Gabriel.

Gabriel	Now I adore Janey, she obsesses my brain
	Alas she married Morris and that gives me pain.
	From Lizzie's grave I must retrieve my poems.
	I leech off my family – oh how I do grieve them.
	And my mistress Fanny expects her keep.
	With all these worries how can I sleep?

Exit Gabriel. Enter Morris.

Morris	Although my designs are new-fangled
	I'm trapped in this love triangle.
	I so love Janey, I can't admit she loves another
	Especially if it's my Pre-Raphaelite brother.

> So I'm off to Iceland as a holiday from work
> If I stay round here, I'll go berserk.

Exit Morris. Enter Janey.

Janey

> Rossetti's a charmer, he conquers my fears
> He's very exciting, and I'm bored to tears.
> While my husband's away, we'll have an affair
> As I've nothing to do, why should I care?

Enter Christina and Maria who form a chorus around Gabriel.

Christina

> My goblin poem's a great best-seller
> Which is more than can be said for this feller.
> He overworks, he's compulsively shaving
> Then he can't sleep and starts raving.

Maria

> We sent him to Scotland for the fresh air
> But he had delusions when he was there.
> We try to help him but it's not enough
> He keeps taking chloral and other stuff.

Gabriel

> All my life I've been a monster of vanity
> Now I begin to fear for my sanity.
> Janey's not mine, even though I'm free
> She won't leave Morris and move in with me.
> Everything's against me, even the songbirds.
> My head is whirling. I haven't the words
> To explain the agony and pain I'm going through
> I'm getting weaker – what can I do?

Janey

> Now my lover's gone mad, he's not much fun
> I'll keep my distance – it's time to run.

Enter Fanny Cornforth.

Fanny Cornforth

> While Janey prepares to do a runner
> In comes Fanny, Gabriel's last stunner.
> He idealised Janey, and now that she's left
> He's nothing to live for, he's a man bereft.
> I visit him and do what he needs
> But it's clear to us all that he's a broken reed.

Gabriel

> I once painted scenes of love and devotion
> That filled my audience with emotion.
> That's in the past, now my death is nigh
> I'm so weary, it's a relief to die.

Gabriel dies. Exit Fanny Cornforth. Enter Morris.

Morris	My patience paid off, my rival is dead Though I can't hope Janey will love me instead. I'll make my cause the people's improvement I think I'll found the Arts and Crafts movement.
Janey	Now Gabriel's dead, life loses its shine. But I'll go back to Morris and try to be kind. He stood by me when I was thoughtless I'll stay at home and look after our daughters. Though we're sad at our recent bereavement Our children are our greatest achievement.

Enter Pre-Raphaelite children.

Pre-Raphaelite children	We're Pre-Raphaelite kids, May and Jenny Morris With the Burne-Jones kids we make up the chorus. We never minded Rossetti's ailments 'Cos he always helped with our entertainments.

They skip with long rope and audience join in.

Exeunt skippers and all adults except Christina. Enter William Rossetti.

William Rossetti	I, William Rossetti, step in to claim my due. Enough children, be off with you.

Exeunt Pre-Raphaelite children.

William Rossetti	I never had the skills of Dante But I made sure we had food in the pantry. In the end I wrote their propaganda up But I'm unknown – it gets my dander up!

Enter Burne-Jones, Millais and Holman Hunt.

Christina	While my brother was wild and fanatic I wrote of secrets in the family attic. Like my sister, I was never a bride It was hard for us keeping our passion inside. But I believe we proved ourselves stronger And what's more, my poetry lasted longer.
Morris	I found painting such a difficult caper That I gave it up to design wallpaper. By the end of the century, in my final acts I was writing socialist tracts.
Holman Hunt	We painted scenes of social history Alongside those of religious mystery. We set the artistic world alight We were proud to be Pre-Raphaelite.

Millais

We became famous and an essential part
Of the curriculum in the history of art
But my paintings were never as good
As when I was in the brotherhood.

Burne-Jones

Our faults and foibles were part of the story
Even if pain and passion made it gory.
But we worked hard painting from the heart
And earned our place in the history of art.

THE END

SIR GAWAIN AND THE GREEN KNIGHT

CAST

Morgan le Fay/Aunt

Handmaid

Chorus 1, 2, 3

Queen Guinevere

Green Knight/Bertilak

Green Lady/Elinor

Galahad

Lancelot

King Arthur

Gawain

Lunette

SCENE 1

In Arthur's court at Christmas time

Enter Morgan Le Fay.

Morgan Le Fay   My name is Morgan Le Fay
I explain the deeper meaning of this play.
I'm Arthur's sister – which I forgot to mention –
And now I'll let you in on my intentions.
I hate his wife, that Guinevere
She's so prissy and insincere.
I want to put her out of sorts
So I've arranged some festive sports.

You'll see me later in disguise
Dressed as an old lady, grizzled and wise.
But just now, off I go.
Handmaid, you can start the show.

Exit Morgan.
Enter Handmaid and Chorus 1, 2 and 3.

Handmaid   Ladies and gentlemen, I beg you take your seats
For this our party of Yuletide treats.
Enjoy the sport that's brought before us.
Now the play starts with the chorus.

Chorus 1   At this Christmas with cares cast aside
We fatten ourselves with food for our feasting.

Chorus 2   Bitter the brunt of the burdens we bear
Weary of winter we welcome respite.

Chorus 3   With singing and sports the seasons we celebrate
With carols in the King's court at Camelot.

Chorus 1	Lightly we lodge with Arthur our liege lord And go as guests of good Guinevere.
Chorus 2	And worship our women as warriors are wont.
Chorus 3	But go gently – our great leader's grumpy.

Exeunt Chorus. Enter Arthur, Guinevere, Galahad, Lancelot and Gawain.

Arthur	I'm Arthur, these my guests, you'll know my name. What I hate about Christmas, it's always the same. There's feasting and jousting, and the usual crew It gets my goat: there's never anything new – A spectacle, a challenge, something I've never seen Some excitement to break up the boring routine.
Guinevere	Husband, dear Arthur, you grumpy old bear Sit with these knights to enjoy our fine fare. Settle for old yarns and tales of past days. Why insist on new tricks to stun and amaze? Be content with your old Christmas stocking – But wait a minute! Do I hear knocking?
Handmaid	Ma'am, I went to answer the door But you won't believe what I just saw. I honestly tried not to stare But these two make a right wicked pair.

Enter Green Knight and Green Lady.

Galahad	Speak of the devil and he will appear I've never seen anything so mightily queer.
Lancelot	Green garments, green pigments, what have we here? A giant of a knight and a figure of fear.
Galahad	Our noble code ordains honour to strangers; But my heart creeps with murmurs of dangers.
Green Knight	Who is the governor of this gang of guzzlers? I'd like to eyeball his highness here! Rise up and utter your regal retort.
Arthur	I'm Arthur, I'm he whom you're seeking You've come to the court of Camelot (To follow your manner of speaking) So sit down and join us and say what you mean. We excuse your manners – they are a bit green.
Green Knight	My mission is not to mince meanings Here in this hall where heroes are hailed.

I grace my game with a garland of greenery.
Enough chatter. I've come to challenge a chap.

Arthur

Now let me see if I've heard this a-right
I think my good fellow, you've come for a fight?

Green Knight

I despise with derision your notion of duels
I could clobber in combat all comers from here
But what I wish for is one who is willing
Unselfishly to swap one strike for another.
I'll bide the first blow with my own battleaxe
But reserve the right in return
To take as toll in a twelvemonth
A knock on the neck of that noble knight.

The company are shocked into silence. Then Arthur speaks.

Arthur

Now you've riled me with all your bluster!
Your challenge is a joke. It won't pass muster.
We're not afraid of your verbal attacks:
I, King Arthur, will take up your axe.

Green Knight gives Arthur axe.

Guinevere

Husband dear, please remember one simple truth:
You're not so young as you were in your youth.

Galahad

Most gracious lord, let me assure you
That I, Sir Galahad will bear arms for you.
Just say the word and I'll take your place
(Unless of course you don't want to lose face).

Lancelot

Arthur, I beg you, appoint a deputy
I'm Lancelot, so let it be me.
I'll see through this challenge without fail,
And then I'll be off for the holy grail.

Gawain

Lord, let me press my claim
Since I am here the humblest in fame.
Let the court say yea if they find it fitting
That Gawain should step forward to do the hitting.

All

Yea.

Gawain steps forward and takes the axe from Arthur.

Green Knight

Then tell me once more the terms of our treaty.

Gawain

I strike the first blow and then in a year
It's your choice of weapons – that's what I hear.

Green Knight	Find me in future in a far-flung fastness And I'll deal you your deadly desserts.
Gawain	I ask you then your place of abode So that when I set off I'll take the right road.
Green Knight	I daresay you'll discover my domain duly. Now banish the blagging: to battleaxe business.

Gawain swings the battleaxe, chops off Green Knight's head with one blow and the head rolls on the floor.

Green Knight picks up his head and holds it aloft.

Green Knight	Remember the rules my knight of romance These walls were witness to your words. To search and seek most seriously And yes to yield in the next new year To the bitter bargain your boldness bought. Find the Green Chapel, or for faint heart be famous!

Exit Green Knight.

Green Lady	Look off he goes. Boys will be boys: At Christmas they like to play with their toys. You won't find a Green Lady in the story books Because they're re-written by sexist crooks.

Exit Green Lady.

Arthur	Good lady wife, knights of the court These strange events were sent for our sport. Why I've just been moaning about the festive routine When who should appear but the chap in green. Personally, I don't think he was altogether sane But he lost his head to our good knight, Gawain.
Guinevere	Brave sir, you've earned a lady's admiration. Now I bid you – on with the celebration.
Lancelot	Coming here with an axe and some holly He got what he asked for, yes sir, by golly.
Galahad	You have to admit, he was a rare crowd-puller. Fancy going round with that sort of colour. And with such deeds disturbing our Christmas table. One thing's for sure – he drinks Carling Green Label.
Gawain	He asked me to hit him. I thought 'He's a goner'. I'm sure I'll be OK if I keep my honour. But privately I can't help feeling a bit of fear For what might happen this time next year.

SCENE 2
Arthur's court, a year later

Enter Chorus 1, 2 and 3.

Chorus 1	The chill Candlemas crept after Christmas The fields were frozen that festival.
Chorus 2	Till the seasons slipped by and sang softly of Spring And the shoots and the sap streamed slowly out.
Chorus 3	The magic of May murmured music And the heat haze held hope of summer horizons Until the dark days drew closer And the calendar kept on with its course.
Chorus 1	All Saints had a sense of a special foreboding And the cold days came creeping to Christmas.
Chorus 2	And moods were marred by memories of last year.
Chorus 3	Till at last Gawain girded himself to go.

Exeunt Chorus.

Gawain	Arthur my lord, the time is upon us When I must depart to win battle honours. Give me your leave to set out tomorrow To face my future, be it glory or sorrow.
Arthur	Let me embrace my knight most courtly. Yes, it's true you must set out shortly On an errand that's kept us all guessing. But you go with our prayers and our blessing.
Guinevere	True knight, it's my belief that your famous bravery Will overcome this green-tinted knavery.
Lancelot	Of course it's against all natural law That a fellow should pick his head off the floor.
Galahad	Me and the lads have thought of the ordeal You let yourself in for, last Christmas meal. We think he's a coward – you won't see him for dust, Once you've artfully parried his thrust. Or, if not, you could cunningly trick him: When he's not looking – up and stick him.
Gawain	Friends, there's no use delaying. I don't believe the Green Knight was playing. Clad me in armour and a strong breastplate That I may appear on the due date.

Handmaid	I'll arm you with spears and your trusty sword
	And dress you in jewels that none can afford
	And though you must ride to places afar
	Take with you the sign of the five-pointed star.
Gawain	Bear witness. I hereby proclaim
	And I'm off to find the green man with no name.

Exeunt all.

SCENE 3
Arrival at the castle

Enter Chorus 1, 2 and 3.

Chorus 1	None can tell of the tasks and travails
	That greeted Gawain as he went on his way.
Chorus 2	The pains and the perils that plagued his passage
	As he fared forth across fields and fells.
Chorus 3	Against bandits and brigands he battled
	Friendless and foodless he fought with foes.
Chorus 1	To Wales and the Wirral he wended his way
	Pleading with people to point out the paladin green.
Chorus 2	Or check out the chapel of comparable colour.
Chorus 3	Frozen he forged forward through forest
	Riding across rivers and down rocky roads.
Chorus 1	Till alone and exhausted in agony
	He hoped for a haven to hold off his hell.
Chorus 2	Till he came on a castle closed in a clearing
	The servants saw his stress and suffered him shelter.

Exeunt Chorus. Enter Gawain.

Gawain	It's a surprise to find a castle in this locality
	But I must welcome their hospitality.
	After such trials and tribulation
	Even a knight needs some recuperation.

Enter Bertilak, Elinor and Lunette.

Bertilak	Greetings, traveller! Hail fellow! Well met!
	You'll be exhausted after your travels, I bet.
	Friend or stranger, you'll join our festive fun.
	We're in for a great time, you son of a gun.

As my guest we'll eat and wassail
Now then, I'm Bertilak, lord of this castle.

Gawain

My lord, I'm glad to accept your proposal.
I'm Gawain. You'll find me at your disposal.

Bertilak

Everyone will be most excited
To have such a visitor: famous and knighted!
But let me present my wife Elinor
I don't think you two have met before.

Bertilak introduces Gawain to Elinor; Gawain bows.

Bertilak

Another of my house guests you won't have met
Is my distant cousin, the lovely Lunette,
Imported to this story from Chrétien of Troyes –
A female part, as we had too many boys.

Gawain bows.

Lunette

Like you I'm a stranger to these parts,
Innocent of all magic arts.
Because I have nothing to hide,
I'm the one in whom you can confide.

Enter Aunt.

Bertilak

Now please do honour to our favourite old Auntie
And bestow on her your gracious bounty.

Bertilak introduces Aunt who is Morgan le Fay in disguise.

Aunt

Oh, I'm just one of those far-off relations
Hanging about at the celebrations.
I just sit quiet and don't make a sound –
Just me and my knitting in the background.

Gawain

Well, as I've come all this distance
I might as well ask your assistance
I'm looking for a chapel in the colour of green
I wonder if that's a place you've ever seen?

Bertilak

Well sir, let's have a toast
The green chapel's only a mile at the most.
This castle is the perfect base
And you shall have the run of the place.
You won't be at all in the way
As I'll be out hunting during the day.
You can entertain the ladies with conversation
While you get your energy conservation.

Gawain	Whichever way your wishes lie As a knight it is my duty to comply.
Bertilak	Then let's give our party a competitive edge And shake hands on a mutual pledge. The fruits of my labours at the chase I'll hand to you with every good grace. In return, your gains you give to me – Whatever you've won. Do you agree?
Gawain	Why this is a most favourable jest: You bag the game, and I'll bag some rest.

SCENE 4
The temptings

Enter Chorus 1.

Chorus 1	Beagles barked and bayed for blood sport The hunters hurrahed with hounds at their heels Far across forests and fields they fared Harassing herds of harts and hinds And in a day's dealing destroying dozens of deer A stag was the symbol of the spoils they slaughtered.

Exit Chorus 1. Enter Gawain and Elinor.

Gawain	Courtly conversation is so refined: Its purpose is to purify the mind.
Elinor	I don't intend to miss the chance For a good chat with a hero of romance. But I'm wondering if you really are a knight so bold If an attractive woman leaves you cold.
Gawain	Excuse me ma'am, am I being dense? What have I said that's caused offence?
Elinor	There really must be something amiss If you don't greet a lady with a kiss.
Gawain *(kisses her)*	Ma'am, I must serve you in a noble fashion So, please, let's have no more talk of passion.

Exit Elinor. Enter Lunette.

Gawain	Lunette, was that the right thing to do? This situation is really quite new.
Lunette	Courtly behaviour suits your fame as a knight What you did was only polite

But next time take another tack
Because look now, here comes Bertilak.

Enter Bertilak.

Bertilak   We've had a hard day at the chase
The stag kept up a terrific pace.
But here's his head as I promised.
Now it's your turn to show you're honest.

Gawain *(kisses Bertilak)* This is all my lord.
I didn't do badly
Though anything more I'd have given gladly.

Bertilak   My goodness, where did you find such treasure
Tell me and I'll go at my leisure.
But later, because now I want to hunt some more
So I'm off to bag some wild boar.
While you entertain the ladies for us
Let's have the intro from the second Chorus.

Exeunt all. Enter Chorus 2.

Chorus 2   Hunters and hounds huddle in half-light
The lords let loose their lurchers
Who speedily sniff the scent of their suspect
A venerable victim, the blackest of boars.
They corner the quarry to kill him in combat
Archers aim arrows to add to his anguish
Bertilak braces himself before the beast
Then slams in his spear to slay the boar – stone-dead.

Exit Chorus 2. Enter Aunt and Elinor.

Aunt   Gawain is stirred not shaken
But thoughts of love begin to waken
Elinor use more of your lady's charm
To bamboozle this knight and do him harm.

Elinor   I don't know how he can have the brass neck
Not to ask for a kiss, or even a peck.

Exit Aunt. Enter Gawain.

Gawain   Elinor please accept my greeting,
What a pleasure to have another meeting.

Elinor   I must say Gawain I'm surprised at you
You just don't listen when you're spoken to.

Gawain	Please don't say that in my haste I'm guilty of some lapse of taste.
Elinor	How is it that you, famous for bravery Champion of virtue, scourge of knavery Will not instruct me in the rites of Cupid? Are you a fraud, or am I stupid? It's well accepted in the courtly code That once a lady's favour is bestowed She'll think something is amiss If she's not greeted with a kiss.
Gawain	I freely put myself at your service To give what you ask, even a kiss.

Gawain kisses Elinor twice who then exits. Enter Lunette.

Gawain	Lunette, give me some advice. I think I've done something that's not nice. I admit that Elinor's a real cracker – But should a knight be giving her a smacker?
Lunette	I'm sure your intentions are of the best But it might put your mind at rest. If you avoid the lady of the palace Or we'll have a drama bigger than Dallas.
Gawain	I can't do right for doing wrong. I'm discourteous if I don't play along. But if I do what she asks, I dishonour my host I don't know which I fear the most.

Enter Bertilak.

Bertilak	Imagine if you please, the forest scene The hounds at bay and a boar so mean With its glinting tusks and piggy eyes We came upon it by surprise And killed it after a struggle Then back here at the double. Here's my gift, the king of boars.

Bertilak gives Gawain the boar's head.

Bertilak	Now Gawain, your turn, what's yours.

Gawain kisses Bertilak twice.

Gawain	Now my lord that clears the score We're level pegging like we were before.

Bertilak   Once more I'm off to the hunt
      Let's see if you can pull another stunt.

Exeunt Bertilak and Gawain. Enter Chorus 3.

Chorus 3   Dogs slavered and stallions shook in their snaffles
      Then with a halloo they heralded the hunt
      Cheering they charged, champions of the chase
      The fox fled before them through field and forest
      White-tipped tail taunting his trackers
      Till they trapped him snarling and snapping
      Fiercely fighting for a feast of fox flesh
      Till Bertilak tore the trophy from their teeth.

Exit Chorus 3. Enter Aunt and Elinor.

Aunt   Gawain's so proper he'll never shift;
      Try and make him accept a gift.
      Something he can't declare.
      First a jewel or perhaps some underwear.

Elinor   Aunt, your suit is far too pressing;
      Gawain just is not one for messing.
      Even though I'm playing tricks,
      I sympathise; he's in a fix.

Exeunt Aunt and Elinor. Enter Gawain.

Gawain   The time draws near
      When I must keep my date with fear.
      And if that wasn't a big enough mess
      With this lady I'm tempted to transgress.

Enter Elinor.

Elinor   This is the third time I've called in love's name
      But I suspect that once more it's in vain.

Gawain   From your servant you may demand a kiss
(kissing her)   But you won't get anymore than this.

Elinor   You only sip at the well of sweetness.
      I've never known a hero show such meekness.
      But even though you're one big booby
      Accept this gift of my red ruby.

Elinor offers ring.

Gawain   Gracious lady, lady fair
      To hurt you I cannot bear.

	But accepting without giving
	Goes clean against my code of living.
Elinor	I understand. A gift of wealth
	Imperils your knightly mental health.
	But at least take this modest girdle
	Surely that won't make your blood curdle.
	Although it may seem of little worth
	Whosoever wraps it round his girth
	Cannot be killed and is immune to blows
	Whoever he fights or wherever he goes.

Elinor gives Gawain her girdle.

Gawain	Well all right I see there's no harm meant
	I accept your undergarment.

Gawain kisses her once on each cheek.

Exit Elinor. Enter Lunette.

Lunette	That girdle may save your life,
	But you can't say you got it from his wife.
Gawain	Far from being constant, I've turned out fickle.
	Love of life has landed me in this pickle.

Exeunt Gawain and Lunette.

Morgan le Fay	Gawain has given a potential lover up;
	Watch now for a knightly cover-up.
	He deems it's wiser to keep mum.
	After all, there's no harm done.

Enter Gawain, Bertilak and Lunette.

Gawain	Bertilak, before we hear about your sport,
	Let me first give my report.
	You might think this is a little bit tame,
	But I've got for you… more of the same.

Gawain kisses Bertilak three times.

Bertilak	Well, more kisses what a surprise!
	I hope you didn't pay more than was wise.
	But I accept them without demur,
	Because all I've got is this fox fur.

Bertilak gives Gawain the fox fur.

Gawain	This exchange has sealed our compact.
	Tomorrow at the Green Chapel I'll play the last act.

SCENE 5
The Green Chapel

Enter Elinor, Lunette, Bertilak and Gawain.

Gawain	What a generous leader and courteous wife. I wish you all joy and freedom from strife. Come forward, please, to point the way I must proceed this New Year's day.
Bertilak	I warn you, that chap at the Green Chapel Is a hell of a man with whom to grapple.
Gawain	Please remember I'm a famous knight. Ducking out now just wouldn't be right.
Bertilak	On your own fate, I'll let you ponder: You'll find the chapel ahead, down yonder.

Exeunt Elinor, Lunette and Bertilak.

Gawain   I see my destiny grows near.
           Still an honest man need nothing fear.
(looking around) It's funny, however I search
           There's nothing that looks much like a church.
           I can't see a message or holy motto.
           But wait!
(finding mound) Over here is some kind of grotto.
           It's dark and surrounded by weeds –
           Less a chapel: more a temple of misdeeds.

           Must I face death or capture
           In this home of evil rapture?
           Brave though I am, my heart is banging.
           Now, what's that unholy clanging?

Gawain hears sounds of Green Knight sharpening his sword. Enter Green Knight and Green Lady.

Green Lady	Now, Green Knight, don your armour This is the climax of the drama. While you act the vanities of male pride, Never forget there's a woman at your side.
Green Knight	Welcome, Gawain, to the wilderness wild. Your timing is true for the tryst we agreed. You tarried a twelvemonth till the turn of the year And the axe's acquaintance, as we arranged. Now, no backchat. Begin our business: Kneel and I'll knock at the nape of your neck.

Gawain   I've come for mercy to plead.
                  I present myself here as we agreed.
(kneels)   A single stroke is all your right,
                  So on with it now, Mr Green Knight.

Green Knight swings axe but Gawain jerks back out of the way.

Green Knight   Ho ho, what a hero we have!
                  The faint heart flinched before the blow fell.
                  I didn't recoil when my cranium cracked.
                  Sir, stand still while I swing.

Gawain   Yes, I admit I withdrew from the pain.

Green Knight swings again but halts the blow an inch above Gawain's neck.

Green Knight   That blow was bravely borne, my beauty.
                  Not a muscle you moved to mock my might.
                  For ducking you deserve a dummy delivery.
                  But next is a new one to knock off your noddle.

Gawain   Suddenly, Green Knight, you're nothing but talk.
                  Are we settling our debts, or out for a walk?
                  I've not forgotten what this is about.
                  Perhaps it's you who's bottling out.

Green Knight strikes a glancing blow, superficially cutting Gawain's neck.

Gawain   Now sir, your advantage is spent
                  My neck is intact, except for a dent.
                  One blow we agreed. Now we are equal.
                  Let's fight, and who knows the sequel?

Green Knight   You've received your reckoning, you can relax.
                  I'm not claiming any more clouts to cleave you.
                  My initial axe blow was for our earliest agreement
                  When you gave me the gains you'd garnered.
                  A prim peck like a proper prince.
                  Second, I swung to see your resolve
                  And acquitted the kisses you gave my consort.
                  Two tests tallied with the truths you told.

                  But the next was iniquity and your neck was nicked,
                  For under your garment is my girl's girdle.
                  You frolicked, you fibbed and you failed, my friend.
                  Loyalty to liege lord you lacked a little.
                  But at least it was love of life let you down,
                  Not lechery or lewdness, that I allow.

Gawain	I'm a miserable failure, I'm covered in shame.
	Your test has undone me, I've lost my good name.
	My honour fell at the final hurdle;
	I curse the day I accepted this girdle.
	I've besmirched the knightly code.
	My courtly career's reached the end of the road.
	I've stayed too long as your guest.
	But tell me the reason I was put to the test.
	Why did you change from the lord of the manor
	To a pagan hero with a green banner?
Green Knight	I've been cursed to this colour
	My might is mandated by Morgan Le Fay
	The aunt who evilly instigates actions.
	Mercilessly she mastered the magic of Merlin
	When she lay with her lover learning his lore.
	She tricked me to test and to taunt
	The courtly Christmas of your king and consort.
	Her gall and her guile were to get Guinevere.
	Anyway, that episode is ended for Elinor and I.
Gawain	Bertilak, you've had a rough time:
	I much preferred it when you spoke in rhyme.
	Because you got caught up in a devilish feud,
	First I was challenged and then I was wooed.
	And though I return alive to Camelot,
	I've tasted the gall of my mortal lot.

Exeunt all. Enter Morgan Le Fay.

Morgan Le Fay	Curses! My plot has turned out a flop
	Guinevere has come out on top.
	Her ideas are so prim and proper!
	But mark my words she'll come a cropper.
	That Elinor was a more lustful beauty
	But Gawain would insist on doing his duty.
	Now let's see what happens when he gets back
	To my brother Arthur and the rest of the pack.

Exit Morgan Le Fay.

SCENE 6

In Arthur's court

Arthur, Guinevere and the knights are assembled.

Arthur	Gawain, welcome back, you warrior brave Come and join our Christmas rave. We can't wait to hear your story. But hold on a moment – you're all gory.
Guinevere	Gawain, my tender knight Let me see, are you all right? What a shocking wound! Just to see it, I nearly swooned.
Galahad	Notwithstanding his long-odds wager He's back more virtuous than John Major.
Lancelot	When he headed out that door We never thought we'd see him more. He's answered the Green Giant's goad – A sight more dangerous than crossing the road.
Arthur	Now Gawain, get to the point at issue – Just where did you get that scar tissue? How did you overcome your green-tinged foe? Tell us the story, blow by blow.
Gawain	As guest of Bertilak I stayed and rested Near the chapel where I'd be tested. Three times his wife tried to seduce me. As a Knight I said, 'No, excuse me'. But before I set out she offered this charm
(holds out girdle)	Which she said would protect me from harm. I took it and hid it, and faced the next day Her husband Bertilak, turned green by Morgan le Fay.
	For punishment his axe blow gave me this gash. Dear friends, I confess I made a right hash. I was guilty of cowardice and deceit. Instead of a knight I turned out a cheat. I can hide the girdle that caused my misery But the scar on my neck is for all to see.
Arthur	Gawain, don't get in such a stew. I say we'll take the contrary view. This was one of our toughest duels, Against a man who broke all the rules.

You were quite entitled to look after yourself
Borrow some magic, and return in good health.

Guinevere   You've got nothing to hide.
I won't hear of your wearing the girdle inside
Your armour. Let it make us remember this fable.
We'll all have one – what say you, round table?

Arthur   This is an emblem of pride
We'll wear it wherever we ride.

Galahad   We'll wear it diagonally across our chest
As part of our armour like all the rest.

Lancelot   Yes, we'll cut quite a dash
Riding to battle with our bright green sash.

Guinevere   That's settled. Now, Gawain, let's celebrate
And forget your close encounter with fate.
But I daresay Arthur will want a concluding word
To help us make sense of what we saw and heard.

Arthur   How kind of you darling to defer to me.
Well, the facts are there for all to see.
Gawain overcame a foe of giant-sized bulk,
A knight who was greener than the Incredible Hulk.
That knight was magicked by my twisted sister.
Yes, Gawain was tempted, but he only kissed her.
And whatever, in the end, his deceit meant,
Was the fault of Morgan, a suitable case for treatment.

It's a bit like cricket, when all's said and done:
Out of the tests, we won two, lost one.
Now we've left the lure of the alliterative lilt,
So let's enjoy our party, up to the hilt.

THE END

THE BUILDING OF THE ST PANCRAS ALMSHOUSES, 1850–1863

CAST

Current Resident 1
Current Resident 2
Dr Donald Fraser (Scottish)
Mrs Fraser, his aged mother (Scottish)
Rev Thomas Dale, vicar of St Pancras until 1860
Canon Champneys, vicar of St Pancras from 1860
Worthy 1
Worthy 2
Baroness Angela Burdett Coutts
Sarah Bickford, retired housekeeper, early resident
Alice Cope, retired housekeeper, early resident
Railway Boss
Henry Baker, architect (Scottish)
Court usher
First Judge
Barrister
Appeal Judge
Timpson, disgruntled builder
Karl Marx
Mrs Marx

Successful candidates for places:

Thomas Markwick, coachbuilder
Lucy Ann Markwick, his wife, *(non-speaking)*
Ellen Lintott, dyer
Rebecca Sprinks, cook

Unsuccessful candidates for places:

Walter Efford
Eliza Efford, *(non-speaking)*
Rebecca Brown, seamstress
Elizabeth Mary Money
Eliza Wakefield, corset maker

Mr Henry Aste, a generous builder
Committee Lady 1, bossy
Committee Lady 2, busy
Committee Lady 3, humble

Audience boo the rail boss, take and give back voting forms, and make hammering noises when required.

PROLOGUE

Enter Current Resident 1 and Current Resident 2.

Resident 1   I live here and I'm intelligent and hearty,
I'd like to welcome you to our party.
(I'm just back from the Lord Southampton pub
That very well-known social hub.)
We've got a surprise for you today:
You're all going to take part in a play.
My neighbour will now tell us more
So that you'll know what's in store.

Resident 2   Let's remember the glory of times past
When things were solid and built to last.
(It was like that when I was in my nursery!)
We're here to celebrate the 150th anniversary
Of the St Pancras almshouses. They're mighty fine
And date from 1859.
Our founder overcame obstacles and disputes
So today we can enjoy the fruits.

Now, let's bring that man of mystery,
Dr Donald Fraser, to reveal our history.

Exeunt Current Resident 1 and Current Resident 2.

SCENE 1
1850–1858

Enter Dr Fraser and his mother Mrs Fraser.

Dr Fraser   I'm a Scottish doctor and St Pancras churchwarden,
I live in Camden in a nice house and garden.
My aged mother lives with me and my wife.
Mother's fed and clothed and has a nice life.

Mrs Fraser   I'm the doctor's ma. Aye, Donald's a good son
But it's not the same for everyone.
Many old people are thrust out in the cold
Just because they're poor and because they're old.

Dr Fraser   They either go to the workhouse or die in the street.
It's 1850 and I plan to give them a treat.
I'll raise money for a haven for their twilight years
Where they can rest after toil without any fears.

Enter Reverend Dale, Worthy 1 and Worthy 2.

Reverend Dale	I'm the Vicar of St Pancras, Reverend Thomas Dale.
	We need social housing on a massive scale.
	It's the fallout from the Industrial Revolution.
	Let's gather some worthies to fund a solution!
Worthy 1	We're willing to support Dr Fraser's latest scheme.
	He needs our contacts to realise his dream.
Worthy 2	To build almshouses to the glory of our patron saint,
	St Pancras, local hero (famous, he ain't).
Reverend Dale	I'll give a stirring sermon with lots of passion
	Now supporting almshouses is in fashion.
Dr Fraser	We must sell subscriptions to the good and the great
	To save old people from an ignominious fate.
Worthy 1	Actually our wives will form a Ladies Committee
	They'll slave away while we're sitting pretty.

Enter Ladies Committee (Lady 1, Lady 2 and Lady 3).

Lady 1	I'm the energetic Lady Number 1.
	Let's work hard but let's have FUN!
Lady 2	I'm Second in command, Lady Number 2,
	Indispensible when there's lots to do.
Lady 3	And I'm humble Lady Number 3.
	No task's too lowly for little me.
Lady 1	We're helping Dr Fraser and this is how:
	Open your wallet and buy a subscription NOW!

Ladies move among the audience handing out forms.

Dr Fraser	A lottery for residents where subscribers vote
	(A bit like Big Brother but on a philanthropic note).
	That's our unique selling point – our U.S.P.
	Subscribe and choose the residents in our lottery!
Reverend Dale	Audience, hold on to your subscription paper
	As you'll get a vote later in this caper.
Dr Fraser	In this parish of St Pancras
	What we need as well is a wealthy banker-ess.
Worthy 1	I know a young spinster with fabulous wealth
	Who takes an interest in the poor and their health.
Dr Fraser	Yes, Angela Burdett Coutts is the woman for us
	We'll make her our first Lady Patroness.

Mrs Fraser	Why can't I be Patroness, I gave you the idea?
Dr Fraser	Ssh, mother, she'll be brilliant, it's very clear.

Exeunt Mrs Fraser, Worthies and Ladies' Committee. Enter Angela Burdett Coutts.

Angela Burdett Coutts	I'm Miss Coutts, shy but with a kind heart. In come I to play my part. Grandad came from Edinburgh – Thomas Coutts (Like Dr Fraser I've got Scottish roots). That's Coutts of Coutts Bank, trusted by royalty. I'm the heir now and I offer you my loyalty. I'll be your patroness for the next 50 years To encourage donations from other rich peers. (Actually I'm connected to the church of St Pancras As that's where grandad secretly married an actress.) I'll start you off with a 50 guineas donation. Please, Dr Fraser, go on with your narration.

Exit Angela Burdett Coutts.

Dr Fraser	We built the first almshouses quite fast. They were in Wilkin Street but they didn't last As they were right in the path of the new railway. Here's the rail boss who wants to have his say.

Enter Rail Boss.

Rail Boss	I'm the boss of the Hampstead and City Junction, I sweep away almshouses without compunction. I'll make an offer for the land – just a paltry sum As I'll soon have the Trustees under my thumb.
Dr Fraser	Don't try to scare us with threatening looks.
Reverend Dale	We can tell you're just a bunch of crooks!
Rail Boss	I'm really only prepared to pay For the sliver of land taken by the railway. So I'm offering you only £2,350. You can manage on that as you're so thrifty.
Dr Fraser	We reject your offer out of hand As we know the whole site's worth at least 6 grand.
Rail Boss	Fools! I'll see you in court, let the judge decide As I stand for 'growth', he'll be on my side.

Exit Rail Boss. Enter First Judge.

First Judge	I'm the Judge who hears this case.
	I intend to put the Trustees in their place.
	Almshouses have had their day
	So I'll let the rail boss have his way.
(bangs gavel)	Next case!

Exit First Judge. Enter Henry Baker.

Henry Baker	I'm Henry Baker, trustee and borough surveyor
	We're in a fix, this setback is major.
	But I'm an architect so I know the value of land
	We'll go to the Appeal Court to get our 6 grand.
Dr Fraser	I'm glad you've got a combative spirit.
	Let's get a barrister of the highest merit.
Reverend Dale	And I wonder how the rail boss will feel
	When we take the case to the Court of Appeal.

SCENE 2
Court of Appeal

Dr Fraser, Henry Baker and Reverend Dale continue on stage.

Enter Court Usher, Barrister and Appeal Judge.

Court Usher	Order! Order! Silence in court!
Barrister	I'm the Trustees' barrister. Consider this thought:
	If you destroy any portion of a property
	So that it can no longer be used properly
	For the purpose for which it was originally intended
	Then compensation must be amended
	To take into account the whole property's value.
Appeal Judge	You're right, lets give the almshouses their due.
	As Appeal Judge, I find in the Trustees' favour.

Exeunt Court Usher, Barrister and Appeal Judge.

SCENE 3
The almshouses

Dr Fraser, Henry Baker and Reverend Dale continue on stage.

Reverend Dale	Hoorah! That barrister was our saviour!
Dr Fraser	We beat the railway in a legal fight
	And got the full value for the site.
	But I hear the residents are worried sick.
	Of course, they want it sorted out quick.

Reverend Dale Here come two residents to let us know
       The various concerns that worry them so.

Enter Sarah Bickford and Alice Cope.

Sarah Bickford I'm Sarah Bickford, a retired nurse from Devon.
       The almshouses are my idea of heaven.
       We're not ungrateful and we don't want to moan
       But where will we live till you build a new home?

Alice Cope I'm a retired housekeeper, Alice Cope.
       The almshouses are my only hope.
       We love our little homes and our regular pensions.
       Please kindly tell us your intentions.

Reverend Dale Bring on the rail boss, we'd better negotiate.

Dr Fraser Audience, boo him, he's the bully we all hate!
(to audience)

Enter Rail Boss. Audience boo.

Rail Boss I concede that you won on a point of law
       Which left me feeling rather sore.
       But I could exploit this situation
       And use it to enhance my reputation.
       I'll let the residents stay two more years –
       Now folks, does that relieve your fears?

Alice Cope We're most grateful, sir. That's very handsome.
       You're a 19th century Richard Branson.

Sarah Bickford Let's go off home and tell the rest
       The future move may be for the best.

Exeunt Alice Cope, Sarah Bickford and Rail Boss.

Angela Burdett Coutts *(from audience)*
       I'm jolly pleased they sorted that out
       So I didn't have to use my clout.
       I've invested heavily in railway shares.
       A conflict of interest would add to my cares.
       It would be such a shame if the 'Age of Steam'
       Were to get in the way of Dr Fraser's scheme.

Dr Fraser Our new homes must be the best
       To give our residents their well-earned rest.
(to Henry Baker) Have you thought how they might be designed?

Henry Baker I think you'll like what I have in mind.
       We don't want it to look 'institutional'

But something recalling the rural idyll:
A row of cottages around a grassy square,
Something pleasing for when they stand and stare.

Dr Fraser It's hard work but I'll raise the lolly
The ladies committee will do something jolly.

SCENE 4
1859

Dr Fraser and Henry Baker continue on stage.

Dr Fraser A year has moved on very fast:
Let's leave that battle in the past.
Now we've bought some acres near at hand
That were part of Lord Southampton's land.
It's a healthy site by fields of goats and sheep
That will gently lull the residents to sleep.

Henry Baker It lies next to the Orphans Working School
Where orphans live on bread and gruel.
So it's in a philanthropic zone
Which ensures the highest moral tone.

Dr Fraser I hate to put a bit of a damp on
But it's next to a pub – the Lord Southampton!

Henry Baker Our rules will stop residents going on a bender.
Meanwhile, put the building contract out to tender.

Dr Fraser Builders' quotes are arriving by the dozen
For this price and that price – my head is buzzing.

Henry Baker Keep calm – we don't have to take the lowest quote.
The most reliable builder will get my vote.

Dr Fraser Mr Batterbury is a dependable man
Who I'm sure will do the best he can.

Henry Baker I fear other builders will kick up a fuss
If we give Mr Batterbury our business.

Enter Mr Timpson, disgruntled builder and Reverend Dale.

Mr Timpson I'm Timpson, a builder with a grudge,
Convinced the Trustees have done a fudge.
So I've called a meeting at the Vestry Hall
For the Trustees to account to one and all.

Reverend Dale As Reverend, I'd better take the chair.
Speak up, Timpson, let's clear the air.

Timpson   Why did you choose Batterbury who was 426 pound
Above the lowest tender? – that's not sound!
The lowest tender usually gets accepted.
I want to know why it was rejected.

Reverend Dale   We're here to publicly explain
That our priority is long-term gain.
We refuse to do building on the cheap
Because what you sow, you reap.
You're disappointed and I'm sorry
But we're employing Mr Batterbury.

Timpson   I just wanted transparency, come what may
So this is where I exit the play.

Exit Timpson.

Dr Fraser   I wonder why Timpson's so upset –
Transparency's not been invented yet.

Henry Baker (*to Reverend Dale*)
Your tact and firmness were inspired.

Reverend Dale   Oh I only did what was required.
Now I'll get back to my master plan
To build ten churches if I can.
Every neighbourhood must have its church,
I'm sorry that I'm leaving you in the lurch.

Exit Reverend Dale.

Dr Fraser   The Reverend Dale has played his part –
He was with us from the very start.
But vicars come and vicars go –
We just have to get on with the show.

Henry Baker   To work, let's proceed with the construction.
And hope we don't have further ruction.

Angela Burdett Coutts (*from audience*)
It's not easy dispensing charity
You need determination and clarity.
You can't avoid conflict, that's the truth.
I fear your path will not be smooth.

SCENE 5
1859–1861

Dr Fraser and Henry Baker continue on stage.

Dr Fraser
At last the building work's begun
On the South Wing and two houses 'on the turn'.
But are the workmen sick or just lazy?
Their delays are driving me crazy!

Henry Baker
First they joined up with the '9 hours movement'
For shorter hours and other improvements.
The strike ended and they're back at their labours
But I fear their hammering annoys the neighbours.
Audience, stamp your feet for the sound of banging
You can be louder, let's hear some clanging.

Audience make sound of hammering.

Enter Karl Marx and Mrs Marx who is weeping loudly.

Karl Marx
I'm Karl Marx, writer of some renown
Unfortunately, we live a few doors down.
Your noise drives my wife around the bend
Can you tell me please when it will end?

Dr Fraser
I regret the work will take the next few years...

Mrs Marx weeps more loudly.

Karl Marx
Oh, drat, you've confirmed our worst fears!

Mrs Marx
If I carry on weeping, I'll lose my looks
While my husband buries himself in his books.

Karl Marx
I'll exit now I've made my contribution
As I'm off to study revolution.

Exit Karl Marx and Mrs Marx.

Dr Fraser
Time passes and two wings are erected.
We've twenty-two inmates yet I feel dejected.
I get so many complaints from dawn till dusk,
Sometimes I feel unequal to the task!

Enter Sarah Bickford and Alice Cope.

Sarah Bickford
We like our new homes but not all the mud
And when it rains it's just like Noah's Flood!

Alice Cope
There are no street signs so our visitors get lost
Please get us signage at whatever the cost!

I'm not one to advise my betters
But how about a gate with the name in letters?

Henry Baker   We note your concern, leave it with us
To be dealt with in due course.

Exeunt Sarah Bickford and Alice Cope muttering 'Whenever'.

Dr Fraser   I'm uneasy that we let some houses out to rent.

Henry Baker   But admit it, the money's heaven-sent!

Dr Fraser   We let dwellings out at four shillings a week
But that's not sheltering the old and the meek!

Henry Baker   You know it's only a temporary measure.

Dr Fraser   Yet I fear we may repent at leisure.

Henry Baker   You're worrying unduly, that's so draining.
Let's have the residents' lottery, it'll be entertaining.
Summon the subscribers, lords and ladies of note.
Audience, you too can have a vote.

Exit Henry Baker.

SCENE 6
The lottery

Dr Fraser remains on stage.

Dr Fraser   Canon Champneys, our new vicar, can preside.
He'll tell us the rules and be our guide.

Enter Canon Champneys.

Canon Champneys   The rules for the lottery are very strict
But it's a sheltering haven if you're picked.
You must be over 60 and have paid your rates
And never queued at the workhouse gates.

Angela Burdett Coutts enters surreptitiously.

Angela Burdett Coutts   I'll slip in here among the crowd
But please don't say my name aloud.
Because I like to be the 'lady unknown'
So I really don't want my cover blown.

Canon Champneys   Who's the first candidate? Let's hear your voice.
Listen carefully audience, then make your choice.

Enter Thomas and Lucy Markwick, Ellen Lintott, Rebecca Sprinks,
Walter and Eliza Efford.

Thomas Markwick	I'm Thomas Markwick, honest working man Fallen into penury with my dear Lucy Ann. I've paid all my bills and worked hard all my life Being a coachbuilder with the help of my wife.
Ellen Lintott	I'm Ellen Lintott, one of the deserving poor. I was a dyer from Kent but I don't work no more. So I go to church and recite all my prayers For rescue from hardship, misery and cares.
Rebecca Sprinks	I'm sober, upright Rebecca Sprinks But desperation may drive me to drinks. I'm a retired cook, going for the sympathy vote: Just look at my rags and the holes in my coat!
Walter Efford	We're the Effords, an unappealing couple, No longer fit, no longer supple. We lack belief in our own worth. We don't expect paradise on this earth.
Canon Champneys	Hurry along, don't dilly-dally If you dawdle, you'll drive us doolally. Who's next? Step up and say who you are. Don't mumble, that won't get you far.

Rebecca Brown, Elizabeth Mary Money and Eliza Wakefield step forward.

Rebecca Brown	I'm the seamstress, Rebecca Brown. I feel the world has let me down. I've always put other people first Now I'm old, I expect the worst.
Elizabeth Mary Money	I'm Elizabeth Mary Money I don't find life very funny. Everyone thinks my name's a joke But it's hard to laugh when you're stony broke.
Eliza Wakefield	I'm Eliza Wakefield, born in Dorset. I've spent my life sewing corsets. I'm tired and weary with limbs that are tottery, Please vote for me in this lottery.
Canon Champneys	Now audience, it's time to make your selection Choose between acceptance and rejection.

Audience wave forms and pass them to Ladies 1, 2 and 3.

Lady 1	Cast your vote, don't delay, House some aged folk today!

Lady 2	Take pity on their sad position,
	Use your vote to improve their condition!
Lady 3	My heart bleeds for the good folk brought low.
	Please save them from a life of woe!

Ladies hand in voting slips to Canon Champneys. He lifts up a scoreboard.

Canon Champneys	Markwicks, Lintott and Sprinks selected
	We regret the others are rejected.
Dr Fraser	Mr and Mrs Efford you were far too modest.
	You won my sympathy, so don't be distressed.
	In April the Trustees can vote you in
	So don't despair or turn to gin.

Exeunt candidates, wailing or cheering as appropriate. Exit Canon Champneys.

SCENE 7
1861–1863

Dr Fraser remains on stage. Enter Henry Baker.

Henry Baker	We've finished two wings, we're on the last lap.
	We need to build the North Wing in that gap.
Dr Fraser	Fundraising is tiring, we need a corporate donor.

Enter Henry Aste.

Henry Aste	Allow me, sir to take on that honour.
	I'm Henry Aste of Upper Park Road,
	A corn merchant in philanthropic mode.
	I've four sons, four daughters and a loving wife.
	Now I want a memorial to my life.
	I want a solid testimonial
	With a portico and arch, something mock-baronial.
	I'll build the front house at my expense
	If you can raise the pounds and pence
	To finally complete the North Wing.
	Do it within six months – now that's the thing!
Henry Baker	I like a challenge, I like a bet.
Dr Fraser	Well, it's by the far the best offer we've had yet.
Henry Baker	Call the Committee Ladies 1, 2 and 3
	To pull out the stops and raise lots of money.

Enter Lady 1, Lady 2, Lady 3.

| Lady 1 | I'll arrange some balls and a participatory drama.
We'll raise more funds than Barack Obama. |

Lady 1   I'll arrange some balls and a participatory drama.
We'll raise more funds than Barack Obama.

Lady 2   And I'll do concerts and a fund-raising dinner
Of the great and the good – it'll be a winner!

Lady 3   I know the local vicars so I'll use my connections.
I'll get the churches to have special collections.

Exeunt Ladies 1, 2 and 3.

Dr Fraser   Within 6 months, though it was touch and go
We got funds to employ the builder, Mr Rowe.
We finished the North Wing at last
Thanks to the challenge from Mr Aste.

Mr Aste   You needed two thousand pounds and you got it all
And now my name's forever on your wall.
It wasn't a pact with the devil.
It was all straight and on the level.
I had a small but significant role
I'll exit now I've achieved my goal.

Exit Mr Aste.

Henry Baker   Dr Fraser, you deserve congratulations.
This is cause for celebration.

Dr Fraser   Together we made a great team.
You helped me realise my dream.
Let's take a pint across the road
As finally we've reaped what we sowed.

Henry Baker   Yes, we can leave now in a blaze of glory
And let the residents finish the story.

Henry Baker and Dr Fraser exeunt to Lord Southampton pub.

Enter current residents, Resident 1 and Resident 2.

Resident 1   It's a gripping tale without a doubt
How these almshouses came about.
Both these men will die in 1878
But Miss Coutts will thrive beyond that date.

Resident 2   She was made a Baroness for her good works,
Funding schools, homes and the Church.
Though at 67 she'll marry a younger man
Who was (scandalously!) American.

Enter Angela Burdett Coutts and Alice Cope.

Angela Burdett Coutts | I enjoy being known as 'Queen of the Poor'.
Charity was my passion, not a chore.
I'll work on till January 1907
When I'll be laid to rest and carried to heaven.
Now Alice Cope will bring us back to the present
Then we'll celebrate, that's always pleasant.

Alice Cope | Remember me? I'm Alice Cope.
I'd like to say it is my hope
That all who'll live here feel truly blessed,
Eat well, live well and take their rest.
So finally I thank you all for taking part
From the very bottom of my heart.

THE END

UNDER THE GREENWOOD:
ROBIN HOOD MAY PLAY

Taken from 'The Early Robin Hood Plays' by David Wiles

CAST

Arthur a Bland	Merry Men
Robin Hood	Friar Tuck
Maid Marian *(non-speaking)*	Friar Tuck's three dogs
Will Scarlett	George a Greene, Pindar of Wakefield
Little John	Beatrice, his beloved

Please take great care with the fight scenes in this play. The authors can take no responsibility for any accidents or injuries arising out of performances of this play.

SCENE 1
In the forest

Enter Arthur a Bland.

Arthur a Bland *(clearing a space for the actors to perform)*
> A room, a room, brave gallants all
> Please give me room to rhyme
> This merry Maying time.
> Activity of youth, activity of age
> Such life was never known or played upon the stage.
> I am a bold tanner,
> From Northamptonshire I came
> Long ago I wrote my name:
> I am bold Arthur a Bland.
>
> As I was walking one summer's morning
> Through the forest merry greenwood
> To view the red deer
> That run here and there
> Then I saw bold Robin Hood.

Enter Robin Hood.

Robin Hood
> Who art thou, bold fellow
> Who comes so boldly here?
> In truth be brief.
> Thou lookest like a thief

Come to steal the King's deer.
I'm the keeper over this forest
And the King put me in trust
To mind the red deer
That run here and there
To stop thee, good fellow, I must.

Arthur   If thou be'st keeper over this forest
And hast any great command
I don't care a peg
For thee looking so big
So mend thyself where thee can.

Robin Hood   Let us measure staves, bold fellow
Before we begin our play.
I won't have my staff
Half a foot longer than thine
Else that will come to foul play.

Arthur   My staff is eight foot and a half
And growed straight on a tree.
An eight foot staff
Will knock down a calf
And I'm sure it will knock down thee.

They fight.

Robin Hood   Oh hold our hands! Oh hold our hands!
And let our quarrels fall.
We shall beat our bones
All to a meat
And get no acquaintance at all.
If thou will leave thy tanning trade
And bide in the greenwood with me.
My name's Robin Hood
And I swear by the wood
I will give thee both gold and a fee.

The two shake hands. Robin pins his livery badge on Arthur.
The Merry Men arrive with Little John and Maid Marian.

Robin   Now stand ye forth my merry men all
And hark what I shall say.
Of an adventure I shall tell
Which befell me the other day.
As I went out on the highway
With a stout friar I met
And a quarter staff in his hand.

                     Lightly to me he leapt
                     And still he made me stand.

                     There were blows two or three,
                     I cannot tell who had the worse.
                     But well I know the whore's son leapt on me
                     And from me took my purse.
                     Is there any of my merry men all
                     That to the friar will go
                     And bring him to me
                     Whether he will or no?

Exeunt Marian and Merry Men.

Little John goes out and brings in Friar Tuck accompanied by three dogs.

Friar Tuck	Deus hic, Deus hic, God be here
(drunk)	Is this not a holy word for a friar?
	God save all this company!
	But am I not a jolly friar?
	For I can shoot both far and near
	And handle a sword and buckler
	And this quarter staff also.
	I come to seek a good yeoman
	In Barnsdale men say is his habitation,
	His name is Robin Hood.

                     And if that he be better man than I
                     His servant will I be and serve him truly.
                     But if I be better man than he
                     By my truth my knave shall he be
                     And lead these dogs all three.

Exeunt dogs. Robin seizes the Friar by the throat.

Robin	Yield Friar in thy long coat!

Friar Tuck	I beg you, hard knave, thou hurtest my throat.

Robin Hood	Of all the men in the morning thou art the worst
	To meet with thee I have no lust
	He who meets with a friar or a fox in the morning
	To speed ill that day he stands in jeopardy!
	Therefore I'd rather meet with a devil of hell
	Than meet with a friar or fox in the morning!

Friar Tuck	Avaunt thou ragged knave this is but a mock
	If you say any more, you shall have a knock!

Robin Hood	Hark Friar to what I say here: Over this water you shall me bear As the bridge is borne away.

Robin climbs onto the Friar's back.

Friar Tuck	Now I'm a Friar within and thou Robin without* To throw you in here I have no doubt!
(throws Robin into the water)	
	Now I'm Friar without and thou Robin within Lie there knave, choose whether to sink or swim
Robin Hood	Why thou lousy friar what hast thou done?
Friar Tuck	Wilt thou fight again with pluck?
Robin Hood	And God send me good luck...
Friar Tuck	Then have a stroke for Friar Tuck!

They fight with staves.

Robin Hood	Hold thy hand Friar, and hear me speak: In this forest I have a hound I would not lose him for a hundred pound. Give me leave my horn to blow That my hound may know.
Friar Tuck	Blow on ragged knave without any doubt Until both thine eyes start out.

Robin blows horn to summon Merry Men.

Friar Tuck	Here come all sorts of ragged knaves Clothed all in Kendal green And to thee they make their way now.
Robin Hood	By adventure they do so.
Friar Tuck	I gave thee leave to blow at thy will Now give me leave to whistle my fill.

Friar summons his dogs.

Friar Tuck	Now cut and thrust Bring forth the clubs and staves And down with those ragged knaves!

The outlaws fight the dogs.

Robin Hood	How sayest thou Friar, wilt thou be my man To do the best service thou can?

Thou shalt have both gold and a fee
And also here is a lady free.

Enter Maid Marian.

Friar Tuck   Here is a huckle duckle an inch above the buckle.
      She is true of trust, to serve a friar at his lust!
      A pricker, a prancer, a tearer of sheets
      A wagger of ballocks when other men sleep!
      Go home you knaves and lay crabs in the fire
      For my lady and I will dance from pure desire!

Friar dances with Maid Marian. Exeunt all.

SCENE 2
In a cornfield

Enter George a Greene and Beatrice.

George   Tell me, sweet Beatrice, how is thy mind content?
      Wilt thou brook to live with George a Greene?

Beatrice   Oh George, how pleasing are these words.
      Came I from Bradford for the love of thee
      And left my father for so sweet a friend?
      Here will I live until my life do end.

Enter Robin Hood, Marian, Will Scarlett and Little John.

George   Happy am I to have so sweet a love,
      But what are these come tracing here along?

Beatrice   Three men come striking through the corn, my love.

George   Back again, you foolish travellers.
      For you are wrong and may not wend this way.

Robin Hood   That were great shame.
      Now by my soul, proud sir
      We be three tall yeomen and thou art but one.
      Come, we will forward in despite of him.

George   Leap the ditch, or I will make you skip.
      What cannot the highway serve your turn
      But you must make a path over the corn?

Robin Hood   Why art thou mad? Darest thou encounter three?
      We are no babes, man. Look upon our limbs.

George   Sir, the biggest limbs have not the stoutest hearts.
      Were ye as good as Robin Hood and his merry men

I'll drive you back the same way that ye came.
Be ye men, ye scorn to encounter me all at once;
But be ye cowards, set upon me all three, to try
The Pindar of Wakefield what he dares perform.

Will Scarlett   Were thou as high in deeds
As thou are haughty in words,
Thou well mightest be a champion for a king.
But empty vessels have the loudest sounds
And cowards prattle more than men of worth.

George   Sir, darest thou try me?

Will Scarlett   Aye, sir, that I dare.

They fight and George a Greene beats him.

Little John   How now! What art thou down?
Come Sir, I am next.

They fight and George a Greene beats him.

Robin Hood   Come Sir, now to me. Spare me not.
For I'll not spare thee.

George   Make no doubt I will be as liberal to thee.

They fight.

Robin Hood   Stay, George, for here I do protest
Thou art the stoutest champion that ever
I laid hands upon.

George   Soft you, sir. By your leave, you lie.
You never yet laid hands on me.

Robin Hood   George, wilt thou forsake Wakefield,
And go with me?
Two liveries will I give thee every year,
And forty crowns shall be your fee.

George   Why, who are thou?

Robin Hood   Why Robin Hood.
I am come hither with my Marian
And these my yeomen for to visit thee.

George   Robin Hood, next to King Edward
Art thou dear to me.
Welcome sweet Robin, welcome Maid Marian
And welcome you my friends.
Will you come to my poor house?

> You shall have wafer cakes to your fill,
> A piece of beef hung up since Martlemas,
> Mutton and veal. If this you like not,
> Take what you find, or what you bring to me.

Robin Hood	Godamercies, good George I'll be thy guest today.
George	Robin, therein thou honourest me. I'll lead the way.

Exeunt all.

THE END

Notes

*'Now I'm Friar Tuck within and thou Robin without' means 'I'm Friar Tuck underneath and you're Robin on top' while the following 'Now I'm the Friar without and thou Robin within' means 'I'm the Friar out of the water and you're Robin in the water'.

Note that Robin Hood actually loses every fight and when he's had enough, he says 'You're good at fighting, you can be in my band'. George a Greene, who wins every fight, cleverly sidesteps the offer to join the band by inviting them all to dinner.

VOTES FOR WOMEN

The story of the suffragettes 1903–1928

CAST

Prologue

Pankhurst family
Mrs Pankhurst, founder of WSPU   Sylvia Pankhurst
(Women's Social and Political Union)   Adela Pankhurst
Christabel Pankhurst   Harry Pankhurst

Politicians
Keir Hardie, member of the ILP   Policeman
(Independent Labour Party)   Curtis Bennett (Magistrate)
Winston Churchill, Liberal politician,
later to join Tories
Lloyd George, Liberal politician

Holloway Prison and suffragette prisoners
Wardress   Mrs Pethick Lawrence
Mary Goulden (Mrs Pankhurst's sister)   Emily Wilding Davison
Jennie Baines   Mary Richardson
Muriel Matters   Ethyl Smyth, composer
Anonymous woman stone thrower   Doctor *(non-speaking)*

Pinner WSPU
Edith Heal
Janie Terrero

Dumbshow
King's horse, Anmer
Derby Day horses
(Emily Wilding Davison, *see above*)

Bromley Baths
Mary Leigh   Second woman *(in audience)*
Chief Rowdy   Third woman *(in audience)*
Chief detective   Kosher Hunt
First woman *(in audience)*

*Audience participate by shouting 'Votes for Women' when Sylvia
Pankhurst waves her banner, and by joining in the singing of 'March
of Women'.*

*In the Bromley Baths scene, audience members (as rowdies) throw fish
heads and (as detectives) chase Sylvia Pankhurst, until the People's Army
– other members of the audience – help her escape.*

At the end the audience join in the final song.

ACT 1
Peaceful protests

SCENE 1
Prologue

Enter Prologue.

Prologue   Today women over 18 vote, and have a voice.
100 years ago they had no choice:
The vote was then exclusively male.
How votes were won for women is our tale.
In the background to our debate
Mrs Fawcett's suffragists were moderate.
But the suffragettes were militant and extreme
How this happened is our theme.

Exit Prologue.

SCENE 2
At the Pankhurst home

Enter Mrs Pankhurst, her daughters Sylvia, Christabel and Adela and son Harry.

Mrs Pankhurst   Mrs Pankhurst is my name
Votes for Women is my aim.
In 1903 I founded the WSPU –
This gave me an awful lot to do.
I had to organise WSPU headquarters
Relying on these faithful daughters.

Sylvia Pankhurst   I'm Sylvia, her devoted daughter.
We may disagree but I always support her.
The politician Keir Hardie is my lover
But he's married, so don't tell my mother.

      Audience, whenever I wave my banner
Shout 'Votes for Women' in a hearty manner.
Have a practice now, don't be shy
You'll grow in confidence by and by.

Sylvia waves banner.

Audience   Votes for Women! Votes for Women!

Mrs Pankhurst	Now meet the jewel in my family's crown One daughter who will never let me down.
Christabel Pankhurst	I'm Christabel. I've studied law And I'm the eldest child of four – A leader of the strongest and best: They carry out orders at my behest.
Sylvia	Christabel's elitist, I want a mass movement To bring working conditions' improvement.
Adela Pankhurst	I'm Adela and I'm a worry to Mother As I'm a financial drain like my brother.
Harry Pankhurst	And I'm Harry the surviving Pankhurst son I wish I was a girl so I'd have more fun.
Adela *(to Harry)*	I'm to study gardening, you'll work on a farm Mother thinks that will keep us safe from harm.
Harry	Oh, let's go to the park on this sunny day I feel I'm just in Mother's way.

Exeunt Adela and Harry.

Sylvia	Now let's begin our principled fight To convince the politicians that we're right.

Exit Sylvia.

SCENE 3
Outside Parliament

Mrs Pankhurst and Christabel remain on stage.

Mrs Pankhurst	It's been so hard to make our mark. We've had lots of rallies in Hyde Park With 3,000 standard bearers, many brass bands And bunting and banners in willing hands: Thousands of women – what a sight! All in suffrage colours (purple, green and white). But only Parliament can extend the vote So we need to enlist politicians of note.

Enter Keir Hardie.

Keir Hardie	I'm Keir Hardie, you can count on me At least until you fall out with the ILP. (We were the origin of New Labour Until Tony Blair lost all socialist flavour.)

Mrs Pankhurst	For your sincerity Mr Hardie we're grateful
	Most MPs are jolly hateful:
	They pledge support before they're elected,
	Then they renege on promises, like we expected.
	Listen to Winston Churchill, an ambitious man.

Enter Winston Churchill.

Winston Churchill	Of women's suffrage, I'm no fan!
	I'm sometimes Liberal but mostly Tory
	The Second World War will bring me glory.
	Whenever I make a political speech…

Sylvia interrupts waving banner from audience.

Sylvia and audience	Votes for Women!

Winston Churchill	That's what they screech.
	My public meetings get suffragette pickets
	So now entry will be names on tickets!

Mrs Pankhurst	We'll forge the tickets, you won't get away
	We'll make you listen to what we say.

Keir Hardie *(to Winston Churchill)*	
	Why won't you back our women's cause?

Winston Churchill	They won't henpeck me into changing laws.
	Come on, let's get back inside Parliament
	And leave these women in their ferment.

Exeunt Keir Hardie and Winston Churchill.

Mrs Pankhurst	We've tried to do things the Parliamentary way
	We march peacefully but we're charged with affray.

Enter Policeman.

Policeman	I've come to arrest Christabel and Mrs P
	You conspired to rush Parliament so follow me
	We'll take you to Bow Street court in the morning
	Where the magistrate's harsh, I give you warning.

Policeman takes Mrs Pankhurst and Christabel away.

SCENE 4
Bow Street Magistrates Court

Enter Magistrate and Lloyd George. Policeman brings in Christabel and Mrs Pankhurst.

Magistrate	I'm Magistrate Curtis Bennett who is on this case I'll ensure the government won't lose face.
Christabel	I'm a barrister so I'll take on our defence And do it with style and confidence. I'll subpoena Lloyd George to the witness box And make him sweat, the cunning old fox.
Lloyd George	I'm Lloyd George, the wily Welsh politician I'd like to keep my prominent position. How dare this suffragette cross-examine me!
Christabel	You witnessed our 'rush' – what did you see? And why won't you bring Votes for Women yet?
Lloyd George	Magistrate, you must gag the insufferable suffragette!
Mrs Pankhurst	That's no way to stop our agitation Remember women are half the nation!
Magistrate	Enough! You'll have three months in jail You can languish there and weep and wail.

Policeman takes Mrs Pankhurst and Christabel out. Enter Sylvia.

Sylvia	I'd better go to HQ and take the lead Until Mother and Christabel are freed.

Exit Sylvia, waving her banner to audience.

Audience	Votes for Women! Votes for Women!
Lloyd George *(to Magistrate)*	
	These suffragettes are out of hand, We hear 'Votes for Women' across the land It's spreading like foot and mouth disease They'll bring the country to its knees.
Magistrate	Even though I send them to Holloway prison They carry on with courage and vision.

Exeunt Lloyd George and Magistrate.

ACT 2
Increased militancy

SCENE 1
In Holloway prison

Enter Christabel and Mrs Pankhurst with Wardress who rattles bunch of keys.
Exit Wardress.

Christabel | Prison conditions are dreadful – is this lawful?
It's so dirty and cold, I feel awful.

Mrs Pankhurst | My dearest Christabel, you're very refined
It's hard for you to be so confined.

Christabel *(aside)* | I won't do this again, no chance!
When I'm released, I'll flee to France.

Mrs Pankhurst | I'm sure I'll be back many times.

Enter Adela and suffragette prisoners.

Mrs Pankhurst | Now hear our family and friends report their crimes.
You start, Adela…

Adela | ….In Manchester I got arrested for leading a crowd
To speak to Winston Churchill – it wasn't allowed.

Mary Goulden *(to Mrs Pankhurst)*
I'm your sister Mary up from Brighton,
Though gentle and frail, I'll always fight on.
I join the marches and get treated rough
Landing in jail, though I'm not very tough.

Jenny Baines | I'm Jenny Baines done for unlawful assembly
I've got five kids so I'm feeling trembly.
I was only speaking to an open air meeting
Now I worry what my kids are eating.

Muriel Matters | I'm Muriel Matters. In Parliament I made a speech
From the Ladies Gallery so I could reach
The MPs, who laugh at our female suffrage bill.
They couldn't move me as I was chained to a grille.
I got a month in Holloway
But I'd do it again any day.

When I'm released I'll hire a balloon
To sail over Parliament, to sing our tune
And call 'Votes for Women' so they won't ignore me
When I see the House of Commons before me.

Anonymous
stone thrower | I'm a stone thrower and I'm anonymous
With increased militancy I'm synonymous.
We hid in offices in Parliament Square
The police had no idea we were there.

When they looked the other way
We crept out in the light of day
And broke government windows with our stones
So now we're here and cold to the bones.

Mrs Pethick Lawrence	I'm Mrs Pethick Lawrence, good at raising cash Being WSPU treasurer is rather rash As the cost of windows smashed by suffragettes Is added to my husband's debts.

Poor Frederick, he was brought to trial
And was sent to prison which was vile.
The bailiffs seized our goods and chattels
As revenge for my suffragette battles.

Emily Wilding Davison   Emily Wilding Davison is my name
Setting fire to pillar boxes is my game.
I pour paraffin on pieces of linen
Find pillar boxes and put them in 'em.
I toss in a match for a lovely blaze
I try to do that every couple of days.

Mary Richardson I'm Mary Richardson who slashed
The Rokeby Aphrodite. It was badly gashed
To the shock and awe of Velasquez lovers.
I got six months so I couldn't do others.

Sylvia *(waving paper and pencils)*
The Rokeby nude was a man-made object
My art makes women the respected subject.
I brought pencils and paper to prison with me
So I can draw the inmates' misery.
I'll invite Keir Hardie to inspect conditions
So he'll press the government with our petitions.

Enter Keir Hardie.

Keir Hardie   These prison cells are grim and squalid
The evidence is pretty solid:
These women are being treated unjustly
I'll insist they're freed; they simply must be.

Exit Keir Hardie.

Ethel Smyth
(waves toothbrush) I'm Ethel Smyth, composer of music
For Mrs P I am quite lovesick.
Now women are roused, we refuse to conform
In 1911 we dared spoil the census form.

'I refuse to be counted' each one of us wrote
'Because I'm a woman without a vote'.
To avoid it, we made all-night entertainment
Concerts and gatherings for women of refinement.

Mrs Pankhurst   I remember you and I stayed up late:
At the Aldwych rink we went for a skate
Then by the Thames we watched the dawn.
We'd outwitted the censors, they have our scorn.

Ethel Smyth   There were too many of us for prosecution
The state was defeated by our resolution.
Watch my toothbrush – don't think 'poor us'
Instead I'll conduct a rousing chorus.

Sylvia   It's the March of Women, we know the song
Come along audience, sing along.

Ethel Smyth conducts with toothbrush cast singing 'March of Women', audience join in.

All   Shout, shout up with your song
Cry with the wind for the dawn is breaking
March, march, swing you along
Wide blows our banner and hope is waking.

Sylvia waves 'Votes for Women' banner.

Audience   Votes for Women! Votes for Women!

Exeunt all except Mrs Pankhurst.

Mrs Pankhurst   The promises of politicians are a dead letter
Things will get worse before they get better.
I'm on hunger strike so I can get out quicker
They think I'll relent – but I'm a sticker.
They force-feed hunger strikers with tubes and clamps
To inflict violence, trauma and cramps.

Wardress enters with doctor.

Wardress   The doctor's here to make you eat
Milk down a nasal tube – what a treat!

Mrs Pankhurst *(waving chamberpot)*
You Satan hounds of hell, withdraw
Or this chamberpot on your heads I'll pour!

Wardress exits swiftly with doctor, chased by Mrs Pankhurst.

SCENE 2
In Sylvia's sitting room

Enter Sylvia.

Sylvia   Mother evaded force-feeding on that occasion
But many suffered oft-times that brutal invasion.
This torture of suffragettes caused consternation
And led to an outcry across the nation.
But let us leave this prison gloom
And go over to my sitting room
Where my siblings have come to visit.
That should be good news but let's see, is it?

Enter Harry.

Harry   Oh Sylvia, I need you to be my nurse
My infantile paralysis is getting worse.

Sylvia   I'll care for you my dear young brother
But how an earth shall we tell Mother?

Harry   I'm dying, my life is at an end
I leave you sadly, dear sister and friend.
You'll go on to fame and renown,
But I'll die, having let the family down.

Harry dies. Enter Adela.

Adela   Harry's dead and mother says I'm a failure
So I'm going off to live in Australia
Christabel's in Paris – say goodbye from me
At least in Melbourne I'll feel free.

Exit Adela.

Sylvia   I feel distraught and so bereft
There's only me and Mother left.

Enter Mrs Pankhurst.

Mrs Pankhurst   And my sister Mary died in the aftermath
Of one of our demos. What a bloodbath!
A double family tragedy – my sister and Harry –
It's a heavy burden for me to carry.

I grieve for both – a sad bereavement,
But I must soldier on. It's our achievement
That everywhere both high and low
Women keenly want to know

Why they are still denied their right
To equal suffrage. I'll lead their fight!

Exeunt all.

SCENE 3
At the home of Edith Heal

Enter Edith Heal with WSPU banner and Janie Terrero.

Edith Heal I'm Edith Heal and I live in Pinner
      I want Votes for Women to be a winner.
      I'm secretary of the local WSPU
      Though my husband Ambrose hasn't a clue.
      I host the committee while he's at the theatre
      He thinks I'm such a gentle creature.

Janie Terrero I'm Janie Terrero, thrown into trouble and strife
      I relish the suffragette's exciting life.
      I threw a stone and went to jail
      Being an artist gives me courage never to fail.

Edith Heal I hear Mrs P has split with Mrs Pethick Lawrence
      Because of the latter's deep abhorrence
      For militant tactics – I know it's like treason
      But the MPs won't listen to reason.

Janie Terrero Lloyd George said we're a fountain of mendacity.

Enter Lloyd George.

Lloyd George You're all a fountain of mendacity!

Janie Terrero You're just annoyed by our tenacity
      Because a suffragette bombed your house.
      You're no more than a political mouse.

Offstage Emily Wilding Davison calls out 'I did it'.

Lloyd George Whoever did it was a female vandal
      Just another suffragette scandal!

Exit Lloyd George.

Janie Terrero And Churchill says now he's one of our friends
      But coming from him, that's just pretence.

Edith Heal Have you heard what happened on Derby Day?
      Emily Wilding Davison got in the way
      Of the King's horse Anmer and was knocked flat
      Just as she raised our banner – fancy that!

The event can be enacted in dumbshow.

Derby horses appear, led by King's horse Anmer.
Emily Wilding Davison enters with banner (which she takes from Edith Heal).

Janie Terrero *(narrates dumbshow)*
        Imagine the scene at that race course
        First, the proud and galloping horse…

Horse gallops.

Janie Terrero   Then Emily trying to grab at the bridle…
        It must have been madness or else suicidal.

Emily Wilding Davison runs in front of and collides with horse.

Janie Terrero   She was trampled down upon the ground
        Then news spread like wildfire all around.
        Alas! The breath of life will depart her!
        Now she'll become our most famous martyr.

Horse runs off. Emily Wilding Davison lies dead. End of dumbshow.

Edith Heal   Now she's dead, we must mourn her loss
        By accompanying her coffin to King's Cross.

Janie Terrero   Yes, we'll honour her in the suffragette manner
(picks up banner) I'll bring along our WSPU banner.

Exeunt Edith Heal and Janie Terrero.

SCENE 4
In Christabel's home in Paris

Enter Sylvia and Christabel.

Sylvia   I always said Christabel was elitist
        I'm summoned to Paris but I won't be defeatist.
        I'll stir up the East End from Bow Road
        To help working women with their heavy load.

Christabel   Why do you want to organise the weakest?
        The WSPU leads the strongest, not the meekest.
        Our troops will march in a dutiful throng
        Following my instructions, singing my song.

Sylvia   But our East End branch takes a broader view
        We empower the poor, that's what we do
        In the East End we'll have the People's Army.

Christabel   Stop! They're riff-raff – and you're barmy!

Sylvia   My resolve couldn't be stiffer
        So Christabel, we'll just have to differ.

I'll found the East London Suffrage Federation
To encourage mass political agitation.

Exit Christabel.

SCENE 5
In the East End Bromley Road baths

Sylvia remains on stage. Enter Mary Leigh.

Sylvia   Mary Leigh, things are even worse, that's a fact
Now they've passed the Cat and Mouse Act
By which they release women on hunger strike
Then re-arrest them whenever they like.

Mary Leigh   Tonight at Bromley Baths there's a meeting
The police will try to give us a beating.
We've had to sneak you into the hall
So your speech can inspire us all.

Sylvia   In this dire political situation
We need more audience participation.
The 'cats' think they've got me in a trap
But you can help this 'mouse' avoid the rap.

Mary Leigh *(to audience)* Some of you can be beastly detectives,
And others rowdies shouting invectives
While the People's Army are the rest.
Your courage and loyalty will be put to the test.

Chief Rowdy   Shout and swear, send fish-heads flying
We'll soon have these women crying.

Rowdies throw fish-heads and shout 'Trollops! Hussies!'

Sylvia   Now sisters throw the fish-heads back,
Shout 'Votes for Women', don't take their flack!

Audience throw fish-heads back.

Audience   Votes for Women! Votes for Women!

Detectives rush in behind Sylvia. Chief detective brandishing a rolled-up newspaper truncheon fights Mary Leigh.

Mary Leigh *(brandishing umbrella)*
I'll thump you with my stout umbrella
Take that, you 'cat', obnoxious fellow.

Chief detective There's Sylvia Pankhurst, she's our quarry
We'll grab her and then she'll be sorry.

Audience help Sylvia escape.

First woman *(in audience)*	Jump, Sylvia, jump! Jump down here We'll get you away, never fear.
Second woman *(in audience)*	Sylvia, take my hat for your disguise We'll hide you from the policemen's eyes.
Third woman *(in audience)*	Sylvia, now swap that hat with mine Then nip out the back into the lane.
Kosher Hunt *(to Sylvia)* *(offers muffler)*	I'm Kosher Hunt, I'm a prize fighter – Of this wrong, I'll be the righter. Hide under my muffler and we'll escape And fade into the East End's landscape.

Sylvia hides under Kosher Hunt's muffler.

Sylvia	I'm glad to say I got away And lived to campaign another day.

Sylvia and Kosher Hunt escape. Exeunt all.

ACT 3
War and aftermath

SCENE 1
1914 Mrs Pankhurst's home

Enter Mrs Pankhurst and Sylvia.

Mrs Pankhurst	It's 1914, World War's broken out We must support the government, I've no doubt In wartime we must suspend our campaign And wait till we have peace again.
Sylvia	Mother that's a great betrayal You've finally given in to the Male! Why is Votes for Women still a crime? Will we ever get the vote in our lifetime?
Mrs Pankhurst	I'm only being realistic.
Sylvia	Well, I'd rather be idealistic. We differed, and the war led to limited reform But I went on fighting for a new dawn.

SCENE 2
Outside Parliament

Enter Sylvia.

Sylvia	It's 1928, and after years of waving my banner We got Votes for Women in a legitimate manner. In the War militant suffragettes went to ground But the moderate suffragists stuck around. So Millicent Fawcett shared some of the glory Though she gets only two mentions in this story.

Enter Lloyd George.

Lloyd George	In 1918 we extended the vote To women householders over 30, take note We delayed female suffrage till 1928.
Mrs Pankhurst	I just lived to see it, it was almost too late.
Sylvia	So it was Lloyd George, first foe, then friend Who brought Votes for Women in the end. I'm sad to say Keir Hardie is dead And I've become a mother unwed. I run a tea-room with my anarchist man. Later I'll fight for Ethiopia as much as I can.

Enter Christabel.

Christabel	Don't forget me, I had a leading role Even from Paris, I helped achieve our goal. After Votes for Women I want Chastity for Men It's nice to have a cause again.
Mrs Pankhurst	To me, sibling rivalry's a mystery As we've all three earned our niche in history.
Sylvia	Remember the women who suffered force-feeding Which left them shocked, badly bruised and bleeding But they held to the cause with courage unspoken And endured this torture with spirit unbroken.
Mrs Pankhurst	That torture was legal but still it was wrong So let's all honour suffragettes in our final song.
Sylvia	If you think you can't sing, just sing extra loudly We like it if you sing out of tune or rowdily Then we'll step back into history and say goodbye Just remember you women, be brave, ORGANISE.

Audience and cast sing suffragette song (to tune of 'Men of Harlech').

All
Women who in every station
Fain would serve your generation
In the councils of the nation
And enfranchised be.

Rise as from a dream awaking
Ease and slothfulness forsaking
In your hearts fresh courage taking
Strike for liberty!

THE END

WAR AND PEACE:
MADAME TOLSTOY'S VERSION
Based on the novel by Leo Tolstoy

CAST

Madame Tolstoy, wife of author
Count Leo Tolstoy, author and sage
Alexandra, daughter of author
Pierre Bezuhoff, illegitimate son of a rich aristocrat
Prince Andrei Bolkonsky, son of a general
Anna Pavlovna, a society hostess
Helene Kuragin, a beauty
Count Rostov
Countess Rostova
Nikolai Rostov, their son
Natasha Rostova, their daughter
Sonia, cousin to Natasha and Nikolai
Boris Dubretski, a careerist
Napoleon
Russian Generals 1, 2 and 3
French Generals 1 and 2
Tsar Alexander
Platon Karyatev, a common soldier

The audience makes the sounds of battle (on Napoleon's cue):

> Boom boom, roar roar
> Listen to the sounds of war.

They can throw cannon balls at the Battle of Borodino and are the flames of Moscow burning. They may waltz as part of the dancing scenes.

The action takes place in Petersburg, Moscow and on the battlefields of Austerlitz and Borodino. It begins at Tolstoy's home at Yasnaya Polanya and ends at Astapovo railway station in Russia.

SCENE 1
Tolstoy's house at Yasnaya Polanya then in a Petersburg salon

Enter Madame Tolstoy.

Madame Tolstoy I'm the much maligned Madame Tolstoy
          I'm married to Leo, my pride and joy.

I copied War & Peace seven times by hand
So I know it as well as my husband.
I bore him thirteen children and I'm the breadwinner
Though Leo calls me a grievous sinnner.
I try to do whatever he wishes
But lately he's got so suspicious.

Here comes Leo with my difficult daughter
I'll exit while you meet the author.

Exit Madame Tolstoy. Enter Tolstoy and daughter Alexandra.

Tolstoy   I am the famous Count Leo Tolstoy
I've written works time can't destroy.

I'm eighty-three and overwhelmed with guilt
As I've deceived my wife up to the hilt
Because I secretly cut her out of my will
And yet my dear wife loves me still.
I'll leave my estate at Yasnaya Polanya
And go abroad with my daughter Alexandra.

Alexandra I'm Papa's favourite, I don't want a quiet life
So I'm beastly to Mama and cause endless strife.
Papa, is it wise to leave when you're weak and old
I fear you'll catch your death of cold.

Tolstoy   Accept it: I'll be gone tomorrow
Yes, I leave my fictional characters with sorrow.
For each character that I gave a part
Is but a fragment of my heart.

Alexandra Natasha Rostova is the star
Some people say she's based on Ma.

Tolstoy   Her brother Nikolai's vainglory
Is just a projection of my own story.
And Pierre Bezuhoff is just like me –
His suffering soul yearns to be free.

Enter Pierre.

Pierre   I'm Count Bezuhoff's son Pierre,
I'm back from abroad but I'm racked with care.

Tolstoy   Prince Andrei is a noble man of action
Who has no truck with frippery or faction.

Enter Prince Andrei.

Andrei	My father's a general and free thinker He expects me to follow him hook, line and sinker. In devotion my religious sister kneels – Frankly, I can't say it appeals. But we can't have so many people in this play So we'll have to save her for another day.
Tolstoy	Now let's see the men at a Petersburg soirée Then at the Rostovs on Natasha's name day. It's all politics, gossip and matchmaking. But both love and war will leave them quaking And each will seek greatness in their own manner. Now Alexandra, let's flee from Yasnaya Polanya Because now my life has one final goal To contemplate my immortal soul.
Alexandra	I'll go with you to the railway station Let them carry on with the narration.

Exeunt Tolstoy and Alexandra. Enter Anna Pavlovna and Helene.

Anna Pavlovna	I'm Anna Pavlovna, queen of parties Here's Helene, one of my lovely smarties. These soirées are gatherings of the élite Let's see who's come to gossip and meet.
Helene	I'm Helene, a stunning head turner, In search of an eligible high earner.
Pierre	These parties put me in a bind No-one here has an open mind. What the French could teach the Russian – Surely that's worth some discussion.
Anna Pavlovna	You'll never fit into Russian society Until you embrace convention and sobriety. I'm sure revolution's a passing craze. Now tell me about your father's malaise.
Pierre	My father's in Moscow at death's brink While here in Petersburg I carouse and drink.
Andrei	Pierre, you must give up wine, women and song. Don't you know that debauchery is wrong?
Pierre	Andrei you're right – you're my hero I'm so weak, my will power is zero! Perhaps the way to end my cares Is to immerse myself in current affairs.

Andrei	The French have given Europe a shake-up Now it's Russia's turn to wake up.
Pierre	Napoleon's a man of vision and destiny Perhaps his ideals will bring out the best in me.

Exeunt Pierre and Andrei.

Anna Pavlovna	Those two won't play by society's rules Typical men – they're only fools.
Helene	I've got my eye on Pierre as a possible beau In case he inherits money, you never know.
Anna Pavlovna	We women learn to survive as we must. Men are fools with politics, cash and lust.

Exeunt Anna Pavlovna and Helene.

Madame Tolstoy *(speaking from audience)*
> Bring on all the Rostov clan
> They're based on my childhood, so I'm a fan.

SCENE 2

The Rostov house

Enter Count Rostov, Countess Rostova, Nikolai, Natasha and Sonia.

Count Rostov	War can't cast its shadow here We can party with good cheer And do things in just the same way To celebrate Natasha's name day.
Countess Rostova	We'll invite all our family and friends Then sit back and see who attends. My darling girls want a lover with dash But I need to find them one with cash.
Nikolai Rostov	I'm Nikolai Rostov, with an honest heart, War's exciting: I can't wait for it to start. I want to join the Hussars and get a commission – Military glory is my ambition.
Natasha	I'm Natasha, I love to dance and sing I'm happy today with everything. I'm never shy and never meek And fall in love about once a week.

Enter Boris.

Boris	I'm Boris, a jumped-up careerist Natasha loves me; I'm her dearest.

Natasha	You're the one on whom I dote
	Boris, you certainly got my vote.
Sonia	I'm Sonia, the penniless cousin
	You know, working thirteen to the dozen.
Nikolai	I've known Sonia all my life.
	One day, my sweet, you'll be my wife.
Sonia	I love Nikolai – I'm besotted
	And wound up till my heart is knotted.
	But my love will never be permitted,
	My heart is sad but my teeth are gritted.
Natasha	True love will always find a way
	You'll come through, come what may.

Enter Pierre.

Count Rostov	Here's Pierre, one of our oldest friends,
	I hear you burn the candle at both ends.
Pierre	Yes, my life seems to have gone to the dogs
	Since my father popped his clogs.
	Petersburg began to pall
	So I thought I'd drop in at your family ball.
Count Rostov	Let's get the dancers in a line
	It's an easy waltz so you'll be fine.
	Natasha and Boris dance together
	Nikolai take Sonia, she's light as a feather,
	My dear wife can dance with me
	So start the music with a sweet melody.

Music plays. Count and Countess, Natasha and Boris, Nikolai and Sonia dance.

Natasha (*to Pierre*)	Even though they say you're a misfit
	I bet you can dance a little bit.

They dance.

Pierre	How quaint and beguiling
	For a moment she had me smiling.

Music stops.

Nikolai	Mother, I'm off to join the army
	I'm determined – war won't harm me.
Sonia	This is the very news I feared
	He's not old enough to have a beard.

Countess	Husband, tell him war's not fun Don't let folly take my darling son.
Count Rostov	Dearest, if he stayed it would bring shame Upon the Rostov family name.
Countess	I despair of men and their foolish dreams Now let's move to one of our warlike scenes. Audience, prepare for your cue Don't forget, we rely on you.

Exeunt all.

SCENE 3

The battlefield at Austerlitz

Enter Nikolai (wearing a military hat).

Nikolai	In the battle I'll be dashing and brave And send the Frenchman to his grave. First meet the generals who'll decide our fates And listen to their wise debates Aided by Boris – who to our surprise Has enjoyed a meteoric rise.

Enter Russian Generals 1, 2 and 3 and Boris.

Boris	I'm Boris, the jumped-up careerist – See a powerful man, and I'll be nearest. Now with my manipulative skill I'd say we're in for a capital kill.

Exit Boris.

Russian General 1 *(with flag)* I'm the one who can win this battle.

Russian General 2	Ignore him and his foolish prattle. My tactics are shock and awe That's the way to win this war.
Russian General 3	Listen: I'll make no bones War is all about the known unknowns.

Enter Napoleon and French General 1 and 2.

Napoleon	My greatness will never cease. My warlike ways have one goal: peace. Today we'll cut the enemy to bits On this field called Austerlitz. I say attack – with my superior tactics The Russians will fall down like matchsticks.

> Audience, go bang and roar
> Give voice to the sounds of war.

Audience   Boom boom, roar roar
                   Listen to the sounds of war.

French Generals and Russian Generals begin to fight. Enter Nikolai.

Nikolai *(charging in)* Here I come, young and naïve.

Nikolai briefly fights French General 1 and retreats.

Nikolai   Oh no, it's too rough – I think I'll leave.

Nikolai runs off and exits.

French   Let's kick the Russian while he's down
General 1   Let's treat him like Gordon Brown.

French   He deserves our wild attacks
General 2   For his mistake on income tax.

French   We'll slay the enemy with sabres
General 1   It'll be a bigger defeat than New Labour's.

Russian   This battle is a free for all –
General 1   Time now for strategic withdrawal.

Drops flag. Exeunt Russian Generals. Enter Andrei.

Andrei   All our troops are retreating
               I can't believe we're taking a beating.
               As I see our resistance sag
               I'll charge forward and save our flag.

Andrei grabs flag, fights French General 1, is wounded and falls.

Andrei   As I lie wounded on the ground
               I've come to realise something profound:
               The sky, the infinite heavens... there is no more
               Why did I never think of that before?

Napoleon   Now I'll tour the battlefield
               Where French victory was sealed.
               The price in bloodshed is appalling.
(indicates Andrei) At least we'll save that man who's fallen.

French Generals 1 and 2 pick up Andrei and carry him away.

Napoleon   Now that France has carried the day
               Let's hear what the Russians say.

Enter Nikolai and Russian Generals 1, 2 and 3, upstage.

Nikolai	I charged forward but then I stumbled Instead of being brave, I was truly humbled. I must admit that war is scary Next time I'll be much more wary.
Russian General 1	I say we achieved our deepest wish And won glory from a skirmish.
Russian General 2	We fought like Russians of great renown What a pity the Austrians let us down.
Russian General 3	On the whole I didn't think much of it I only care to make a private profit.

Exeunt Nikolai and Russian Generals 1, 2 and 3.

Napoleon	I won this battle – so I'm off home you see To rule Europe by diplomacy. I'll let Russia enjoy some years of peace And then I'll bring her to her knees.

SCENE 4

Petersburg

Enter Anna Pavlovna, Helene and Pierre.

Anna Pavlovna	Count Bezuhoff, I hear your spending Is carrying on and never ending.
Helene	You're a well-known man about the town Don't you want a wife, to settle down?
Pierre	I can't resist your worldly charms I think I'd like you in my arms.
Helene	I know just how a man feels Held in the grip of lofty ideals.
(aside)	He's so easily guided But soon he'll be derided.
(to Pierre)	Pierre, let's drink from the wedding cup
(aside)	Just don't ask for a pre-nup.
Pierre	I set myself high ideals And now I know how true love feels.
Anna Pavlovna	Our campaign has won a victory! Yes, it seems a fine trick to me.

Exeunt Anna Pavlovna and Helene.

SCENE 5
Petersburg

Pierre remains on stage. Enter Andrei.

Andrei
: After the battle of Austerlitz
Military life lost its glitz.

Pierre
: I was foolish and blinded by lust
Alas my marriage has turned to dust.

Andrei
: To serve the Tsar was my ambition
Following in the autocratic tradition.
I'm fed up with polite society
There's no place for a man like me.

Pierre
: I wanted to live for the happiness of others
And believed that underneath we're all brothers.
But my head and my heart are in such a muddle
Do I seek honour or just a cuddle?
I'd like to be idealistic
But in politics is that realistic?

Andrei
: Men are weak: God will judge.
That's my view – I won't budge.

Pierre
: I've got the message loud and clear
To change my attitude of doubt and fear
Though its hard because I'm set in my ways
Of wandering around in a puzzled daze.

Exeunt Pierre and Andrei.

Madame Tolstoy *(from audience)* Bring on the Rostovs for some sanity
They've got both good looks and humanity.

SCENE 6
The Rostov house

Enter Nikolai, Natasha and Sonia.

Enter Count and Countess Rostov, who remain upstage.

Nikolai
: Natasha, how's your paramour?
Don't you love him anymore?

Natasha
: Well, Boris had his pluses –
Just a pity about the bendy buses.

Sonia
: I was so worried about Nikolai
I thought he'd gone away to die.

Nikolai	Sonia, my childhood sweetheart I hate it when we're apart. But as a loyal military gent I must spend time with the regiment.
Natasha	I'm looking forward to this society ball I might meet someone handsome and tall.

Enter Pierre and Andrei.

Natasha	But here's Pierre, our family friend With a war hero on the mend.
Pierre	This is Andrei, the Bolkonsky heir You'll find him honourable and fair.
Andrei	Please don't look askance If I ask you for a dance.

The dance begins. Nikolai and Sonia, Natasha and Andrei dance.

The dance ends. Andrei returns to Pierre. Natasha returns to Nikolai and Sonia.

Andrei *(to Pierre)*	She's as fresh as the morning dew My careworn heart loves anew.
Natasha	Thank goodness I'm alive today This man takes my breath away.
Andrei	To cut a very long story short I suddenly find I'm the marrying sort. Now I've glimpsed the promised land I must ask your father for your hand.
Count Rostov	Prince, I'm quite at your disposal Dare we hope for a betrothal?
Andrei	Unfortunately I'm due to go away So we'll wed in a year and a day.
Natasha	To spend such a very long time apart May break my lovelorn tender heart. Who knows what a year may bring, I may even have a little fling.
Andrei	Alas I must give second place to my heart Duty impels me to play a soldier's part.

Exit Andrei.

Natasha	How can my fate be so hard? To find true love and then be barred.

Exit Natasha.

Countess Rostova	If she lands him in her net We could escape from our mounting debt. But before they can be united I fear there's the French to be fighted. Soon, audience, once more We'll hear the raucous sounds of war.

Exeunt all.

SCENE 7
War – the battlefield at Borodino

Enter Alexander, Tsar of all Russia and Boris.

Tsar Alexander	I'm Tsar Alexander Romanoff. Go on, cheer, admit you like a toff.
Boris	I'm Boris, the jumped-up careerist fool It doesn't matter as I went to a good school.

Exit Boris. Enter Nikolai and Russian Generals 1, 2 and 3.

Nikolai	The Tsar makes war a religious duty Transcending all the gore and booty.
Tsar	Generals of the Imperial Army Make sure that Napoleon cannot harm me.
Russian General 1	The motherland is very devout We'll unite to keep Napoleon out.
Russian General 2	We'll uphold the Orthodox faith And fight to keep our homeland safe.
Russian General 3	Get ready for the battle of Borodino It'll be the biggest you've ever seen-o.
Nikolai	This is what I'm waiting for Let's enjoy the thrill of war. My heart feels quite unsteady As all around the troops get ready.

Enter Prince Andrei and Pierre.

Pierre	I must say, I'm very surprised It all seems so badly organised.
Andrei	I fear our leaders deserve contempt Each one of them – there's none exempt. All their talk of bravery Amounts to nothing but knavery.

Enter Napoleon and French Generals 1 and 2.

Pierre	I say, here is our fearsome foe Perhaps it's time for me to go.
Napoleon	I like power and I like danger I'm an inveterate regime-changer. What we need is one world realm With myself, Napoleon, at the helm. Audience, clear the decks Let me hear your sound effects. Then throw a cannon ball Watch both French and Russian fall.
Audience	Boom boom, roar roar Let us hear the sound of war.

Audience throw cannon balls at all the generals and Andrei. Pierre wanders around but is not hit.

Pierre	This battle has a great human cost I do declare I am quite lost. But I mustn't stand here musing When all around me is confusing.

Exit Pierre. Audience continue to throw cannon balls.

Andrei	For Russia this battle's a mighty one.

Andrei is hit by a cannon ball.

Andrei	Oh no, I've got a blighty one. So much for ideals and honour Soon I fear I'll be a goner.

Exit Andrei, wounded.

Russian General 1	It's hard to know who's won the battle When men are slaughtered just like cattle.

Exeunt Russian Generals 1, 2 and 3.

Napoleon	I'll cut the Tsar down to size When I seize Moscow as my prize.

Exeunt Napoleon and French Generals 1 and 2.

Madame Tolstoy *(from audience)*
      The horror of war could send us past caring
      But let's see how the Rostovs are faring.

SCENE 8
Moscow – the Rostovs

Enter Nikolai, Sonia, Count and Countess Rostov.

Nikolai	War has put me through the mangle
	Now I see life from a different angle.
	Sonia's nice but has no bridal gift
	I can't marry her, so she'll be miffed.

Exit Nikolai.

Sonia	Nikolai's back but he's not like of old
	It's as I feared – his love's gone cold.
Natasha	I haven't had a letter from Andrei
	I only hope I'll see him one day.
Countess Rostova	The French are coming, let's get cracking
	I need all your help to do the packing.
	Pile up our furniture and our plate
	Let's take them off to our country estate.

Exeunt Sonia and Natasha.

Count Rostov	My sweet, as we load our baggage train
	Let's make room for the halt and lame.
Countess Rostova	This is another of your foolish schemes!
	You men always live beyond our means.
Count Rostov	Countess, don't let our hearts be hard
	There's wounded soldiers in the yard.

Enter Nikolai.

Nikolai	Andrei is among the wounded
	I'm told he will soon be dead.
Countess Rostova	Don't let Natasha know
	It would deal her a terrible blow.

Exeunt Count Rostov and Countess Rostova. Enter Natasha.

Natasha	Sonia told me Andrei is here
	Wounded, and his time is drawing near.
	I'll nurse him while he has living breath
	I'll face up to his impending death.

Enter Prince Andrei.

Andrei	We fell in love at society dances
	Alas, life has changed our circumstances.

Natasha	Andrei, you are the love of my life Without the war I'd have been your wife.
Andrei	Thank God! My heart is deeply blessed Before I go to eternal rest. Natasha your spirit was rather wild But as I die, we are reconciled.

Andrei dies. Exit Natasha.

SCENE 9

The retreat from Moscow

Enter Napoleon.

Napoleon	I could have taken a thousand Kremlins If it wasn't for my supply-line gremlins. Truth is, I've come as far as I can Since I invaded without an exit plan. Audience, set Moscow ablaze To show Russians the error of their ways.

Audience wave their flames.

Napoleon	Now with no more reference to Iraq I'll take prisoners and march my army back.

Exit Napoleon. Enter Pierre guarded by French General 1.

Pierre	Cruel fate! You've brought me down low Captured by the French, taken from Moscow. Forced to march on the long retreat I must confess I feel dead beat.

Enter Karyatev guarded by French General 2.

Pierre	Then I met this humble fellow Whose good soul can make me mellow.
Karyatev	I'm the peasant Platon Karyatev I arrive quite late in this narrative. Note that everything I say Distils the meaning of this play.
Pierre	The French are deep-dyed blackguards Without mercy they shoot laggards.
Karyatev	You expect a bed of lovely roses But life is as the Lord disposes. Expectations just deceive us Accept sad events will always grieve us.

(eats)	It simply doesn't do to brood So let's enjoy these scraps of food.
Pierre	To hear this poor fellow in such harmony Brings about a kind of calm in me.
Karyatev	God's grace is in all we do Each morning we wake anew.
Pierre	As I despair at Moscow's burning Let me confess my heart's true yearning. In this extremity I see clearly Truth is, I love Natasha dearly.
Karyatev	Sir, I congratulate you on your happiness It'll take our mind off all this crappiness. But now I can't walk any more So let the French enforce the law.

Karyatev sits down.

French General 1	I'm sorry to shoot you but I must. Another Russian bites the dust.

Shoots Karyatev who dies.

French General 2	Audience, dry your eyes No use crying over his demise.

Exeunt French Generals 1 and 2.

Madame Tolstoy *(from audience)*	
	Audience, are you still following the story? We never said it would be hunky-dory Let's visit the Rostovs for the final time For Pierre to press his suit in rhyme.

SCENE 10
The Rostov house

Enter Pierre.

Pierre	The French would have shot me too But they sensed my blood was blue. As society got back to normal I've come to visit – not too formal. I'm here at the Rostov house Determined to be braver than a mouse.

Enter Natasha.

Natasha	Pierre, you've always been a friend
	I was reconciled with Andrei at the end.
	Now I am at peace with myself
	Happy to be left on the shelf.
Pierre	The book is long, but I'll be snappy
	My life's goal is to make you happy.
Natasha	I now depart this play and scoot off
	To begin life as Mrs Pierre Bezuhoff.
	I give flirtation and dancing a miss
	And settle for domestic bliss.

Enter Sonia.

Natasha	For my nanny I'll take Sonia
	What a shame my brother didn't wan'ya.
Sonia	Unrequited love and rejection was tough
	But I'll care for your kids – for me that's enough.
Pierre	I think of Karyatev who kept his humanity
	In the midst of war's insanity.
	As I take Natasha to be my wife
	Will she help calm my inner strife?
	Or will I take headstrong risks
	And join up with the Decembrists?
	Who as historians report
	Challenged the Tsar but then got caught.
	A century on, has Tolstoy, my begetter
	In his flight fared any better?
	Let's take you to Astapovo, a station backwater
	For some last words from Tolstoy's daughter.

Exeunt Pierre, Sonia and Natasha.

SCENE 11
Astopovo station

Enter Tolstoy and Alexandra.

Alexandra	'War and Peace' ends with Pierre still alive
	His new wife loves him, his children thrive.
	But my father's stuck here, old and ailing
	The train is late and his body's failing.
(aside)	I haven't told him the press and Mamma's outside
	She's still the one person I can't abide.

Tolstoy   I'm a hero of the Russian nation
        Slowly dying at this railway station.
        I left home in such a hurry
        How is my wife? Tell her I'm sorry...

Tolstoy dies.

Alexandra   I'll just inform the media pack...

Exit Alexandra. Enter Madame Tolstoy.

Madame Tolstoy   ...While I steal in behind her back.
        When he left, I threw myself in the pond
        Because he betrayed our marital bond,
        We left it too late to make amends
        Why did he not trust me instead of his 'friends'?
        I loved him for nearly fifty years
        Though often plagued by doubts and fears.
        But now let's leave affairs of the heart
        It's time for cakes and delicious tart.

THE END

XMAS MUMMERS PLAY

Adapted from variations of the traditional play, performed around England

CAST

Sweep

Father Christmas

King of Egypt

Prince George

Turkish Knight

Doctor Slack

Fair Sabra

Beelzebub

Humpty Jack

Dragon

Enter Sweep with a broom.

Sweep
I am the Sweep with my busy broom.
Let's clear a space. Make room, make room.
We are mummers, here to perform a play.
So step in, Father Christmas and have your say.

Enter Father Christmas.

Father Christmas
I'm Father Christmas, believe it or not.
Let's hope Father Christmas will never be forgot.
As days grow short and nights grow dark
Prince George must battle with the Turk.
George is Day, the Turkish Knight is Night (Get it?)
The Solstice is the moment for their ritual fight.
But first, step in, the King of Egypt, take a seat
Or if no chair is found, stay on your feet.

Enter the King of Egypt.

King of Egypt
I am the mighty King of Egypt so beware.
I'm in charge here, so you all take care.
Prince George is my prospective son-in-law.
He's good at killing monsters by the score.

Enter Prince George.

George
I am Prince George, a noble champion bold.
I killed the Dragon and won the crown of gold.
I fought him and I gave him no quarter
Now I claim Fair Sabra, the King of Egypt's daughter.

Enter Turkish Knight.

Turkish Knight
Not so fast with your nuptial plan
First you have to fight this man.

I am the Turkish Knight from sunny Afrikee
I challenge your claim to sovereign-ity!

Turkish Knight fights Prince George and Turkish Knight is killed.

George   Alas, alack for I have killed my brother.
Alas, alack, I will never get another.

King of Egypt   The Turkish Knight has now been slain.
Who can bring him to life again?

Father Christmas   We need to call on Doctor Slack
Let's hope he's good and not a quack.

Enter Doctor.

Doctor   You need me? Slack my nature, slack by name
Peddling potions is my game.

King of Egypt   Are you NHS or do you charge a fee?
Or are you paid by a drugs company?

Doctor   My finances are confidential
Please just trust my credentials.
(to Turkish Knight) Here's my special little bottle
Come, I'll pour this down your throttle.

Turkish Knight revives.

King of Egypt   Doctor, if you expect a fee, you'll get nowt
Because we're going to kick you out.

Exit Doctor chased by other players.

Enter Fair Sabra who dances towards Prince George to become his wife.

George   I swear to you dearest Sabra
If you will be my wife,
That I will do my best
To make you happy all my life.

They embrace.

Fair Sabra   To make the party crack
And to bring us all good cheer
We need Beelzebub, Dragon and Jack
So let them enter here.

Enter Beelzebub, Humpty Jack and Dragon.

Beelzebub   In steps I, Beelzebub
You'll usually find me in the pub.

I'll go back there as quick as I can
Don't you think me a jolly old man?

Humpty Jack | In comes I, Humpty Jack
With my wife and family on my back
Out of nine I've got but five
All the rest have been starved alive.
Times have been hard and my family's small
I work hard to find bread and cheese to feed them all.

Dragon | In comes I, the Dragon bold
I'm not a myth as you've been told.
I've got strong teeth and snapping jaws
Mighty muscles and very sharp claws!

Father Christmas | Our play is concluded with George and Sabra wed
Our fights are all fought and our lines have been said.
We'll say Merry Christmas and be going along
We bid you adieu with this well-known song:

All sing: | We wish you a Merry Christmas
We wish you a Merry Christmas
We wish you a Merry Christmas
And a Happy New Year.

Good tidings we bring
To you and your kin.
We wish you a Merry Christmas
And a Happy New Year.

THE END

YULETIDE WOMEN'S MUMMERS PLAY

Adapted from the 'Ladies Mumming Play' by John Boyd Hyland

CAST

Witch of Winter

Lady of Misrule

St Joan of Arc

Mary Read

Pope Joan

Anne Bonny

Doctor Cut

Dame Spring

Little Devil Doubt

Enter Witch of Winter.

Witch of Winter   Room, room, gallons of room
Pray give us room to rhyme;
We come to entertain you
This merry Christmas time.
I'm Morrigan, the Witch of Winter,
When days are dark and gloomy;
I'm as craggy as the bare old oak
Lashed by the winds so stormy.

Now winter surely is the time
For rest and recuperation,
Like animals we snuggle up
For a bit of hibernation.
So here we are to weave a tale
A quite unusual story:
Of how St Joan fought Mary Read
We hope it's not too gory.

St Joan's a pious lass,
She's holy with a mission
And she's going to clash with Mary
Who's got no inhibition.
And now good people clear the way
Walk in the Lady of Misrule I say.
Pray show the people sport and play
Before tonight we'll go away.

Enter Lady of Misrule.

Lady of Misrule   Welcome to you good people
And a Merry Christmas too;

> I am the Lady of Misrule
> Come to play some tricks on you.
> I'm still at large to have some fun;
> Watch out or I'll pinch your bum.
> Life's often not what it seems
> And now we've got our first surprise:
> St Joan wasn't burnt at the stake
> Here she stands before our eyes.

Enter St Joan.

St Joan   In comes I, St Joan of Arc,
                A noble champion bold;
                I raised the siege of Orleans
                As in history it is told.
                I was a poor peasant girl of Lorraine
                Who won the Dauphin's ear,
                And here comes Joan, the female pope,
                Who'll be my second here.

Enter Pope Joan.

Pope Joan   I'm Pope Joan who made it to the top
                And I really wasn't beastly,
                I was indeed the first to prove
                That women can be priestly.
                I'm still the one and only Papess
                Who fooled all the Church;
                I'll fight gallantly by your side
                And not leave you in the lurch.

Lady of Misrule   Well spoken, noble champions,
                Now gaze upon your foes:
                Here come the fearsome challengers
                Of whom you must dispose.
                They flew the Jolly Roger
                Though they were both with child;
                They terrorised the Spanish Main
                And all their enemies beguiled.

                Now let the pirate foes appear
                Walk in bold challengers, walk in.

Enter Mary Read and Anne Bonny (both pregnant).

Mary Read   My name it is brave Mary Read,
                I live on gin and brandy;

The gin it keeps my temper short
And the brandy makes me randy.
With my mate Anne Bonny I come in spite
To fright this silly saint tonight.
We've sailed with Captain Rackham,
We've ruled the Spanish Main,
With our babies in our bellies,
We've killed for plunder and gain.

Anne Bonny   We've freebuckled and swashbooted,
I couldn't count the churches we've looted.
The Bond Street lights are tawdry,
We've jewels which will bedazzle,
So come on leave your boring jobs
And join us on the razzle!

St Joan   I am St Joan just come from France
With my swords I'll make this pirate dance.
Like I did to the English, I'll cut her down to size
And send her back to Jamaica to make mince pies.

Mary Read   I'll slay this insipid champion,
I'll show this saint no quarter;
And then I'll liven up the rest of you
And many more I'll slaughter.

Pope Joan   Nay, stay thy hand thou mean pirate,
Harm not two holy ladies;
Else we'll strive to lay thee low
And send thy soul to Hades.

Anne Bonny   Brave words my worthy pope
From such a one as you,
I laugh to hear your lofty boasts…

Mary Read   … And I'll prove that they're not true.
For if Joan of Arc, you dare fight with me
I soon will run you through.

St Joan and Mary Read fight. St Joan kills Mary.

Lady of Misrule   Oh cruel St Joan what have you done?
You've killed my only daughter!
I know she wasn't very nice
And didn't do what she oughta.
(to Witch)   Oh help me, Witch
Have you got the magic potion

	To pick my Mary up And set her back in motion?
Witch of Winter	I'm sorry, dear, it's Christmas So we're closed for the duration. When days are short, witches shut up shop For rest and recuperation. Perhaps there is a doctor to be found To cure this deep and deadly wound?

Enter Doctor Cut.

Doctor Cut	Yes, I'm Doctor Cut who can save This girl a-lingering in the grave. For all my medicines are sure And death's a sickness I can cure.
Witch	Where do you come from, tell me plain?
Doctor Cut	From Italy, Greece, France and Spain Around the world and back again. There's nowhere that I haven't been And no disease I haven't seen. I'm familiar with the Chinese ways; Gout, depression and malaise, Even the hangover from the gin, Can be treated with a pin. (Just show me where to stick it in!)
Lady of Misrule	Doctor, if you can cure my daughter fair Who lies prostrate before you there, Ten pounds will I gladly give To you if you can make her live.
Doctor Cut	Thank you, now I'll perform A little of my science. This magic brew, a drop of which Sets death all at defiance. Its name is El-e-can-pim-pom-pane And it brings the dead to life again. A drop on her head, a drop on her heart Rise up old girl and play your part.

Mary rises.

Mary Read	Oh mother, your face I'm glad to see, I thought that was the end of me. I'll give up all my wicked ways And help the poor and meek.

I'll do that till my dying day
Well at least for about a week.

St Joan   And now you know I'm best of all
Come, Pope Joan, let's leave the hall.

Enter Dame Spring.

Dame Spring   Not so fast! Beware St Joan of my dread power!
I'm Dame Flora, Goddess of the Spring.
A thousand times I'll fight the Church
Yet never you shall win.
Churchmen may think they've conquered me
And overthrown me quite,
But with the springtime I'll return
And leap up to the light.

St Joan   I'll never fear thy might Dame Spring
Though many flee thy power;
I'll battle with the pagan gods
For ever and an hour.

Dame Spring   Let thee and I the battle try!

St Joan   If thou dost conquer, I must die.

They fight. Dame Spring falls.

St Joan   See how quickly Dame Spring fell
For all her boasted fettle.
She couldn't conquer bold St Joan
For I'm a woman of mettle.

Dame Spring rises.

Dame Spring   Nay, nay, St Joan beware of pride
Dame Spring is well and lusty,
If you're a woman of mettle
Then I fear your metal's rusty!

They fight again and St Joan falls.

All   Doctor! Doctor!

Enter Doctor Cut.

Lady of Misrule   Here's the Doctor that I crave
He brought my Mary from the grave.

Doctor Cut   Alright, I'll do this one for free
Since you paid 10 times my normal fee.

Doctor Cut cures St Joan.

St Joan
:   I'm glad that I am back alive
    And have been cured of my sin of pride.

Witch
:   And now we must send for little Devil Doubt
    To collect some money or we'll leave with nowt!

Enter Little Devil Doubt (with broom).

Little Devil
Doubt
:   In comes I, little Devil Doubt
    With my petticoat hanging out;
    Five yards in and five yards out.
    Money I want and money I crave
    If you don't give me money
    I'll sweep you into the grave.

Lady of Misrule
:   And now our play is over
    And Mary has fought St Joan,
    We bid farewell to these players
    And thank them every one
    As they step back through the centuries
    For they must slip away,
    While we celebrate Christmas
    So give us your applause, we pray.

THE END

ZENDA: THE PRISONER OF SIBLING RIVALRY

A state of the nation play

CAST

Sisterband 1, 2, and 3, who are the prologue and epilogue
Ediband, a political aristocrat, the younger brother
Locals 1 and 2
Daviband, another political aristocrat, older brother to Ediband
Ms Spin, a spin doctor
Baron Rupert, media baron and tyrant
Lady Greed, his mistress
Bishop Rowan
Theresa May, coronation guest
Angela Merkel, coronation guest
Princess Fabia, a socialist beauty
Cleggiband, a henchman
Count David of Hentzau, an adventurer

The action takes place in England, Zenda, and the capital of Politania.

The audience boo Baron Rupert, shout socialist slogans for Princess Fabia, and vote on Ediband's dilemma.

Slogans can include 'Vote Ken', 'Join the general strike', 'Save the NHS', timeless socialist slogans such as 'To each according to his means', 'The people united will never be defeated', and the audiences' own favourites.

SCENE 1
Prologue

Enter Sisterband 1, 2 and 3.

Sisterband 1 We're Sisterband, a sort of chorus
    Life's currently disappointing for us.
    There's unemployment and delayed pensions
    Divorce, fear of crime and workplace tensions.

Sisterband 2 When the nation is in such a bad way
    Let's imagine an adventure far away.
    We'll escape the Coalition's mania
    In the tranquil kingdom of Politania.
    Where Daviband's preparing for coronation –
    So let's send Ediband as our delegation.

Sisterband 3	Yet there is a malign power in that land: Baron Rupert and his media band. They seek to control it all: Alas, Politania lies in thrall.
Sisterband 1	Good Daviband has a regal air Alas, poor Ediband, it's not fair: While Davi claims his patrimony Edi can't even do his matrimony.
Sisterband 2	Come in, Ediband, to go for the ride And watch while Daviband claims his bride – That's Princess Fabia, the socialist dream Who will be their future queen.

Enter Ediband.

Ediband	I'm the cadet of an intellectual house Though you may think me a political mouse. This will be an opportunity for public exposure To flaunt my boyish looks and suave composure. Yet when there's a question of leadership Audience, don't doubt I'm up for it. On the way to see Davi crowned I'll visit a place much renowned: Zenda – Castle of Electoral Reform Where democracy can be reborn.
Sisterband 3	But audience take heed: Who is that mysterious Lady Greed?

Enter Lady Greed.

Lady Greed	I don't know what my part's for I think I'm some kind of caricature. Although I'm selfish at the start By the end I have a golden heart.

Exeunt Sisterband 1, 2 and 3 and Lady Greed. Enter Baron Rupert.
Audience boo.

Baron Rupert	I want world domination I won't show mercy to any nation. I've got my eyes on the BBC And its juicy licence fee. I'll grab all the power I need Then spend my time with Lady Greed.

Exit Baron Rupert.

SCENE 2
Zenda

Ediband remains on stage. Enter Locals 1 and 2.

Local 1	Welcome stranger. Us locals are all a-goggin To see the crown on Daviband's noggin. Mind, you've an uncanny resemblance To the man who'll be our prince.
Local 2	Of Daviband you're the spit – Or maybe to the left a bit. But Baron Rupert is the one we fear His influence spreads far and near.
Ediband	I want to see your castle and its towers They say it has magic powers.
Local 1	Alas, its claims to electoral reform Are treated by all with bitter scorn. Anyway it's in Baron Rupert's control.
Ediband	Even so, I think I'll take a stroll To the edge of town To see that place of great renown.

Exeunt Locals 1 and 2. Enter Daviband and Ms Spin.

Daviband	In comes I, the future king Daviband And suitor for Princess Fabia's hand. I'll be a leader beyond compare I'll steer a course between Brown and Blair.
Ms Spin *(to audience)*	I'm mistress of the art of spin It's your votes I aim to win. I'll see that popularity's flames are fanned To guarantee victory for Daviband.
Ediband	Excuse me if it seems like quibbling What about the younger sibling?
Daviband	As senior male I'm the one that must prevail And be liberty's defender. Though Baron Rupert has bought Zenda – Just like he bought *The Times*, Another of his takeover crimes – I've done some political horse trading Before tomorrow's victory parading.

	When I've climbed to the summit You'll read: IT'S THE SUN WOT WON IT.
Ediband	I say good luck – You'll need it against that schmuck.
Daviband	I believe my statesmanlike arts Can defeat Baron Rupert's darts. Why, when I'd appeased his wrath Rupert gave me this drink to quaff.
Ms Spin	Now let me propose a toast To the brother who has the most.

Daviband drinks.

Ediband	Cheers! You're a first-born winner Whereas I'm just a political beginner.
Daviband	I found success came easy Wait! I'm feeling queasy. Promised fame has gone to my head Now I think I must go to bed.

Daviband falls over, drugged.

Ms Spin	Thanks to Baron Rupert's media scheming Daviband is drugged and sweet-dreaming. He will miss tomorrow's coronation Edi, you must step in and save the nation – Otherwise Baron Rupert will claim the crown And kick our country while it's down. The people won't know which is which – After a day we'll reverse the switch.
Ediband	A gentleman must step forward and be gallant No matter if he has a meagre talent. Even though I'm nobody of note I've won victory by the alternative vote.
Ms Spin	Leave Daviband drugged in a hunting lodge Let's go and foil Rupert's dodge.

SCENE 3
The capital of Politania

Ediband and Ms Spin remain on stage. Enter Locals 1 and 2, Baron Rupert and Lady Greed.

Local 2	We want a ruler to lead us to the promised land Yes, it's you King Daviband!

Baron Rupert *(to audience)*	My plan was that Daviband would not appear And so fall victim to my media's smear. But events are taking a different route Somehow they've found a substitute.

Enter Bishop Rowan with crown. He prepares to crown Ediband.

Bishop Rowan *(crowns Ediband)*	Daviband, I hope you have the grace To make Politania a better place, And that you won't be noted for Policies that no one voted for.
Local 1	We agree with Bishop Rowan Daviband, save us, go on!

Audience cheer.

Bishop Rowan	Let's meet some political leaders So we can bite the hands that feed us.

Enter Theresa May and Angela Merkel.

Theresa May	I'm Home Secretary, Theresa May I'm grateful for a small part in this play Just like in the Cabinet, I'm a token woman A millionaire, but *not* Old Etonian. I wear kitten heels, smart and slinky But that doesn't mean I'm strange or kinky. Here is the heroine of our circle The redoubtable Chancellor Merkel.
Angela Merkel	I started life in research chemistry Now I'm Chancellor of the United Germany. I'm not known for effervescence I just exude a calming presence.

Exeunt Theresa May and Angela Merkel.

Local 2	I know where next we're heading: To yet another royal wedding.
Ediband	The population bow and kneel They accept me as if I'm real. I have assumed my brother's crown I hope I don't let the people down.
Baron Rupert *(aside)*	My men have now kidnapped Daviband That will give me the upper hand. He will wake to have his luncheon In Zenda's electoral dungeon.

Enter Princess Fabia.

Princess Fabia	In comes I, Princess Fabia
	With my beauty I'll enslave ya.
	I'm an ideal socialist dream
	Looking for a leader to make me queen.
Local 1	Audience, shout out slogans and aspirations
	In favour of socialist nations.

Audience shout slogans.

Princess Fabia	Whatever politics' ins and outs,
	About Daviband I have my doubts.
	Although he considered me a beauty
	I always found him rather snooty.
Lady Greed	Alas, I must be a dupe
	To have fallen for Baron Rupe.

Exit all except Ediband and Ms Spin.

SCENE 4

Ms Spin	Bad news about the switch: there's a bodge
	Daviband's missing from the hunting lodge.
	Rupert's put him in jail
	Our one-day ruse must now fail.
Ediband	Our plans are in ruins
	They'll realise our mischievous doings!
	Baron Rupert will see right through me
	He won't believe I'm a 'new me'.
Ms Spin	Hold on. The populace has yet to note
	The switch made by the alternative vote.
	We must keep on with our pretence –
	It's our only means of defence.
	Baron Rupert must be stewing:
	He can't expose his own wrong-doing.
	You must carry on as king
	No one will notice a thing.
Ediband	I suppose I may just last out fine
	If I avoid Prime Minister's Question Time.
	I'll just carry on quietly
	Enjoying Politania's society.

Enter Princess Fabia.

Ms Spin *(to Ediband)* She's as sweet as Princess Kate
    Go and ask her for a date.
    Mind you must be on your best behaviour
    If you're to deceive Princess Fabia.

Fabia
    Before the crowning you were away some weeks:
    Do I see a change in the colour of your cheeks?

Ediband
    An alteration in complexion
    Is no cause for introspection.
    You are as pure as mountain snow
    Come, and let our courtship grow.

Exeunt Ediband and Princess Fabia. Enter Baron Rupert.

Baron Rupert *(to audience)* I'll organise a double homicide
    And compel Fabia to be *my* bride.
    Then all power will come to me
    And I can privatise the BBC.
    Where's the person to do what I have planned?
    Come in my henchman, Cleggiband.

Enter Cleggiband.

Cleggiband
    I've sent Ediband a note to discuss a pact
    He won't suspect he'll be attacked.

Exit Baron Rupert. Enter Ms Spin and Ediband.

Ms Spin
    Hmm, I smell a rat
    A lying Liberal Democrat!

Cleggiband *(to Ediband)* You're not who you say you are –
    Prepare for your last hurrah.

Cleggiband draws sword.

Ediband *(drawing sword)* Ms Spin come to my aid
    Demonstrate why you're paid.

Ms Spin *(drawing sword)* Cleggiband, we see through your tricks
    You're just one of Rupert's sidekicks.

Ediband
    We'll fight – let's see who counts the most
    The winner is 'first past the post'.

Ediband and Ms Spin fight Cleggiband. Cleggiband retreats.

Cleggiband
    Even though I've lost to you and your spinner
    I may yet turn out the winner.

Exit Cleggiband.

Ediband	We've seen off Rupert's crony But they know that I'm a phony.
Ms Spin	Perhaps it might be wise For you to stay on in disguise. What would it cost ya To maintain your imposture?
Ediband	There's one strong reason to maintain deceit Princess Fabia's swept me off my feet. She's won my own true heart I cannot bear for us to part. Yet I must take the honorable course And free Daviband by force. Yes, I must return to Zenda To put Baron Rupert through the blender.
Ms Spin	Should Ediband risk a fight To do what is morally right Should he put his principles first Even though his heart would burst? Let's have vote to see Don't worry it's not AV. Those who would follow the heart's command Now's the time to raise your hand.

Audience vote.

Ms Spin	Those who would restore Daviband from harm And take the righteous cause, lift your arm.

Audience vote.

Ms Spin	I'm afraid elections don't matter a jot: He's going, whether you like it or not.

Enter Princess Fabia with ring. Exit Ms Spin.

Ediband	Your love has put me in a daze. I have set aside my former ways. Now I must seek your permission To go off on a secret mission. I loved you with all my heart But on state business I must depart.

Princess Fabia *(aside)* Sometimes it's best to hedge
(to Ediband, giving ring) Let me leave you with this pledge.

Exeunt Ediband and Princess Fabia.

SCENE 5
Zenda

Enter Daviband, Baron Rupert and Cleggiband.

Cleggiband	I guard the king and do my master's bidding He's at my mercy, I'm not kidding
Daviband	All this time I'm kept in purdah While Baron Rupert plots hate and murder. I'm beginning to turn pale – Powerless, my health will fail. I regret the day I was born I hate this Castle of Electoral Reform!
Baron Rupert	Soon I'll kill the younger son Then Daviband, your days will be done. I will bring about disaster And privatise the state broadcaster: All the lefty media shower Will be brought within my power. I've enlisted a political opportunist To get the foul deed done the soonest.

Exeunt Daviband and Cleggiband. Enter Count David.

Count David	I'm Count David of Hentzau. Eton is where I went, so I am snobbish and aloof And don't give a fig for the truth. Rupert, your wish is my command I'm out to get that Ediband.
(to audience)	You may think Rupert is very bad But I am a political cad. What's more – and don't tell Sam – I'm a bit of a ladies' man.

Exit Count David. Enter Ediband and Ms Spin.

Ediband	We are waiting outside Zenda But Rupert is a tough defender.

Enter Count David.

Ms Spin	Count David approaches on a mission Surely not a coalition?
Count David	Rupert offered to buy you off I didn't agree because I'm a toff.

> So prepare to be unmasked, impostor!
> As for Fabia, you'll have lost her –
> I've seen her at royal dances
> I must say I fancy my chances.

Ediband   Such taunts are insolent and cruel
            David, you've let down your public school.
            Play it fair at the ballot box
            Win or lose, then take the knocks.

Count David *(makes to stab Ediband)*
            Let me make a playful thrust
            We'll fight again, I know we must.

Exit Count David.

Ediband *(to Ms Spin)* I want revenge, spin doctor.
            I love Fabia. That cad knocked her!

Ms Spin   Secret messages from Lady Greed reveal
            The king is ill – the danger's real.
            He's kept in the castle jail
            Where Cleggiband is the guardian male.
            If attacked, Rupert has left a note:
            'Kill Daviband and dump the body in the moat'.

Ediband   This is a hard nut to crack,
            But I've planned how I will attack:
            Ms Spin, *you* stage a diversionary thrust
            Meanwhile *I* will go for bust.
            You distract Rupert and wicked Dave
            I'll send Cleggiband to his grave.

Exit Ediband.

SCENE 6

Baron Rupert's apartments

Ms Spin remains on stage.

Ms Spin   One thing may help our plan succeed
            We've had a message from Lady Greed.
            Her love for Baron Rupert wavers
            Count David now seeks her favours.
            Regardless of the danger
            We'll storm her bed chamber.

Exit Ms Spin. Enter Lady Greed and Count David.

Count David	Rupert's aims are for power worldwide He'll use you and cast you aside. Why don't you and I enter coalition?
Lady Greed	Be gone, you'll cause suspicion. Rupert's scheming fills me with disgust But I won't allow your treacherous lust.

Enter Baron Rupert.

Baron Rupert	Count David, confound your lechery Now you'll suffer for your treachery.
Count David	I have no ideology All I care about is me.

Baron Rupert and Count David fight. Rupert is fatally wounded.

Baron Rupert	I am to damnation hurled Sent there by the *News of the World.* Yet my death will not end my hatred Of pathetic nation-statehood.

Baron Rupert dies.

Count David	Now I've survived this scrape It's time for me to escape.

Exit Count David. Enter Ms Spin.

Ms Spin	The villains' quarrel with each other Has saved me a lot of bother.
Lady Greed	For me this is no happy ender: I curse the day that I saw Zenda.
Ms Spin	Be off. I know it's not very nice But you were only ever a plot device.

Exeunt Ms Spin and Lady Greed.

SCENE 7
The dungeon in Zenda's castle

Enter Ediband, Cleggiband who has Daviband captive.

Ediband	Audience, imagine the danger I swam the moat like Stewart Granger – But all those scenes of tension I must leave to your invention.
(to Cleggiband)	We meet again, Cleggiband Now we'll see who is unmanned.

Cleggiband   With coalition I hoped to launch a new era:
              In this electoral dungeon, my end is nearer.

Ediband and Cleggiband fight.

Ediband *(lands a blow)* You loved power enough to defect for it
              That will teach you to betray the electorate.

Cleggiband *(wounded)* If only I hadn't been such a tease
              Over those tuition fees!

Cleggiband dies.

Ediband *(to Daviband)*
              I saved you, my flesh and blood
              I only hope that I've done good.

Daviband   Don't expect any thanks from me
              As elder son, that's the way it has to be.

Enter Ms Spin.

Ms Spin   David and Rupert argued over Greed
              I didn't know where it would lead
              But Rupert's life is spent, so
              You next must fight David of Hentzau.
              As a fighter you're his equal
              But that must wait for the sequel.

Exeunt all except Ms Spin, who remains on stage.

SCENE 8
Outside the castle

Enter Princess Fabia.

Ms Spin *(aside)* Here's the man with first place in your heart.
              I don't think she'll tell them apart.

Enter Daviband.

Daviband   Politania's safe: Baron Rupert's dead
              You and I can enjoy the life ahead.

Princess Fabia Even though you've killed that blackguard
              You've returned drawn and haggard.

Daviband   I must go: affairs are pressing
              It's a comfort to have your blessing.

Princess Fabia I will play the dutiful wife
              While you attend to political strife.

Exeunt Daviband and Ms Spin.

Princess Fabia	There was one funny thing He wasn't wearing my ring.

Enter Ediband.

Ediband	Fabia, you haven't been seeing double I'm the cause of all the trouble. I confess I am your true lover The other one is my brother. Alas, our hearts are broken: The proof is this love token.

Ediband shows ring.

Princess Fabia	Now it's my turn to face a choice, But I listen to my conscience's voice And know my duty is to back a winner. As a statesman, you're just a beginner.
Ediband	Alas, I haven't got what it takes To sort out this pit of snakes. It's time to leave Politania I'm a gent: I won't detain ya.
Princess Fabia	Although my character is artless Please know I am not completely heartless. We must all suffer fate's cruel blows But each year, expect this day a lover's rose.

Fabia gives Ediband a red rose. Exeunt Princess Fabia and Ediband.

SCENE 9
Epilogue

Enter Sisterband 1, 2 and 3 and Angela Merkel.

Angela Merkel	Now you've sorted your ruling male out, I daresay you'll want a bail out But after these events, I am cancelling all bets We'll refuse to pay Politania's debts.
Sisterband 1	I think this fantasy went to the authors' head All they wanted was a play beginning with zed.
Sisterband 2	Sibling rivalry is just family politics You can hang on to resentments or 'pick and mix'. If you learn to tolerate your sister or brother, You'll become a better father or mother.

Sisterband 3   With humour you appreciate the shared history
That you share with siblings – that's the key.
Now let's get on with our cakes and tea.

THE END

Notes

Well-known stories can inspire plays about topical events, as well as about timeless themes, in keeping with the one-off, in-the-moment character of domestic theatre. Usually we have been content with topical references, and rarely bring on living characters, except sometimes the Queen. But in summer 2011 we were looking for way to celebrate finishing this book, and hit on the idea of a play beginning with 'Z'.

More or less the only literary work that came to mind was *The Prisoner of Zenda*, written at the end of the 19th century by the novelist and establishment figure, Anthony Hope. Set in the imaginary kingdom of Ruritania, it remained popular in the 20th century through film and television adaptations. We decided it could be a vehicle for a topical spoof, linking to the febrile political climate of 2010 and 2011, covering the 2010 general election, Coalition government, Labour Party leadership contest and the referendum on the Alternative Vote as a means of electing Members of Parliament. The press had recently begun to reiterate its favourite theme of sibling rivalry between Ed and David Miliband, the former having unexpectedly won the Labour leadership through the Alternative Vote, and the latter disappearing from the political scene.

Our intention was to create a light-hearted riff for a summer afternoon on themes of political chicanery, socialist hopes and sibling rivalry. But although dated, this play shows how domestic theatre can be a way of addressing a theme which is on everyone's minds – perhaps a local protest over the closure of a shop, post office or library – adapting traditional motifs like the wicked baron, mysterious castle or unrequited lovers. It can be extended into a sort of 'humane agit-prop' – celebrating values of community, acceptance, and joy in struggle.

Of course topical references can cut both ways. We were delighted a few weeks after our party when the News International scandal drew attention to the activities of the media baron Rupert Murdoch – but almost from the moment the performance closed, it became increasingly evident that we should have switched the ending – like the 1979 film adaption with Peter Sellers – so that the prisoner Daviband departs to live privately, and his unlikely substitute Ediband carries on to fight the battles of Politiania and win his socialist sweetheart.

Glossary to plays

The plays have many references to products, topics, personalities, TV programmes and jokes in common usage at the time of their first performance. You can change them to your own topical references, but we have included this glossary to help make them comprehensible. Names are in alphabetical order of surname.

Reference	Play (A–Z)	Description
ASBO	K	Anti-Social Behaviour Order, a civil order introduced in 1998. In 2010, the Coalition Government announced its intention to abolish ASBOs
Laura Ashley	R	Manufacturer of flower-printed dresses
AV	Z	Alternative Vote – system rejected by 2011 referendum
Big Brother	T	Television reality programme
Big Issue	G	Weekly magazine sold by homeless people
Birkenstocks	O	Fashionable sandals and footwear
Tony Blair	A, G, O, V, Z	New Labour Prime Minister, 1997–2007
David Blunkett	R	New Labour Home Secretary, 2001–2004, also held other Cabinet posts
Bond Street	Y	West End street famous for Christmas lights and expensive clothes shops
Richard Branson	T	Entrepreneur, owner of Virgin Rail
Brasso	P	Cleaning fluid for brass
Gordon Brown	A, G, W, Z	New Labour Chancellor, 1997–2007 and Prime Minister, 2007–2010
Beau Brummel	G	George Bryan Brummel (1778–1840) was a friend of the Prince Regent, the future King George IV. His name was a by-word for fashion
Sam (Cameron)	Z	Spoof reference to Sam, wife of David Cameron, Tory Prime Minister 2010
Carling Green Label	S	Carling Black Label is a much advertised lager
Castlemaine 4X	G	Australian beer
Chloral	R	Once a widely used sedative and hypnotic substance

Winston Churchill	V	Entered Parliament as a Conservative in 1900, joined Liberals in 1904 and after periods in Cabinet Office, formally rejoined Conservatives in 1925. Subsequently Prime Minister
Nick Clegg	G, Z	Liberal Democrat Leader and Deputy Prime Minister in 2010 Coalition
Cowabunga	N	Catchphrase from 1980s comics and television programme *Teenage Mutant Ninja Turtles* and before that in *The Howdy Doody Show* in America in the 1950s. (Originally 'Kowabonga')
Dallas	S	American television soap
Count David	Z	Spoof character for David Cameron, Tory Prime Minister 2010
Decembrists	W	The army officers who led a failed uprising against Tsar Nicholas I in December 1825
Furuncle	K	A boil
Gladiators	O	Television programme, film
Gazza	A	Paul Gascoigne, footballer, wild character
Gortex	O	Brand of waterproof outdoor wear
Stewart Granger	Z	Actor (1913–1993) who played lead in 1952 film of *The Prisoner of Zenda*
Gunners	R	Arsenal football team who won both the FA Cup and Premiership in 2002
Glen Hoddle	A	Footballer, steady character, captained England and later managed national team (1996–1999)
Michael Howard	G	Tory Home Secretary, 1993–1997
Hutton Enquiry	Q	Public enquiry in 2003 (published 2004) which investigated the circmstances surrounding the death of Dr David Kelly, including allegations that a government dossier on Iraq's alleged weapons of mass destruction had been 'sexed up'.
Iraq war	G	Unpopular war started in 2003 by US President George Bush and Tony Blair on grounds that Saddam Hussein President of Iraq had weapons of mass destruction. Also know as Second Gulf War
Boris (Johnson)	G, W	Second Mayor of London, vowed to get rid of bendy buses
Ken (Livingstone)	G, Z	First Mayor of London, defeated by Boris Johnson in 2008

Luftwaffe	P	World War Two German airforce
Theresa May	Z	Conservative politician, made Home Secretary in 2010
MD	M	Qualification for medical doctor
Angela Merkel	Z	First woman Chancellor of Germany (in 2005)
David and Ed Miliband	Z	Political brothers, cabinet members in Labour government, David 2005–2010 and Ed 2007–2010
'Mind the Gap'	G	Announcement on tube trains to mind the gap between the tube train and the platform
Mogadon	M	Anxiolytic drug with sedative properties
News of the World	Z	British Sunday newspaper, closed 2011
NHS	H, X, Z	National Health Service, beleaguered publicly funded health service
Barack Obama	T	United States President from 2010
Panorama	G	BBC current affairs televison programme
Quasimodo	A	Bellringer in novel 'The Hunchback of Notre Dame' and later film adaptations
Quorn	P	Meat substitute
Rigoletto	B	A highly emotional opera by Giuseppe Verdi, first performed in 1851
Scud	N	Type of missile in operational use in the second half of the 20th century
Tom Stoppard	H	Playwright, author of *Rosencrantz and Guildenstern are Dead* and other plays
Jack Straw	G	New Labour Home Secretary, 1997–2001 and Justice Minister, 2007–2010
Margaret Thatcher	G, N	Tory Prime Minister 1979–90 who said 'The lady's not for turning'
Mary Ward	H	Adult Education Centre in London
WD40	H	Lubricant which drives out moisture
Anne Widdecombe	G	Outspoken Tory politician, Minister of State for Prisons in Home Office 1995–1997 under Michael Howard, whom she described as having 'something of the night' about him
Rowan Williams	Z	Archbishop of Canterbury from 2003 who commented on the Coalition policies in 2011

Sources, references and further reading

Sources

Aucassin and Nicolette and Other Tales trans. Pauline Matarasso, Penguin, Harmondsworth, 1971

Hesiod, *The Homeric Hymns and Homerica*, trans. Evelyn-White, Hugh G., Heinemann, London, 1959 (first publ.1914)

Hope, Anthony, *The Prisoner of Zenda*, Penguin Popular Classics, London, 1994 (first publ. 1894)

Sir Gawain and the Green Knight – available in several translations. We recommend the verse translation by J.R.R. Tolkien, in *Sir Gawain and the Green Knight, Pearl, Orfeo*, George Allen and Unwin, London, 1975

Sutton, Shaun, *The Queen's Champion*, Edward Arnold, London, 1961

Wiles, David, *The Early Plays of Robin Hood*, D.S. Brewer, Cambridge, 1981

References

Boyd Hyland, John *We're Jolly Boys: An introduction to mumming and pace-egging*, published by the author in Oldham, 1978 (available in Cecil Sharp House Library)

Daniel, Samuel, *Vision of the Twelve Goddesses: A royal masque*, available as an e-book or published by BiblioBazaar LLC, Charleston, SC, USA, 2009

Growing Old Disgracefully: A network for older women. www.growingolddisgracefully.org.uk

Helm, Alex, *Eight Mummers Plays*, Ginn and Co, Aylesbury, 1971

Iles, Norman, *Who killed Cock Robin? Nursery rhymes and carols restored to their original meanings*, R. Hale, London, 1986

King, Sue and Clifford, Angela, *England in Particular*, Common Ground/ Hodder and Stoughton, London, 2006

Klinger, Samuel, *Graveyard Laughter*, Satellite Books, London, 1979

Lower Shaw Farm, Old Shaw Lane, Shaw, Swindon, Wiltshire, SN5 5PJ. Tel: 01793 771080 enquiries@lowershawfarm.co.uk

Red House, Red House Lane, Bexleyheath, Kent, DA6 8JF. Tel: 020 8304 9878. www.nationaltrust.org.uk/main/w-redhouse

Rowe, Doc and Robson, Carolyn, *The English Folk Dance and Song Society Resource Packs 1: May. 2: Midwinter. 3: Plough Monday to Hocktide*, EFDSS, London, 1993 (Pack 1), 1994 (Pack 2), 1995 (Pack 3)

St Pancras Almshouses website link to *Dr Fraser's Dream* http://www.stpancrasalmshouses.org/node/46

Thiel, Lisa, *Spirit of the Plants*, © 1984 www.sacreddream.com

Vaughan Williams Library, English Folk Dance and Song Society (EFDSS), Cecil Sharp House, 2 Regent's Park Road, London, NW1 7AY. Tel 020 7485 2206 www.efdss.org

Women's Library, London Metropolitan University, 25 Old Castle Street, London, E1 7NT. Tel: 020 7320 2222. www.londonmet.ac.uk/thewomenslibrary

Further reading

Coult, Tony and Kershaw, Baz, eds, *Engineers of the Imagination: The Welfare State handbook*, Methuen, London, 1990 – especially the inspiring graphics coordinated by Tony Lewery

Gassner, John, ed, *Medieval and Tudor Drama*, Applause, New York, 1987

Hole, Christina, *A Dictionary of British Folk Customs*, Paladin, London, 1978

Mayfield, Beatrice, *Apple Games and Customs*, Common Ground, London, 1994

Opie, Iona and Peter, *The Singing Game*, Oxford University Press, Oxford, 1985